# Information Security Policies, Procedures, and Standards

## Guidelines for Effective Information Security Management

### THOMAS R. PELTIER

# AUERBACH PUBLICATIONS

A CRC Press Company

Boca Raton   London   New York   Washington, D.C.

## Library of Congress Cataloging-in-Publication Data

Peltier, Thomas R.
   Information security policies, procedures, and standards : guidelines for effective
      information security management/Thomas R. Peltier.
         p.   cm.
   Includes bibliographical references and index.
   ISBN 0-8493-1137-3 (alk. paper)
   1. Computer security. 2. Data protection. I. Title.

QA76.9.A25 P46 2001
005.8--dc21
                                                                        2001045194

**Visit the  Auerbach Publications Web site at www.auerbach-publications.com**

© 2002 by CRC Press LLC
Auerbach is an imprint of CRC Press LLC

No claim to original U.S. Government works
International Standard Book Number 0-8493-1137-3
Library of Congress Card Number 2001045194
Printed in the United States of America          4  5  6  7  8  9  0
Printed on acid-free paper

# Information Security Policies, Procedures, and Standards

## Guidelines for Effective Information Security Management

# OTHER AUERBACH PUBLICATIONS

**ABCs of IP Addressing**
Gilbert Held
ISBN: 0-8493-1144-6

**Application Servers for E-Business**
Lisa M. Lindgren
ISBN: 0-8493-0827-5

**Architectures for E-Business Systems**
Sanjiv Purba, Editor
ISBN: 0-8493-1161-6

**A Technical Guide to IPSec Virtual Private Networks**
James S. Tiller
ISBN: 0-8493-0876-3

**Building an Information Security Awareness Program**
Mark B. Desman
ISBN: 0-8493-0116-5

**Computer Telephony Integration**
William Yarberry, Jr.
ISBN: 0-8493-9995-5

**Cyber Crime Investigator's Field Guide**
Bruce Middleton
ISBN: 0-8493-1192-6

**Cyber Forensics:
A Field Manual for Collecting, Examining, and Preserving Evidence of Computer Crimes**
Albert J. Marcella and Robert S. Greenfield, Editors
ISBN: 0-8493-0955-7

**Information Security Architecture**
Jan Killmeyer Tudor
ISBN: 0-8493-9988-2

**Information Security Management Handbook, 4th Edition, Volume 1**
Harold F. Tipton and Micki Krause, Editors
ISBN: 0-8493-9829-0

**Information Security Management Handbook, 4th Edition, Volume 2**
Harold F. Tipton and Micki Krause, Editors
ISBN: 0-8493-0800-3

**Information Security Management Handbook, 4th Edition, Volume 3**
Harold F. Tipton and Micki Krause, Editors
ISBN: 0-8493-1127-6

**Information Security Policies, Procedures, and Standards: Guidelines for Effective Information Security Management**
Thomas Peltier
ISBN: 0-8493-1137-3

**Information Security Risk Analysis**
Thomas Peltier
ISBN: 0-8493-0880-1

**Information Technology Control and Audit**
Frederick Gallegos, Sandra Allen-Senft, and Daniel P. Manson
ISBN: 0-8493-9994-7

**New Directions in Internet Management**
Sanjiv Purba, Editor
ISBN: 0-8493-1160-8

**New Directions in Project Management**
Paul C. Tinnirello, Editor
ISBN: 0-8493-1190-X

**A Practical Guide to Security Engineering and Information Assurance**
Debra Herrmann
ISBN: 0-8493-1163-2

**The Privacy Papers:
Managing Technology and Consumers, Employee, and Legislative Action**
Rebecca Herold
ISBN: 0-8493-1248-5

**Secure Internet Practices:
Best Practices for Securing Systems in the Internet and e-Business Age**
Patrick McBride, Joday Patilla, Craig Robinson, Peter Thermos, and Edward P. Moser
ISBN: 0-8493-1239-6

**Securing and Controlling Cisco Routers**
Peter T. Davis
ISBN: 0-8493-1290-6

**Securing E-Business Applications and Communications**
Jonathan S. Held and John R. Bowers
ISBN: 0-8493-0963-8

**Securing Windows NT/2000:
From Policies to Firewalls**
Michael A. Simonyi
ISBN: 0-8493-1261-2

**TCP/IP Professional Reference Guide**
Gilbert Held
ISBN: 0-8493-0824-0

## AUERBACH PUBLICATIONS

www.auerbach-publications.com
To Order Call: 1-800-272-7737 • Fax: 1-800-374-3401
E-mail: orders@crcpress.com

# Dedication

To Lisa, my editor and life compass

# Contents

# Acknowledgments

It seems that I have spent the greatest part of my working life writing policies and procedures. As the result of an ongoing audit at the company where I was working, I was asked to step in and develop a set of information security policies and procedures. Because I had taken courses in writing fiction and poetry and had a poem published in the school literary journal, I felt I was highly qualified for this task. Little did I know. After a couple of attempts, I took everything I had learned about image development, character development, complex sentences and threw it all away. I had to go back to the basics and I had a lot of questions. These questions were answered by a tremendous group of professionals who have become my friends.

First in my list of acknowledgments is my mentor and friend, John O'Leary, the Director of the Computer Security Institute–Education Resource Center. No matter what the subject, John seems to have some experience in all areas of information security, and he is always ready to lend an opinion and direction. It was his encouragement to "try it; if they don't stone you, then you're onto something." John's approach is always a bit more formal than mine, but he encouraged me to find the path of least resistance. John and his wonderful wife Jane have always been available to bounce ideas off of or just to listen and offer advice.

Lisa Bryson is my friend, fellow information security professional, editor, and now my wife. We have known each other for almost 15 years and have had many a lively discussion on how security should be implemented. She always reminds me that not many people can see the smile on your face through your writings. Say what you mean, and do not be a wise guy. I hate it when she is always right.

Next on my list is Pat Howard. I must have been a very good person in a previous life to be afforded the opportunity to meet and work with Pat. He is able to take some of my ramblings, my very bad drawings on flipcharts, and turn them into finished products. He keeps me on track and provides insight on the new standards and other requirements.

John Blackley and Terri Curran are two dear friends who have allowed me to review and research their materials, and they did the same for me. Before we were consultants, we worked at organizations that required policies, procedures, and standards, but did not want anything to impede the business process. John, Terri, and I spent many hours discussing how to get management to understand just how bright we were and that our documents were going to save our companies in spite of themselves.

Who can leave out his publisher? Certainly not me; Rich O'Hanley has taken the time to discuss policies and procedures with numerous organizations to understand what their needs are and then presented these findings to me. A great deal of my work here is a direct result of what Rich discovered the industry wanted.

Others who have helped me along the way include:

- Justin Peltier, my son, fellow information security professional, and best friend
- William H. Murray, the first person I heard speak on the security needs of organizations, and who has inspired me ever since
- Hal Tipton, the steady voice of reason in this crazy profession
- Charles Cressen Wood, fellow writer
- Harry DeMaio, whose book (*Information Security and Other Unnatural Acts*) gave great insight into just how difficult our task is
- Mike Corby, my friend and now boss. (I have known Mike for over 25 years, and he has always given the best and most honest advice. If you would like the prototype for the honest man, you could stop the search when you meet Mike Corby.)
- Rich O'Hanley, not only the world's best editor and task master, but a good friend and source of knowledge. How he keeps his sanity while working with writers is totally beyond me. Thanks Rich!

# Introduction

The purpose of an information security program is to protect the valuable information resources of an enterprise. Through the selection and application of appropriate policies, standards, and procedures, an overall security program helps the enterprise meet its business objective or mission charter. Because security is sometimes viewed as thwarting business objectives, it is necessary to ensure that effective, well-written policies, standards, and procedures are implemented.

When writing information security polices, standards, and procedures, it is necessary to make certain that proper grammar and punctuation are used. Part of an effective book on writing should discuss these topics. The importance of an effective topic sentence to the overall success of a policy statement must be addressed.

Since I came into the information security profession in 1977, we have discussed the need for standardization of the practice. We saw the beginnings of this process when the National Institute of Standards and Technology (NIST) began publishing such documents as *An Introduction to Computer Security: The NIST Handbook* (NIST Special Publication 800-12).

Now the International Organization of Standardization (ISO) has published the recently adopted *Information Technology — Code of Practice for Information Security Management* (ISO 17799) and its parent British Standards (BS 7799). These documents and others, such as *Banking and Related Financial Services — Information Security Guidelines* (ISO/TR 13569), the Health Insurance Portability and Accountability Act (HIPAA), Privacy of Consumer Financial Information (Graham-Leach-Bliley Act), and the Generally Accepted Information Systems Security Practices (GASSP), have stepped into the void and provided all security professionals with a map of where to take the information security program.

Although the title of this book is *Information Security Policies, Procedures, and Standards: Guidelines for Effective Information Security Management,* security is not the end product of these documents. Good security must be measured in how well the assets of the enterprise are protected while the mission and business objectives are met. This book will teach the reader how to develop policies, procedures, and standards that can be used in all aspects of enterprise activities.

# *Chapter 1*

# Overview: Information Protection Fundamentals

The purpose of information protection is to protect the valuable resources of an organization, such as information, hardware, and software. Through the selection and application of appropriate safeguards, security helps the organization to meet its business objectives or mission by protecting its physical and financial resources, reputation, legal position, employees, and other tangible and intangible assets. We examine the elements of computer security, employee roles and responsibilities, and common threats. We also examine the need for management controls, polices and procedures, and risk analysis. Finally, we present a comprehensive list of tasks, responsibilities, and objectives that make up a typical information protection program.

## 1.1   Elements of Information Protection

Information protection should be based on eight major elements:

1.  Information protection should support the business objectives or mission of the enterprise. This idea cannot be stressed enough. All too often, information security personnel lose track of their goals and responsibilities. The position of ISSO (Information Systems Security Officer) has been created to support the enterprise, not the other way around.

2.  Information protection is an integral element of due care. Senior management is charged with two basic responsibilities: a *duty of loyalty*, which means that whatever decisions it makes must be made in the best interest of the enterprise, and a *duty of care*, which means that senior management is required to protect the assets of the

1

enterprise and make informed business decisions. An effective information protection program will assist senior management in performing these duties.

3. Information protection must be cost-effective. Implementing controls
   based on edicts is counter to the business climate. Before any control
   can be proposed, it is necessary to confirm that a significant risk exists.
   Implementing a timely risk analysis process can accomplish this. By
   identifying risks and then proposing appropriate controls, the mission
   and business objectives of the enterprise will be better met.

4. Information protection responsibilities and accountabilities should be
   made explicit. For any program to be effective, it is necessary to publish
   an information protection policy statement and an information protection group mission statement. The policy should identify the roles and
   responsibilities of all employees. To be completely effective, the language of the policy must be incorporated into the purchase agreements
   for all contract personnel and consultants.

5. System owners have information protection responsibilities outside their
   own organization. Access to information often extends beyond the
   business unit or even the enterprise. It is the responsibility of the
   information owner (normally the senior-level manager in the business
   that created the information or the primary user of the information). A
   main responsibility is to monitor usage to ensure that it complies with
   the level of authorization granted to the user.

   If a system has external users, its owners have a responsibility to share
   appropriate knowledge about the existence and general extent of
   control measures so that other users can be confident that the system
   is adequately secure. As the user base expands to include suppliers,
   vendors, clients, customers, shareholders, and the like, it is incumbent
   upon the enterprise to have clear and identifiable controls. For many
   organizations, the initial sign-on screen is the first indication that there
   are controls in place. The message screen should include three basic
   elements:
   a. That the system is for authorized users only
   b. That activities are monitored
   c. That by completing the sign-on process, the user agrees to the
      monitoring

6. Information protection requires a comprehensive and integrated
   approach. To be as effective as possible, it is necessary for information
   protection issues to be part of the system development life cycle.
   During the initial or analysis phase, information protection should
   include a risk analysis, a business impact analysis, and an information
   classification document. Additionally, because information is resident
   in all departments throughout the enterprise, each business unit
   should establish an individual responsible for implementing the information protection program to meet the specific business needs of the
   department.

7. Information protection should be periodically reassessed. As with anything, time changes the needs and objectives. A good information protection program examines itself on a regular basis and makes changes wherever and whenever necessary. This is a dynamic and changing process and therefore must be reassessed at least every 18 months.

8. Information protection is constrained by the culture of the organization. The ISSO must understand that the basic information protection program will be implemented throughout the enterprise. However, each business unit must be given the latitude to make modifications to meet its specific needs. If your organization is multinational, it is necessary to make adjustments for each of the various countries. These adjustments will have to be examined throughout the United States. What might work in Des Moines, Iowa may not fly in Berkeley, California. Provide for the ability to find and implement alternatives.

Information protection is a means to an end and not the end in itself. In business, having an effective information protection program is usually secondary to the need to make a profit. In the public sector, information protection is secondary to the services the agency provides. Security professionals must not lose sight of these tenets.

Computer systems and the information processed on them are often considered critical assets that support the mission of an organization. Protecting them can be as important as protecting other organizational resources, such as financial resources, physical assets, and employees. The cost and benefits of information protection should be carefully examined in both monetary and nonmonetary terms to ensure that the cost of controls does not exceed the expected benefits. Information protection controls should be appropriate and proportionate.

## 1.2 More Than Just Computer Security

Providing effective information protection requires a comprehensive approach that considers a variety of areas both within and outside the information technology area. An information protection program is more than establishing controls for the computer-held data. It should address all forms of information. In 1965, the idea of the "paperless office" was first introduced. The advent of the third-generation computers brought about this concept. However, today the bulk of all the information available to employees and others is still found in printed form. To be an effective program, information protection must move beyond the narrow scope of IT and address the issues of enterprisewide information protection. A comprehensive program must touch every stage of the information asset life cycle, from creation to eventual destruction. The fundamental element to this corporate-wide program is an Information Security Policy that is part of the corporate policies and does not come from IT.

### *1.2.1    Employee Mind-Set toward Controls*

Access to information and the environments that process it are dynamic. Technology and users, data and information in the systems, risk associated with the system, and security requirements are ever-changing. The ability of information protection to support business objectives or the mission of the enterprise may be limited by various factors, such as the current mind-set toward controls.

A highly effective method of measuring the current attitude toward information protection is to conduct a "walkabout." After hours or on a weekend, conduct a review of the workstations throughout a specific area (usually a department or a floor) and look for just five basic control activities:

1.  Offices secured
2.  Desk and cabinets secured
3.  Workstations secured
4.  Information secured
5.  Diskettes secured

Conducting an initial walkabout in the typical office environment will reveal a 90 to 95 percent noncompliance rate with at least one of these basic control mechanisms. The result of this review should be used to form the basis for an initial risk analysis to determine the security requirements for the office environment. When conducting such a review, employee privacy issues must be considered.

## 1.3   Roles and Responsibilities

As discussed before, senior management has the ultimate responsibility for the protection of the organization's information assets. One responsibility is the establishment of the function of Corporate Information Officer (CIO). The CIO directs the day-to-day management of information assets of the organization. The ISSO and Security Administrator should report directly to the CIO and are responsible for the day-to-day administration of the information protection program.

Supporting roles are performed by the service providers and by the Systems Operations team that designs and operates the computer systems. They are responsible for implementing technical security on the systems. The telecommunications department is responsible for providing communication services, including voice, data, video, and fax. Security mechanisms must be implemented to protect these communication services.

The information protection professional must establish strong working relationships with the audit staff. If the only time you see the audit staff is when they are in for a formal audit, then you probably do not have a good working relationship. It is vitally important that this liaison be established and that you meet to discuss common problems at least each quarter.

Other groups include the physical security staff and the contingency planning group. These groups are responsible for establishing and implementing controls and can form a peer group to review and discuss controls. The group responsible for application development methodology will assist in the implementation of information protection requirements in the application system development life cycle. The quality assurance group can assist in ensuring that information protection requirements are included in all development projects prior to movement to production.

The Procurement group can work to get the language of the information protection policies included in the purchase agreements for contract personnel. Education and Training can assist in the development and implementation of information protection awareness programs and in training supervisors on how to monitor employee activities. Human Resources will be the organization responsible for taking appropriate action on any violations of the organization information protection policy.

An example of a typical job description for an information security professional is shown in Exhibit 1.

**Exhibit 1    Typical Job Description**

Director, Design and Strategy

Location:            Anywhere, World
Practice Area:   Corporate Global Security Practice
Grade:

**Purpose:**
To create an information security design and strategy practice that defines the technology structure needed to address the security needs of its clients. The information security design and strategy will complement security and network services developed by the other Global Practice areas. The design and strategy practice will support the clients' information technology and architecture and integrate with each enterprise's business architecture. This security framework will provide for the secure operation of computing platforms, operating systems, and networks, both voice and data, to ensure the integrity of the clients' information assets. To work on corporate initiatives to develop and implement the highest quality security services and ensure that industry best practices are followed in their implementation.

**Working Relationships:**
This position reports in the Global Security Practice to the Vice President, Global Security. Internal contacts are primarily Executive Management, Practice Directors, Regional Management, as well as mentoring and collaborating with consultants. This position will directly manage two professional positions: Manager, Service Provider Security Integration; and Service Provider Security Specialist. Frequent external contacts include building relationships with clients, professional information security organizations, other information security consultants, vendors of hardware, software, and security services, and various regulatory and legal authorities.

*(continued)*

**Exhibit 1    Typical Job Description (continued)**

**Principal Duties and Responsibilities:**

The responsibilities of the Director, Design and Strategy include, but are not limited to, the following:

- Develop global information security services that will provide the security functionality required to protect clients' information assets against unauthorized disclosure, modification, and destruction. Particular focus areas include:

    Virtual private networks
    Data privacy
    Virus prevention
    Secure application architecture
    Service provider security solutions

- Develop information security strategy services that can adapt to clients' diverse and changing technological needs.

- Work with Network and Security practice leaders and consultants, create sample architectures that communicate the security requirements that will meet the needs of all client network implementations.

- Work with practice teams to aid them from the conception phase to the deployment of the project solution. This includes quality assurance review to ensure that the details of the project are correctly implemented according to the service delivery methodology.

- Work with the clients to collect their business requirements for electronic commerce, while educating them on the threats, vulnerabilities, and available risk mitigation strategies.

- Determine where and how you should use cryptography to provide public key infrastructure and secure messaging services for clients.

- Participate in security industry standards bodies to ensure strategic information security needs will be addressed.

- Conduct security focus groups with the clients to cultivate an effective exchange of business plans, product development, and marketing direction to aid in creating new and innovative service offerings to meet client needs.

- Continually evaluate vendors' product strategies and future product statements and advise which will be most appropriate to pursue for alliances, especially in the areas of:

    Virtual private networks
    Data privacy
    Virus prevention
    Secure application architecture
    Service provider security solutions

- Provide direction and oversight of hardware and software-based cryptography service development efforts.

**Accountability:**

Maintain the quality and integrity of the services offered by the Global Security Practice. Review and report impartially on the potential viability and profitability of new security services. Assess the operational efficiency, compliance to industry standards, and effectiveness of the client network designs and strategies that are implemented through the company's professional service offerings. Exercise professional judgment in making recommendations that may impact business operations.

**Exhibit 1    Typical Job Description (continued)**

**Knowledge and Skills:**
- ■ 10 Percent Managerial/Practice Management
  Ability to supervise a multidisciplinary team and a small staff; must handle multiple tasks simultaneously; ability to team with other Practice Directors and Managers to develop strategic service offerings
  Willingness to manage or to personally execute necessary tasks, as resources are required
  Excellent oral, written, and presentation skills
- ■ 40 Percent Technical
  In-depth technical knowledge of information-processing platforms, operating systems, and networks in a global distributed environment
  Ability to identify and apply security techniques to develop services to reduce clients' risk in such an environment
  Technical experience in industrial security, computer systems architecture, design, and development, physical and data security, telecommunications networks, auditing techniques, and risk analysis principles
  Excellent visionary skills that focus on scalability, cost-effectiveness, and implementation ease
- ■ 20 Percent Business
  Knowledge of business information flow in a multinational, multiplatform networked environment
  Solid understanding of corporate dynamics and general business processes; understanding of multiple industries
  Good planning and goal-setting skills
- ■ 20 Percent Interpersonal
  Must possess strong consulting and communication skills
  Ability to work with all levels of management to resolve issues
  Must understand and differentiate between tactical and strategic concepts
  Must be able to weigh business needs with security requirements
  Must be self-motivating

**Attributes:**
Must be mature, self-confident, and performance oriented. Will clearly demonstrate an ability to lead technological decisions. Will establish credibility with personal dedication, attention to detail, and a hands-on approach. Will have a sense of urgency in establishing security designs and strategies to address new technologies to be deployed addressing clients' business needs. Will also be capable of developing strong relationships with all levels of management. Other important characteristics will be the ability to function independently, holding to the highest levels of personal and professional integrity. Will be an excellent communicator and team player.
Specific requirements include:
- ■ Bachelor's degree (Master's degree desirable), advanced degree preferred
- ■ Fifteen or more years of information technology consulting or managerial experience, eight of those years spent in information security positions

*(continued)*

**Exhibit 1    Typical Job Description (continued)**

■ CISSP certification preferred (other appropriate industry or technology certifications desirable)

**Potential Career Path Opportunities:**
Opportunities for progression to a VP position within the company

## 1.4   Common Threats

Information processing systems are vulnerable to many threats that can inflict various types of damage resulting in significant losses. This damage can range from errors harming database integrity to fires destroying entire complexes. Losses can stem from the actions of supposedly trusted employees defrauding a system, from outside hackers, or from careless data entry. Precision in estimating information protection-related losses is not possible because many losses are never discovered, and others are covered up to avoid unfavorable publicity.

The typical computer criminal is an authorized, nontechnical user of the system who has been around long enough to determine what actions would cause a "red flag" or an audit. The typical computer criminal is an employee. According to a recent survey in the "Current and Future Danger: A CSI Primer on Computer Crime & Information Warfare," more than 80 percent of the respondents identified employees as a threat or potential threat to information security. Also included in this survey were the competition, contract personnel, public interest groups, suppliers, and foreign governments.

The chief threat to information protection is still errors and omissions. This concern continues to make up 65 percent of all information protection problems. Users, data entry personnel, system operators, programmers, and the like frequently make errors that contribute directly or indirectly to this problem.

Dishonest employees make up another 13 percent of information protection problems. Fraud and theft can be committed by insiders and outsiders, but are more likely to be done by employees. In a related area, disgruntled employees make up another 10 percent of the problem. Employees are most familiar with the information assets and processing systems of the organization, including knowing what actions might cause the most damage, mischief, or sabotage.

Common examples of information protection-related employee sabotage include destroying hardware or facilities, planting malicious code (viruses, worms, Trojan horses, etc.) to destroy data or programs, entering data incorrectly, deleting data, altering data, and holding data "hostage."

The loss of the physical facility or the supporting infrastructure (power failures, telecommunications disruptions, water outage and leaks, sewer problems, lack of transportation, fire, flood, civil unrest, strikes, etc.) can lead to serious problems and makes up eight percent of information protection-related problems.

The final area is malicious *hackers* or *crackers*. These terms refer to those who break into computers without authorization or exceed the level of authorization granted to them. Although these problems receive the largest amount of press coverage, they only account for five to eight percent of the total picture. They are real and they can cause a great deal of damage. But when attempting to allocate limited information protection resources, it may be better to concentrate efforts in other areas. To be certain, conduct a risk analysis to see what your exposure might be.

## 1.5   Policies and Procedures

An information protection policy is the documentation of enterprisewide decisions on handling and protecting information. In making these decisions, managers face hard choices involving resource allocation, competing objectives, and organization strategy related to protecting both technical and information resources as well as guiding employee behavior.

When creating an information protection policy, it is best to understand that information is an asset of the enterprise and is the property of the organization. As such, information reaches beyond the boundaries of IT and is present in all areas of the enterprise. To be effective, an information protection policy must be part of the organization asset management program and must be enterprisewide.

There are as many forms, styles, and kinds of policy as there are organizations, businesses, agencies, and universities. In addition to the various forms, each organization has a specific culture or mental model of what a policy is, how it is to look, and who should approve the document. The key point here is that every organization needs an information protection policy. According to the 2000 CSI report on Computer Crime, 65 percent of respondents to its survey admitted that they do not have a written policy. The beginning of an information protection program is the implementation of a policy. The program policy creates the attitude of the organization toward information and announces internally and externally that information is an asset and the property of the organization and is to be protected from unauthorized access, modification, disclosure, and destruction.

This book leads the policy writer through the key structure elements and then reviews some typical policy contents. Because policies are not enough, this book teaches the reader how to develop standards, procedures, and guidelines. In each section the reader is given advice on the structural mechanics of the various documents as well as actual examples.

## 1.6   Risk Management

Risk is the possibility of something adverse happening. The process of risk management is identifying those risks, assessing the likelihood of their occurrence, and then taking steps to reduce the risk to an acceptable level. All risk analysis processes use the same methodology. Determine the asset to be reviewed. Identify the risk, issues, threats, or vulnerabilities. Assess the probability of the risk occurring and the impact to the asset or the organization should the risk be realized. Then identify controls that would bring the impact to an acceptable level.

The 2001 CRC Press book titled *Information Security Risk Analysis* discusses effective risk analysis methodologies. The book takes the reader through the theory of risk analysis:

- Identify the asset
- Identify the risks
- Prioritize the risks
- Identify controls and safeguards

The book helps the reader understand qualitative risk analysis and then gives examples of this process. To make certain that the reader receives a well-rounded exposure to risk analysis, the book presents eight different methods, ending with the Facilitated Risk Analysis Process (FRAP).

The primary function of information protection risk management is the identification of appropriate controls. In every assessment of risk, there will be many areas for which it will not be obvious what kind of controls are appropriate. The goal of controls is not to have 100 percent security. Total security would mean zero productivity. Controls must never lose sight of the business objectives or mission of the enterprise. Whenever there is a contest for supremacy, controls lose, productivity wins. This is not a contest, however. The goal of information protection is to provide a safe and secure environment for management to meet its duty of care.

When selecting controls, you will need to consider many factors, including the information protection policy of the organization, the legislation and regulations that govern your enterprise, along with safety, reliability, and quality requirements. Remember that every control will require some performance requirements. These performance requirements may be a reduction in user response time, additional requirements before applications are moved into production, or additional costs.

When considering controls, the initial implementation cost is only the tip of the cost iceberg. The long-term cost for maintenance and monitoring must be identified. Be sure to examine any and all technical requirements and cultural constraints. If your organization is multinational, control measures that work and are accepted in your home country might not be accepted in other countries.

Accept residual risk. At some point management must decide if the operation of a specific process or system is acceptable, given the risk. There can be any number of reasons that a risk must be accepted. These include but are not limited to:

- The type of risk may be different from previous risks.
- The risk may be technical and difficult for a layperson to grasp.
- The current environment may make it difficult to identify the risk.

Information protection professionals sometimes forget that the managers hired by our organizations have the responsibility to make decisions. The job of the ISSO is to help the information asset owners identify risks to the assets. Assist them in identifying possible controls and then allow them to determine their action plan. Sometimes, they will choose to accept the risk, and this is perfectly permissible.

## 1.7 Typical Information Protection Program

Over the years, the computer security group responsible for access control and disaster recovery planning has evolved into the enterprisewide information protection group. Included in their ever-expanding roles and responsibilities are:

- Firewall control
- Risk analysis
- Business impact analysis
- Virus control and virus response
- Computer emergency response
- Computer crime investigation
- Records management
- Encryption
- E-mail, voice-mail, Internet, video-mail policy
- Enterprisewide information protection program
- Industrial espionage controls
- Contract personnel nondisclosure agreements
- Legal issues
- Internet monitoring
- Disaster planning
- Business continuity planning
- Digital signature
- Secure single sign-on
- Information classification
- Local area networks
- Modem control
- Remote access
- Security awareness programs

In addition to these elements, the security professional now has to ensure that standards, both in the United States and worldwide, are examined and acted upon where appropriate. This book discusses these new standards in detail.

## 1.8 Summary

The role of the information protection professional has changed over the past 25 years and will change again and again. Implementing controls to be in compliance with audit requirements is not the way to run such a program. There are limited resources available for controls. To be effective, information owners and users must accept the controls. To meet this end, it will be necessary for information protection professionals to establish partnerships with their constituency. Work with your owners and users to find an appropriate level of controls. Understand the needs of the business or the mission of your organization. Make certain that information protection supports those goals and objectives.

# Chapter 2

# Writing Mechanics and the Message

This chapter first discusses writing mechanics; and then it examines what the new standards identify as content material for a security policy. When we have provided the infrastructure for policy writing, we then examine the policy structure (this is done in Chapter 3).

We begin this chapter with a discussion on attention spans. Most of us can understand that attention spans seem to have shrunk over the years. We then examine the reading and comprehension level of employees. These two elements lead us to the need to develop an effective "grabber" to gain the readers' attention and then to keep them interested.

The final elements discussed in this chapter are the mechanics of a topic sentence and why it is important. We also review the thesis statement, which is part of our discussion on *topic-specific policies*. When you are writing policies, standards, and procedures, many of the covenants of writing will be abandoned, but an effective topic sentence or thesis statement is vitally important to retain and enhance.

## 2.1 Attention Spans

There are clear and compelling reasons an effective topic sentence is important in catching the reader's attention and keeping it. The first of these is time constraints. Employees do not have a lot of time to search for the meaning of a policy. They need to see it right up-front, and it must explain why it is important to them. Calvin Coolidge was a man of few words, but he got his point across. During a dinner at the White House, sitting next to him was a woman who needed only a warm body to have a "conversation." After nattering on for a long period of time, she said to President Coolidge, "I have a bet that I can make you say more than three words." Coolidge looked at her and said, "You lose."

It is not the number of words that you say or write; in fact, most of our employees tune out long before there is an end to the topic. Have you ever found yourself thinking about other things when someone else is talking or while attempting to read something? To get the message to our employees requires the proper selection of words to gain maximum impact. You no longer have unlimited time to get the message out. To survive in business today, you must be able to get you message to your employee in less than a minute.

Along with time, the next constraint is attention span. Recently, I attended a training session on the attention span of individuals. As a trainer, I always like to keep up on what will make me better in getting my ideas out. During this session we were shown a film clip of the old *Jack Benny Show,* a program that ran during the late 1950s through the early 1960s. We were asked to count the number of seconds between camera angle changes. We were able to count seven or eight seconds between changes. Then we were shown a clip of the *Brady Bunch* (1970s). The change time was about four seconds. Then we were shown a music video and counted one second between camera angle changes.

When I was growing up, the average television commercial ran 60 seconds. Today, the average commercial runs 15 to 30 seconds. If you sit through a 60-second commercial today, you will think you have just sat through *War and Peace.*

According to Milo O. Frank, the author of *How to Get Your Point across in 30 Seconds or Less*, the attention span of the average individual is 30 seconds. To match this limited time frame of attention span, the writer needs to get the message out to the reader in an average of 100 words. Now some of us read faster than others and some read slower, but the average of 100 words will put you pretty much on target.

With the limited time frame and the concept of attention span now revealed to you, it will be necessary for you to understand some key concepts (see Exhibit 1).

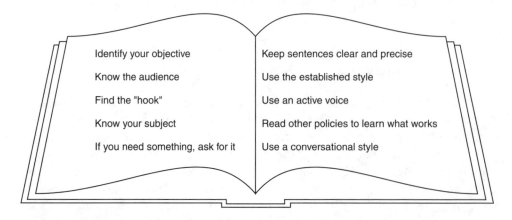

**Exhibit 1   Key Concepts**

## 2.2  Key Concepts

- *Identify your objectives* — Before you begin to develop a policy, standard, or procedure, you will have to know what it is that you are going to discuss. It cannot be some abstract concept. You will need a clear vision of what needs to be accomplished in the document before you.
- *Know your audience* — As important as it is to know what you are going to write about, it is also necessary to know who your audience is. When writing a policy, the audience will often be the general employee population (all employees); when writing procedures, the audience will be much narrower. The success or failure of your policies, standards, and procedures will depend on how well you focus in on the intended audience.
- *Find the hook* — Employees need to know how the document impacts their life. So establish quickly why it is important to the intended reader. This kind of statement is generally used to get people's attention. The hook must relate to the objective and how they are affected.
- *Know your subject* — The best-written policies, standards, and procedures are those that properly address the topic. Research how others have addressed the topics you need to address. The best place to find this kind of information is through your local chapter of the Information Systems Security Association (ISSA), which can be found by accessing its Web site (www.issa.org) or by searching the Internet. Whatever it takes, it is necessary for you to know as much as possible about your topic.
- *If you need something, ask for it* — A policy or procedure without a specific objective is a wasted opportunity. If there is a need for a response or a compliance issue, make certain that the reader is told what is expected and what the time frame is.
- *Keep sentences clear and precise* — Now is not the time to create your doctoral thesis. Keep the message brief and to the point. Do not use unnecessary words or show off your newfound vocabulary. This concept harks back to knowing your audience. Use the language of your enterprise when developing a general policy statement and the language of the specific department for a topic-specific policy or procedure.
- *Use the established style* — Research the style and format of existing policies and procedures. Do not become innovative; stick to what is expected. The policy or procedure will be better accepted if it looks like what the readers are used to.
- *Use an active voice* — A sentence in which the performer of the action is the subject of the verb is said to be in the active voice. In passive sentences, the subject is acted upon; passive sentences use passive voice. For example:

    Passive voice: The software is written by the programmer.

    Active voice: The programmer writes the software.

The choice between using the active or passive voice in writing is a matter of style, not correctness. However, most handbooks recommend using active voice, which they describe as more natural, direct, lively, and succinct. The passive voice is considered wordy and weak.

- *Read other policies* — Not just information security policies, but as many policies as possible. When I was traveling to Malaysia, the airline staff passed out landing documentation forms and among them was a policy statement for a country that read "Drug smuggling is punishable by death." Later, I was teaching a class on policy writing and asked my students if this was a policy. I was informed that not only was it a policy, but it was enforced. The key point here is that a policy does not have to be a large document. So read other policies and procedures and see how they handle the topic.
- *Use a conversational style* — This is a matter of preference, but over the years I have found that using a style that is most like a conversation is the best way to get the message out to the audience.

## 2.3   Topic Sentence and Thesis Statement

During the development of policies and procedures, we will be using two key writing terms: topic sentence and thesis sentence. So before we can begin to discuss the structure of policies, it is important to take a few minutes to cover these most important topics.

A *topic sentence* is a general statement that expresses the main idea of a paragraph. A paragraph is a group of sentences that develop one main idea. The main idea is the general statement that the other sentences support or explain.

The topic sentence has two main parts:

- *Subject* — What the paragraph is about
- *Focus* — What the paragraph will say about the subject

Examples:

Most adults/find learning a foreign language difficult.
   subject   /                    focus

Telephones/intrude into the privacy of our daily lives.
   subject   /                    focus

Parents of teenagers/often feel unappreciated.
   subject              /                    focus

A topic sentence sets up one paragraph, which is usually less than a page of text; therefore, the topic sentence should be general, but not too general.

| Too general: | Security is important. |
|---|---|
| Still too general: | Information security is important for the business. |
| Much better: | Business-related information is an asset of the enterprise and is the property of the company and all employees are responsible for protecting this asset. |

General guidelines for creating effective topic sentences are as follows:

- A topic sentence should always be a complete sentence.
- A topic sentence should not merely state a single fact.
- A topic sentence should be a general statement, but should not be too broad or too vague.

A topic sentence may come at the beginning, as the second sentence, at the end, or may be implied. In academic writing assignments, many instructors (but not all) seem to prefer that the topic sentence come at the beginning of the paragraph. To be most effective, it is strongly recommended that it be the opening sentence of any policy or procedure.

The other writing element is the *thesis statement*. We will use this form of writing when we discuss the topic-specific policy statement. By discussing it here, we will be able to move through the structure elements of policies more quickly.

Everything you write should develop around a clear central thesis. Your thesis is the backbone of your policy or procedure. Ask yourself, "What is the main point of this document?" Your answer should resemble the thesis statement of your policy and should focus your central ideas into one or two sentences.

When developing a thesis statement, it is best to avoid starting your thesis sentence with "It is the policy of…." Furthermore, tackling two topics at once (even if they seem related) should be avoided as much as possible. Pick one and stick with it.

## 2.4  The Message

A few years ago I took a speed-reading class, and one of the things we learned was how to read a textbook for review. When reviewing a chapter, read all the captions, graphs, and illustrations first; then read the opening paragraph in its entirety, the opening sentence of the other paragraphs, and the closing paragraph in its entirety. The message must come through clearly and precisely and be reinforced in each of the subsequent paragraphs.

It cannot be stressed enough that the opening one or two sentences must grab the readers and tell them what is important and why it impacts them. As we begin to discuss the structure of the policy statement in Chapter 3, you will begin to see examples of where this has been done successfully and where it needs more work.

## 2.5  Writing Don't's

Over the years, I have taught a number of classes on writing policies and procedures. To ensure that the students maintain an effective attention span, I use bits of humor to get the point across. The following is an example of this kind of writing humor, but the statements are true.

### 2.5.1  How to Write Well

1. Avoid alliteration. Always.
2. Prepositions are not words to end sentences with.
3. Avoid clichés like the plague. (They are old hat.)
4. Employ the vernacular.
5. Eschew ampersands & abbreviations, etc.
6. Parenthetical remarks (however relevant) are unnecessary.
7. It is wrong to ever split an infinitive.
8. Contractions aren't necessary.
9. Foreign words and phrases are not apropos.
10. One should never generalize.
11. Eliminate quotations. As Ralph Waldo Emerson once said: "I hate quotations. Tell me what you know."
12. Comparisons are as bad as clichés.
13. Do not be redundant; do not use more words than necessary; it is highly superfluous.
14. Profanity sucks.
15. Be more or less specific.
16. Understatement is always best.
17. Exaggeration is a billion times worse than understatement.
18. One-word sentences? Eliminate.
19. Analogies in writing are like feathers on a snake.
20. The passive voice is to be avoided.
21. Go around the barn at high noon to avoid colloquialisms.
22. Even if a mixed metaphor sings, it should be derailed.
23. Who needs rhetorical questions?

## 2.6  Summary

In this chapter we discussed the writing mechanics and concepts to use to get the message out to the reader. Included in this discussion were:

- Attention span
- Keeping the topic up-front
- Amount of time before we lose the reader
- Writing concepts
- Identifying the objective

- Knowing the audience
- Finding a hook
- Knowing the subject
- Asking for what is needed from the reader
- Keeping sentences clear and precise
- Using established forms of documents
- Using an active voice
- Reading other policies
- Using a conversational style
- Topic sentence and thesis statements
- Writing don't's

When you need to write policies, standards, and procedures, you will have an overwhelming desire to start writing. But take the time to determine what needs to be done and how you will do it. Do your research. There are no new policies. Whatever you need to write about, you should be able to find an example that can be used to guide you along in your development. Try to avoid the temptation of taking an existing policy and just changing the names. It might work, but the odds that this kind of quick fix will meet the specific business objectives of your organization are very small.

In Chapter 3 we discuss the policy statement, its structure, and ISO 17799 suggested contents.

# Chapter 3

# Policy Development

The cornerstone of an effective information security architecture is a well-written policy statement. This is the wellspring of all other directives, standards, procedures, guidelines, and other supporting documents. As with any foundation, it is important to establish a strong footing. As will be discussed, a policy performs two roles: one internal and one external.

The internal portion tells employees what is expected of them and how their actions will be judged. The external portion tells the world how the enterprise is run, that there are policies that support sound business practices, and that the organization understands that protection of assets is vital to the successful execution of its mission.

In any discussion regarding written requirements, the term *policy* has more than one meaning. To some, a policy is the directive of senior management on how a certain program is to be run, what its goals and objectives are, and to whom responsibilities are to be assigned. The term *policy* may refer to the specific security rules for a particular system such as ACF2 rule sets, RACF permits, or intrusion-detection system policies. Additionally, policy may refer to entirely different matters, such as specific management decisions that set an organization's e-mail privacy policy or Internet usage policy.

This chapter examines three different forms of policy statements: the general program policy, the topic-specific policy, and the system/application-specific policy.

## 3.1 Policy Definitions

### 3.1.1 Policy

A *policy* is a high-level statement of enterprise beliefs, goals, and objectives and the general means for their attainment for a specified subject area. A policy should be brief (which is highly recommended) and set at a high level.

### 3.1.2    General Program Policy

A *general program policy* sets the strategic directions of the enterprise for global behavior and assigns resources for its implementation. This includes such topics as information management, conflict of interest, employee standards of conduct, and general security measures.

### 3.1.3    Topic-Specific Policy

*Topic-specific policy* addresses specific issues of concern to the organization. Topic-specific policies might include e-mail policy, Internet usage policy, phone usage, physical security, application development, system maintenance, and network security.

### 3.1.4    System/Application-Specific Policy

*System/application-specific policies* focus on decisions taken by management to protect a particular application or system. System/application-specific policy might include controls established for the financial management system, accounts payable, business expense forms, employee appraisal, and order inventory.

## 3.2    Frequently Asked Questions

### 3.2.1  What Is a Security Policy?

Security policy is defined as a high-level statement of organizational beliefs, goals, and objectives and the general means for their attainment as related to the protection of organizational assets. A security policy is brief, is set at a high level, and never states "how" to accomplish the objectives.

Because policy is written at a high level, organizations must develop standards, guidelines, and procedures that offer those affected by the policy one or more possible methods for implementing the policy and meeting the business objectives or mission of the organization.

### 3.2.2    What Should Be in a Policy?

When developing the policy, there is as much danger in saying too much as there is in saying too little. The more intricate and detailed the policy, the more frequent the update requirements and the more complicated the training process for those who must adhere to it.

The policy should define the goal or business purpose for its existence, the policy statement, the scope or affected parties/locations/legal entities, and the individual responsibilities of those charged with the implementation and enforcement of the policy. The policy, because it is at the highest level, provides for management discretion in the actual implementation of processes to meet the intent of the policy.

### 3.2.3    Why Should an Enterprise or Service Provider Implement an Information Security Policy?

In the absence of an established policy, the current and past activities of the organization become the *de facto* policy. Where there is no formal policy, the organization may be in greater danger of a breach of security, loss of competitive advantage, loss of customer confidence, and increased governmental interference. By implementing policies, the organization takes control of its destiny and reduces the likelihood that the internal or external auditors or courts will step in to set policy that may stifle the business instead of supporting it.

### 3.2.4    Can the Enterprise or Service Provider Get Along with Unwritten Policy?

Many organizations, especially new ventures, seem to get along with informal policies. These exist, much like folklore and customs, and are passed from one employee to another through word of mouth. Why, then, are written and published policies necessary? Information, the intangible asset of every organization, is a unique asset. There is often a great deal of confusion about how to handle information, how to classify information, and who has the ultimate responsibility for the information.

There may be legal or regulatory reasons an information security policy must be published. But the primary reason for having a written and published policy is that only a written policy can be used to prove the management standard of "due diligence" to a court of law, in a customer contract, in vendor relations, in acquisitions, and for public relations.

### 3.2.5    Are There Regulatory Reasons for Policy Implementation?

The International Organization for Standardization, founded in 1947, is a worldwide federation of national standards bodies from approximately 100 countries, one from each country. Among the standards it fosters is Open Systems Interconnection (OSI), a universal reference model for communication protocols. Many countries have national standards organizations, such as the American National Standards Institute (ANSI), that participate in and contribute to ISO standards development.*

A new ISO standard has been adopted for information security. This new standard, published in December 2000, is noted as ISO 17799. Registration to

---

\*    "ISO" is not an abbreviation. It is a word, derived from the Greek *isos*, meaning "equal," which is the root for the prefix "iso-" that occurs in a host of terms, such as "isometric" (of equal measure or dimensions) and "isonomy" (equality of laws, or of people before the law). The name ISO is used around the world to denote the organization, thus avoiding the assortment of abbreviations that would result from the translation of "International Organization for Standardization" into the different national languages of members. Whatever the country, the short form of the organization's name is always ISO.

ISO 17799 will provide the guidelines for security information management systems. Further, it promotes a managerial system for safeguarding information and its confidentiality and integrity. Registration will objectively demonstrate that a management system has implemented internationally recognized business controls for information security.

The ISO 17799 standard discusses ten areas, and item number one is an *information security policy*. The objective is to provide management direction and support for information security. Enterprise senior management should set clear direction and demonstrate its support for and commitment to information security through the issue of an information security policy across the entire enterprise.

The U.S. Federal Sentencing Guidelines for Criminal Activities define executive responsibility for fraud, theft, and anti-trust violations and establish a mandatory point system for U.S. federal judges to determine appropriate punishment. Because much fraud and falsification of corporate data involves access to computer-held data, liability established under the guidelines extends to computer-related crime as well. What causes concern for many executives is that the mandatory punishment could apply to them even when intruders enter a computer system and perpetrate a crime.

In addition to the mandatory scoring system for punishment, the guidelines also have an incentive for proactive crime prevention. The requirement is for management to show "due diligence" in establishing an effective compliance program. There are seven elements that capture the basic functions inherent in most compliance programs:

1. Establish policies, standards, and procedures to guide the workforce.
2. Appoint a high-level manager to oversee compliance with the policy, standards, and procedures.
3. Exercise due care when granting discretionary authority to employees.
4. Assure compliance policies are being carried out.
5. Communicate the standards and procedures to all employees and others.
6. Enforce the policies, standards, and procedures consistently through appropriate disciplinary measures.
7. Establish procedures for corrections and modifications in case of violations.

### 3.2.6 Are There Other Reasons to Implement Policies?

Information is a unique enough asset to warrant a written statement regarding its protection. Although there are legal and regulatory reasons to implement policies, standards, and procedures, the bottom line is that good controls make good business sense. Failing to implement controls can lead to financial penalties in the form of fines and costs. Such activities can lead to loss of customer confidence, competitive advantage, and ultimately, loss of business. By implementing proper controls, documenting them in writing, and communicating them to all affected individuals and entities, the organization can realize real cost benefit by avoiding public criticism and saving time on the investigation and subsequent disciplinary process.

Most importantly, only a written policy can be convincing in courts of law, customer contracts, vendor relations, acquisitions, and public relations.

## 3.3  Policies Are Not Enough: A Preliminary Look at Standards, Guidelines, and Procedures

A general program policy (GPP) is written at a broad level and, as such, will require supporting standards, procedures, and guidelines. Standards, procedures, and guidelines provide a clearer direction for employees, managers, and others by offering a more-detailed approach to implementing policy and meeting the business objectives or mission of the organization.

A policy is not a specific and detailed description of the problem and each step that is needed to implement the policy. For example, a policy on requiring access control for remote users has exceeded its scope if there is a discussion about passwords, password length, password history, etc. Standards and guidelines (which are discussed in Chapter 5) specify technologies and methodologies to be used to secure systems. Procedures are the detailed steps required to accomplish a particular task or process.

Enterprise standards specify a uniform suite of specific technologies, parameters, or procedures to be used by those wishing to access enterprise resources. Enterprise standards should not be confused with British Standards 7799 (BS 7799), the ISO 17799 (published in December 2000), the Australian-New Zealand 44 44 (ANZ 44 44), the Generally Accepted System Security Principles (GASSP), or other national or international documents.

Enterprise guidelines are implemented to assist the user community, support personnel, and others in secure access to enterprise information and system resources. Guidelines, however, attempt to provide business units and others with alternatives to increase levels of control where deemed appropriate. Where a standard is mandatory, a guideline is a suggestion.

Enterprise procedures normally assist with compliance to applicable policies, standards, and guidelines. They are the detailed steps to be followed by users, support personnel, or others to accomplish a particular task.

Many organizations issue overall information security manuals, regulations, handbooks, practices and procedures, or other similar documents. These documents are a closely linked mix of policy, standards, guidelines, and procedures. Although such documents serve as a useful tool, it is important to distinguish between a policy and its implementation elements. Policy requires approval of management, while standards, guidelines, and procedures can be modified as needed to support changing environments. Standards, guidelines, and procedures promote flexibility and cost-effectiveness by allowing alternative approaches to the implementation process.

## 3.4   Policy, Standards, Guidelines, and Procedures: Definitions and Examples

### 3.4.1  Definitions

*Policy* — A policy is a high-level statement of enterprise beliefs, goals, and objectives and the general means for their attainment for a specified subject area.

*Standards* — Standards are mandatory activities, actions, rules, or regulations designed to provide policies with the support structure, and specific direction they require to be meaningful and effective. They are often expensive to administer and, therefore, should be used judiciously.

*Guidelines* — Guidelines are more general statements designed to achieve the policy objectives by providing a framework within which to implement procedures. Where standards are mandatory, guidelines are recommendations.

*Procedures* — Procedures spell out the specifics of how the policy and the supporting standards and guidelines will actually be implemented in an operating environment.

### 3.4.2   Example 1 — Access to Company Information Is Restricted

*Policy:* Access to company information systems is restricted to authorized users only.

*Standard:* Users are required to have a unique UserID and a confidential password.

*Guideline:* Passwords should be five to eight alphanumeric characters

*Procedure:* UserID and password requests must contain a signature of the authorized information owner. Approval signatures shall be verified against the company *Authorized Signatures Reference Manual.*

### 3.4.3   Example 2 — Custodians Should Provide a Safe and Secure Environment

*Policy:* Information *custodians* are responsible for providing a safe and secure processing environment in which information can be maintained with integrity.

*Standard: Custodians* of information processing systems must ensure that the system is free from destructive software elements (such as viruses), which would impair the normal and expected operation of the system.

*Guidelines:* Where available, a virus prevention, detection, and recovery package should be installed. Employees with access to computer systems should attend a training session on the virus threat to understand

**Exhibit 1   Policy Diagram**

the damage a virus infection can inflict and understand their personal responsibility for protecting their own systems.

*Procedures:* Viruses are often transmitted through public-domain software. Software that is public domain (i.e., non-licensed software also called "shareware" or "freeware") or the employee's personal property shall not be permitted on company equipment without the explicit authorization of organization management and after being certified as virus-free.

Employees are to turn off or lock up desktop systems at the end of the workday to prevent unauthorized access and possible virus contamination.

Employees are to use the "write protection" tabs on diskettes whenever possible.

Employees are to report any type of unauthorized access, theft, or virus infection to the Information Protection group or the Help Desk upon discovery.

## 3.5   Policy Key Elements

To meet the needs of an organization, a good policy should:

- *Be easy to understand.* As discussed in Chapter 2, it is important that the material presented meet the requirements of the intended audience. All too often, policies, standards, and procedures are written by subject matter experts and then given to a general-use audience. The material is often written at a college level when the average reading and comprehension level in the workplace is that of a sixth grader (a 12-year-old).
- *Be applicable.* When creating policy, the writer may research other organizations and copy that document verbatim. However, it is important to ensure that whatever is written meets the needs of your specific organization.

- *Be doable.* Can the organization and its employees still meet business objectives if the policy is implemented? I have seen many organizations that have written the ultimate security policy, only to find out that it was so restrictive that the mission of the organization was placed at risk.
- *Be enforceable.* Do not write a self-defeating policy. A policy may state, "Use of the company-provided telephone is for business calls only." For most organizations, this may in fact be the policy, but almost every phone in the facility is used daily for personal calls. What might make a better policy is one that says, "Company-provided telephones are to be used for management-approved functions only." This opens up some latitude and still meets the business need.
- *Be phased in.* It may be necessary to allow the organization to read and digest the policy before it takes effect. Many organizations publish a policy and then require the business units to submit a compliance plan within a specific number of days after publication. This provides the business unit managers a period of time to review the policy, determine where their organization may be deficient, and then submit a timetable for compliance. These compliance letters are normally kept on file and are made available to the audit staff.
- *Be proactive.* State what has to be done. Do not get into the routine of making pronouncements — "Thou shalt not!!!!" Try to state what can be done and what is expected of the employees.
- *Avoid absolutes.* Never say never. Be diplomatic and understand the politically correct way to say things. When discussing sanctions for noncompliance, some organizations have stated, "Employees violating this policy will be subject to disciplinary sanctions up to and including dismissal without warning," when the policy could better have stated something like, "Employees found in noncompliance with this policy will be deemed in violation of the Employee Standards of Conduct." The Standards of Conduct state that employees will suffer disciplinary sanctions up to and including dismissal. Use the kinder, gentler approach.
- *Meet business objectives.* Security professionals should remember that the controls must help the organization reach an acceptable level of risk. A 100 percent security program could mean zero percent productivity. Whenever controls or policy impact the business objectives or mission of the organization, then the controls and policy will lose. Work to understand that the policy exists to support the business, not the other way around.

## 3.6  Policy Format and Basic Policy Components

The actual format (layout) of a policy will depend on what policies look like within a specific organization. It is very important that any policy developed look like published policies from the organization. Some members of the review panel will be unable to read and critique the new policy if it does not look like a policy.

Policies are generally brief (in comparison to procedures and practices), usually not much more than a page or two of material.

> Information is an asset and the property of the organization. All employees are responsible for protecting that asset from unauthorized access, modification, disclosure, or destruction.

When creating policies, it is helpful to understand that there are generally three types of policies that will be used during the development of a security document:

1. *General policy* — This is used to create the overall information security vision of an organization.
2. *Topic-specific policies* — These address specific topics of concern. There will normally be a topic-specific policy for each section of an information security document.
3. *Application-specific policies* — These focus on decisions taken by management to protect particular applications or systems.

### 3.6.1   *Program Policy*

Senior management is responsible for issuing a program policy to establish the information security policy of the organization and its basic construction. This high-level policy defines the intent of the information security program and its scope within the organization. It also assigns responsibilities for implementation and compliance with the policy.

The components of a program policy should include:

- *Topic* — The topic portion of the policy normally defines the goals of the program. When discussing information, most program policies concentrate on protecting the confidentiality, integrity, availability, and authenticity of the information resources. Additionally, it will attempt to establish that information is an item of value to the enterprise and, as such, must be protected from unauthorized access, modification, disclosure, and destruction, whether accidental or deliberate.
- *Scope* — The scope is a way to broaden or narrow the topic, such as "all information wherever stored and however generated." This could expand the topic on information security, whereas a statement like "computer-generated data only" would sharply narrow the topic scope. The scope statement can also broaden or narrow the audience affected by the policy. For example, the statement, "the policy is intended for all employees," pretty much takes in all of the people working for the enterprise, whereas, "that personnel with access to top-secret information" would limit the audience.
- *Responsibilities* — Typically, this section of the policy identifies three or more specific roles and their responsibilities. The first role discussed is that of management and it is typically charged with implementing

and supporting the program. Employees are responsible for adhering to the policy and reporting any suspected problems to management. The policy could also establish an office responsible for day-to-day administration of the policy.

- *Compliance* — The policy will generally discuss two issues regarding compliance:

  a. Who is responsible for ensuring compliance to the policy objectives. Two specific groups are usually identified:

     i.   First-line supervision and its role in monitoring employee activities

     ii.  The internal audit staff and its responsibility to conduct formal reviews

  b. What happens when the policy is violated. When developing and implementing the policy, keep in mind that violations of the policy may be unintentional. The violation could be a result of lack of training and awareness. Therefore, it will be necessary to establish a review process for each violation case-by-case, as opposed to creating mandatory sanctions. Allow management some leeway when reviewing problems.

### 3.6.2  Topic-Specific Policy

In each section of the procedure document, the material begins with the policy statement of the organization. Unlike the program policy, the topic-specific policy narrows the focus to one issue at a time. Hence, we discuss creating a procedure document to support the policy statement. It will be in this document or, in some cases, in stand-alone policies where this approach will be used.

The basic components of a topic-specific policy include the following:

- *Thesis statement* — To establish a policy on a specific topic, the writer must interview management and determine the relevant issues to be addressed. As in the *Intent* section of the program policy, the goals and objectives of the policy should be identified.
- *Relevance* — The topic-specific policy also needs to establish to whom the policy applies. In addition to whom, the policy will want to clarify where, how, and when the policy is applicable. Is the policy only enforced when employees are in the work-site campus or will it extend to off-site activities?
- *Responsibilities* — The establishment of roles and responsibilities is usually included in the topic-specific policy. When responsibilities are documented in a policy or procedure, it is always best to identify the position or job title rather than an individual by name. Job functions are usually more permanent than people.
- *Compliance* — Here it may be appropriate to describe in some detail the behavior that is unacceptable and the consequences of that behavior. The responsibility for monitoring compliance should also be identified.

- *Additional information* — For a topic-specific policy, a list that identifies individuals (by job title) and departments that the user can contact for additional information should be made available. Where to obtain copies of associated procedures should also be included.

### 3.6.3   Application-Specific Policy

Program-level and topic-specific policy both address policy from a broad level; they usually encompass the entire enterprise. The application-specific policy focuses on one specific system or application. As the construction of security architecture for an organization takes shape, the final element will be the translation of program and topic-specific policies to the application and system levels.

Many security issue decisions apply only at the application or system level. Some examples include:

- Who has the authority to read or modify application data?
- Under what circumstances can data be read or modified?
- How is remote access to be controlled?

To develop a comprehensive set of system security policies, use a process that determines security rules (policy) based on business and mission objectives.

- Define the business objectives; then establish which security tools will support those objectives.
- Establish the rules for operating the application or system. Determine who has access to what resources and when.
- Determine if automated security tools can help administer the policy.

## 3.7   Policy Content Considerations

A policy document should be approved by management, published, and communicated, as appropriate, to all employees. It should state management commitment and set out the organization's approach to managing information security. As a minimum, the following guidance should be included:

- A definition of information security, its overall objectives and scope, and the importance of security as an enabling mechanism for information sharing
- A statement of management intention, supporting the goals and principles of information security
- A brief explanation of specific security policies, standards, and compliance requirements, including:
  Compliance with legislative and contractual requirements
  Security awareness and education requirements

Prevention and detection of viruses and other malicious software
Business continuity planning
Consequences of security policy violations
- A definition of general and specific responsibilities for information security management, including security incident reporting
- References to documentation that may support the policy, e.g., more detailed security policies and procedures for specific information systems and security rules with which users should comply

This policy should be communicated throughout the enterprise in a form that is relevant, accessible, and understandable to the intended reader.

## 3.8  Program Policy Examples

The following are actual program policy statements for information security. As you read through them, examine them for the key element structure:

- Topic
- Scope
- Responsibilities
    Senior management
    Line management or supervision
    Employee
- Compliance
    Business unit noncompliance
    Employee noncompliance

We examine a number of actual information security policy statements. As we examine each one, please use the above four items as a checklist to determine the completeness of each policy.

### 3.8.1  Example 1 — A Utility Company

Information is a valuable corporate asset. Business continuity is heavily dependent upon the integrity and continued availability of certain critical information and the means by which that information is gathered, stored, processed, communicated, and reported. As such, steps will be taken to protect information assets from unauthorized use, modification, disclosure, or destruction, whether accidental or intentional.

The protection of these assets is a basic management responsibility. Employing officers are responsible for:

- Identifying and protecting computer-related information assets within their assigned area of management control
- Ensuring that these assets are used for management-approved purposes only

- Ensuring that all employees understand their obligation to protect these assets
- Implementing security practices and procedures that are consistent with the Company Information Asset Security Manual and the value of the asset
- Noting variance from established security practice and for initiating corrective action

Example 1 addresses the checklist as follows:

- *Topic* — "Information is a valuable corporate asset.... As such, steps will be taken to protect information...."
- *Responsibilities* — "The protection of these assets is a basic management responsibility."
- *Scope* — "Ensuring that all employees understand their obligation to protect these assets."
- *Compliance* — "Noting variance from established security practice and for initiating corrective action."

This policy is a good start. However, the topic is vague, and that is not acceptable. The most important goal of any writing is to quickly identify the topic. Without the title, we have only a vague idea of where the document is leading us.

There are key points to remember when writing or editing a policy or procedure. Every enterprise has a specific way of identifying itself in print. Make certain that you find this information and use only the accepted forms. For example, General Motors Corporation might be referred to as GMC. However, GMC is a division of General Motors. The accepted forms of reference to the entire corporation are General Motors or GM.

When identifying levels of management, most organizations have established a scheme for how differing levels are referred to in print. Normally, *Management*, with an uppercase M, refers to senior management and lowercase *management* refers to line management or supervision.

In the policy above, the writer referred to the "employing officer." For many enterprises, an officer is the most senior level of management. Officers may rank up there with the board of directors. The Chief Executive Officer, Chief Financial Officer, etc. are examples of this level of management. It is pretty safe to assume that the writer was not intending for such a high-ranking individual to be involved in this policy.

### *3.8.2   Example 2 — A Medical Service Organization*

The Medical Service Association shall provide an appropriate level of security to:

- Maintain the reliability, integrity, and availability of its assets
- Prevent and detect misuse
- Protect information assets against unauthorized modification, disclosure, or destruction (whether accidental or intentional)

- Satisfy legal and contractual requirements for security
- Provide enforcement and recovery guidelines (including insurance coverage) for instances when a compromise of security is detected
- Protect and provide a secure and safe work environment for its employees

Expenditures for security generally shall not exceed the value of the asset being protected.

The Management Analysis Department's Security Unit shall be the central authority for developing, monitoring, and enforcing association-wide policies, procedures, and guidelines.

Management of each department shall be responsible for:

- Ensuring adherence to all Association security policies, procedures, and guidelines
- Continually assessing the department's specific security risk
- Developing and maintaining a disaster recovery plan that both defines and protects department assets from unauthorized access and ensures their recovery from any misuse or destruction by human or natural means
- Providing adequate security training of department personnel based on the Association Security Training Plan

All new product or system development shall include adequate security internal control, and disaster recovery elements.

Any use of Association assets for other than their intended purpose is considered a misuse and is a violation of this policy.

Violations or suspected violations of any Association policy or procedure must be reported immediately to department management and the Association Security Officer or his appointed representative(s). Violators may be subject to immediate disciplinary action up to and including termination of employment and criminal prosecution, if appropriate.

Example 2 addresses the checklist as follows:

- *Topic* — Eventually the policy establishes that the "Association shall provide an appropriate level of security ... of its assets ... and protect information assets...."
- *Responsibilities* — The policy does establish that "Management of each department shall be responsible...." and then lists a number of items.
- *Scope* — The policy does not seem to establish whether this is Association-wide; the scope of the policy is not clear.
- *Compliance* — The policy does establish that "Management ... is responsible for ... ensuring adherence to all Association security policies, procedures, and guidelines."

This policy meets most of the checklist guidelines, but it misses some others and then adds pieces of information, such as the discussion on expenditures, that probably belong somewhere else. Again, a strong topic sentence is missing.

You need the attention of readers; the place to get them hooked is the first sentence. Sell the policy in the opening sentence. The policy does make a strong statement about what can occur if noncompliance is found.

### 3.8.3   Example 3 — A Power Company

*Policy Statement*

It is the policy of the Power and Light Company to protect all company information from disclosures that would violate company commitments to others or would compromise the competitive stance of the company.

*Employee Responsibilities*

Employee responsibilities are defined in Company Procedure AUT 15. Violations of these responsibilities are subject to appropriate disciplinary action up to and including discharge, legal action, and having the matter referred to law enforcement agencies.

Example 3 addresses the checklist as follows:

- *Topic* — The policy statement establishes that "company information … that would violate company commitments … or compromise … competitive stance…" must be protected.
- *Responsibilities* — The policy does establish "employee responsibilities."
- *Scope* — Here the policy makes a mistake in the first section; the policy actually narrows the scope of the material to be protected by stating that "company information … that would violate company commitments … or compromise … competitive stance…." This statement in fact narrows the overall policy direction.
- *Compliance* — Straight out: you violate, you pay the penalty.

Although this policy does meet one of the main requirements of a policy — that it be brief; it appears to be too brief. Some very important elements are left out, especially what role management will play in this policy and how compliance will be monitored. The policy also seems to exclude information about personnel.

The opening sentence discusses the "policy" of the company. The document was drafted as a policy statement, so it is not necessary to add the term "policy" to the text. Let the words establish what the policy is.

### 3.8.4   Example No. 4 — A Manufacturing Company (International)

*Basic Policies*

The Company relies heavily on various kinds of information resources in its daily operations. These resources include data-processing systems, electronic mail, voice-mail, telephones, copiers, facsimile machines, and other information-generation and exchange methods. It is very important for users to recognize that these resources are made available to them to help the company meet short- and long-term goals, objectives, and competitive challenges. Any improper use of any resource **is not** acceptable and **will not** be permitted.

The company policies listed here form the basis for the Information Resources Protection Policy (IRPP):

1. Data and information about the operation of the company and its employees are collected and retained only to satisfy legitimate business purposes or as required by law.

2. Protecting company information is every employee's responsibility. Company people share a common interest in ensuring information is not intentionally, accidentally, or improperly disclosed, lost, or misused.

3. Positive steps must be taken to prevent improper disclosure of company information and unauthorized access to company information resources.

4. Data, information, and processing resources are company assets that may be used only for management-approved company business purposes and not for personal or any other kinds of use of gain.

5. Like any company asset, the company reserves the right to inspect information resources and their use at any time.

6. Company records and information are available to individuals only on a need-to-know basis. Access or attempted access to information and the use of information resources outside one's authority are prohibited.

7. Established corporate and unit procedures are to be used for budgeting, approval, and acquisition of information-processing facilities, equipment, software, and support services.

8. Protective measures must be provided to control access and to protect the integrity of all information systems that process information.

9. Appropriate safeguards must be built into information-processing facilities. These safeguards should minimize the extent of loss of information or processing support that could result from such hazards as fire, water, or other natural disasters while maintaining operational effectiveness. Business recovery plans must provide for a continuation of vital business functions if loss failure should occur.

10. Independent reviews to ensure that program objectives are being met are an integral part of this effort. These reviews may be conducted by Corporate Auditing, the internal audit staff of a unit, or external auditors.

11. Deliberate unauthorized acts against Company or customer automated information system(s) or facilities, including but not limited to misuse, misappropriation, destruction of information or system resources, the deliberate and unauthorized disclosure of information, or the use of unauthorized software/hardware, will result in disciplinary action as deemed by management.

Example 4 addresses the checklist as follows:

- *Topic* — Items 4, 5, and 8 can be used and modified to form the text of what is to be protected.
- *Responsibilities* — Item 2 seems to address this issue.
- *Scope* — The policy identifies "users" but does not relate this term to actual employees.
- *Compliance* — Item 10 addresses formal review.

Basically, this is a good policy. It can be improved by moving the big-ticket items to the top. Whenever a policy is developed, begin with what the topic to be discussed is all about. Lead with this information in the first sentence.

### 3.8.5 Example 5 — An Insurance Company

Business information is an essential asset of the Company. This is true of all business information within the Company, regardless of how it is created, distributed, or stored and whether it is typed, handwritten, printed, filmed, computer-generated, or spoken.

All employees are responsible for protecting corporate information from unauthorized access, modification, duplication, destruction, or disclosure, whether accidental or intentional. This responsibility is essential to Company business. When information is not well protected, the Company can be harmed in various ways, such as significant loss to market share and a damaged reputation.

Details of each employee's responsibilities for protecting Company information are documented in the Information Protection Policies and Standards Manual. Management is responsible for ensuring that all employees understand and adhere to these policies and standards. Management is also responsible for noting variances from established security practices and for initiating corrective actions.

Internal auditors will perform periodic reviews to ensure ongoing compliance with the Company information protection policy. Violations of this policy will be addressed as prescribed in the Human Resource Policy Guide for Management.

Example 5 addresses the checklist as follows:

- *Topic* — Paragraph 1 addresses this issue.
- *Responsibilities* — Paragraph 2 addresses employee responsibilities and paragraph 3, sentence 2 establishes the management role.
- *Scope* — Paragraph 1 addresses the scope of the policy.
- *Compliance* — Paragraph 3 refers employees to a company document that provides more detail on the responsibilities. Paragraph 4 establishes the formal review process.

I like this policy. It is clear, crisp, and concise. However, it needs work. There is too much *why* the policy was developed in it. I like policies to stick to the facts and not add information that is not relevant to the actual policy.

Also, the first line of the fourth paragraph actually limits who can perform a review of the policy compliance levels. The policy specifically identifies the internal audit staff as having this responsibility. Technically speaking, no other entity can perform a review task. So be careful with your words. They can and will be used against you at a later time.

Appendix B has additional program policy statements. The next section contains examples of topic-specific policy statements.

## 3.9    Topic-Specific Policy Examples

The following topic-specific policies address various areas of concern. Notice whether the basic components — thesis statement, relevance, responsibilities, compliance — and additional information are included.

### 3.9.1    *Example 1 — Internet Security Policy*

#### Introduction

The Company, through the Internet, provides computing resources to its staff to access information, communicate, retrieve, and disseminate organization and business-related information. Use of the public Internet by Company employees is permitted and encouraged where such use is suitable for business purposes in a manner that is consistent with the Company standards of business conduct and as part of the normal execution of an employee's job responsibilities. In addition, the Company provides intranet facilities as a means of sharing timely organization and business-related information throughout the company.

As with all Company policies, this policy applies to all employees, contractors, consultants, as well as any other individuals utilizing the Company-provided Internet connection.

#### Policy Objectives

The Internet Security Policy has been implemented to:

- Provide direction for the protection of Company-owned and controlled information assets.
- Establish standards for providing desktop access to the Internet.
- Identify safeguards to enable the exchange of Company information with other Internet users while protecting the business interests of the Company and the privacy right of the employees.
- Identify enterprise responsibilities in regard to local, state, federal, or international regulations and laws governing electronic information exchange and commerce.

## Internet Access Standards

- The use of Company-provided access to the Internet is intended exclusively for management-approved activities.
- All access to the Internet by employees must be done through the Company-provided method.
- All publications/content files not classified as PUBLIC in accordance with the Company Information Classification Policy, must be approved by Corporate Communications.
- All business cases for Internet initiatives must be submitted to ES Network Control and ES Information Security.
- Company Internet users must report all security-related incidents to appropriate management upon discovery.
- Company policies regarding Employee Standards of Conduct, Conflict of Interest, Company Ethics Policy, Equal Employment Opportunity and Diversity in the Workplace, Communication and Information Protection also apply to the Internet.
- Employees must submit a completed *Internet Usage and Responsibility Agreement* prior to Company-provided Internet access (Exhibit 2).

**Exhibit 2   Internet Usage and Responsibility Agreement**

---

### *Internet Usage and Responsibility Agreement*

I, _____, acknowledge and understand that access to the Internet, as provided by the Company, is for Management approved use only. This supports Company policies on Standards of Conduct and Equal Employment Opportunity and Diversity, and among other things, prohibits the downloading of games, viruses, inappropriate materials or picture files, and unlicensed software from the Internet.

I recognize and accept that while accessing the Internet, I am responsible for maintaining the highest professional and ethical standards, as outlined in Company policy on Standards of Conduct.

I have read and understand the Company policies mentioned above and accept my responsibility to protect the Company's information and good name.

Name _____      Date _____

---

## 3.9.2   *Example 2 — A Telecommuting Policy*

### Policy

The Company allows telecommuting where there are opportunities for improved employee performance, reduced commuting miles, and/or potential for savings for the Company or business unit.

## Provisions

Business Units may implement telecommuting as a work option for certain employees based upon specific criteria and procedures consistently applied throughout the agency. Business Units opting to implement a telecommuting policy for their departments shall ensure that each employee request is considered in relation to the departmental operating requirements and customer needs.

- Consideration may be given to employees who have demonstrated work habits and performance well suited to successful telecommuting.
- Telecommuting criteria and procedures shall be evaluated to ensure its benefits and effectiveness.

The telecommuter's conditions of employment shall remain the same as for non-telecommuting employees. Employee salary, benefits, and employer-sponsored insurance coverage shall not change as a result of telecommuting.

- Business visits, meetings with Your Company customers, or regularly scheduled meetings with co-workers shall not be held at the home worksite.
- Telecommuting employees shall not act as primary caregivers for dependents nor perform other personal business during hours agreed upon as work hours.
- Tele-worksites shall be in the same state as the central worksite.

The Company shall provide tele-worksite office supplies. Equipment and software, if provided by the business unit for use at the tele-worksite, shall be for the purposes of conducting Company business.

The telecommuter shall normally provide home worksite furniture and equipment. The employee shall maintain a clean, safe workspace. In the case of injury occurring during telecommuting work hours, the employee shall immediately report the injury to the supervisor.

## Responsibilities

Employees shall sign and abide by a telecommuting agreement between the employee and the supervisor. A model agreement, an addendum to this policy, may require modification to fit individual tele-worksite circumstances (Exhibit 3).

- Telecommuting shall be voluntary. Unless otherwise provided in the agreement, either the Business Unit or the employee may discontinue the arrangement at any time, generally giving one week's notice.
- The agreement shall specify individual work schedules.

**Exhibit 3  Model Telecommuting Agreement**

### MODEL TELECOMMUTING AGREEMENT

TELE-WORKSITE
Travel between the tele-worksite and the central worksite shall not be reimbursed.
___ Home (Specify location in home)
___ Satellite
___ Other (Specify)
Address:
Phone:

CENTRAL WORKSITE
Will there be any sharing of or changes in work space when telecommuting begins?
___ Yes ___ No

If yes specify:

SCHEDULE
Telecommuting days: ___ Mon. ___ Tue. ___ Wed. ___ Thur. ___ Fri.

If telecommuter must come into the office on a scheduled telecommuting day, may another day be substituted? ___ Yes ___ No

Telecomutting time: Start _____ Finish _____ Total Hours Per Day _____
Lunch _____ to _____

EQUIPMENT
The Company is not responsible for any private property used, lost, or damaged. The Company may pursue recovery from the employee for property that is deliberately or negligently damaged or destroyed while in the employee's care, custody, or control. The Company is responsible for the deductible on Company property unless otherwise specified in this agreement under OTHER ARRANGEMENTS. Employees are advised to contact their insurance agent and a tax consultant for information regarding home worksites.

In the event of equipment failure, the employee may be assigned to another project and/or work location. The employee shall surrender all Company-owned equipment and data documents immediately upon request.

What equipment will be used?
ITEM ----------------------- INVENTORY NO. ------------------- OWNER

(list)

Will there be a modem connection to a state LAN or mainframe? ___ Yes ___ No
Is there any other computer security issue? ___ Yes ___ No

(*continued*)

**Exhibit 3   Model Telecommuting Agreement (continued)**

If yes to either question, has advice been obtained from Information Protection? ___ Yes ___ No

COMMUNICATION
Will the following be utilized:
Call forwarding? ___ Yes ___ No
Answering machine or voice mail? ___ Yes ___ No
Receptionist or co-workers take calls? ___ Yes ___ No

How will incoming calls to the central worksite be answered on telecommuting days?
The employee agrees to call the office to obtain messages at least ___ times a day. Call in times: (list)

The employee shall promptly notify the supervisor when unable to perform work assignments due to equipment failure or other unforeseen circumstances.

Other procedures: (list)

ARRANGEMENTS
Date telecommuting to begin: _____
Intervals for telecommuting agreement review: _____
Agency policy for payment of business telephone and data calls from the tele-worksite: (attach)

The employee and supervisor plan to participate in ODOE-sponsored training and assistance?
___ Yes ___ No

TERMINATION
Unless specified in OTHER ARRANGEMENTS, the Company and/or employee may discontinue this arrangement at anytime generally giving one week's notice.

OTHER ARRANGEMENTS
Additional conditions agreed upon by the employee and supervisor: (list)

I have read and understand both the telecommuting policy and this agreement and agree to abide by and operate in accordance with their terms and conditions. I agree that the sole purpose of this agreement is to regulate telecommuting and that it neither constitutes an employment contract or an amendment to any existing contract.

Employee _____ Supervisor _____ Date _____

## Compliance

Company management has the responsibility to manage corporate information, personnel, and physical property relevant to business operations, as well as the right to monitor the actual utilization of all corporate assets.

Employees who fail to comply with the policies will be considered to be in violation of Your Company's *Employee Standards of Conduct* and will be subject to appropriate corrective action.

### 3.9.3   Example 3 — Information Classification

### Policy

Information is a company asset and is the property of the Your Company. Your Company information includes information that is electronically generated, printed, filmed, typed, stored, or verbally communicated. Information must be protected according to its sensitivity, criticality, and value, regardless of the media on which it is stored, the manual or automated systems that process it, or the methods by which it is distributed.

### Provisions

To ensure the proper protection of corporate information, the Owner shall use a formal review process to classify information into one of the following classifications:

- *Public:* Information, that has been made available for public distribution through authorized company channels. (Refer to Communication policy for more information.)
- *Confidential:* Information, that, if disclosed, could violate the privacy of individuals, reduce the competitive advantage of the company, or could cause significant damage to Your Company.
- *Internal Use:* Information, that is intended for use by employees when conducting company business. Most information used in Your Company would be classified Internal Use.

### Declassification

The Owner is to establish a review process for all information classified as Confidential, and reclassify it when it no longer meets the criteria established for such information.

### Responsibilities

Employees are responsible for protecting corporate information from unauthorized access, modification, destruction, or disclosure, whether accidental or intentional. To facilitate the protection of corporate information, employee responsibilities have been established at three levels: *Owner*, *Custodian*, and *User*.

1. *Owner:* Your Company management of an organizational unit, department, etc. where the information is created, or that is the primary user of the information. Owners are responsible to:
   a. Identify the classification level of all corporate information within their organizational unit.
   b. Define and implement appropriate safeguards to ensure the confidentiality, integrity, and availability of the information resource.
   c. Monitor safeguards to ensure their compliance and report situations of noncompliance.
   d. Authorize access to those who have a business need for the information.
   e. Remove access from those who no longer have a business need for the information.
2. *Custodian:* Employees designated by the Owner to be responsible for maintaining the safeguards established by the Owner.
3. *User:* Employees authorized by the Owner to access information and use the safeguards established by the Owner.

## Compliance

Company management has the responsibility to:

- Manage corporate information, personnel, and physical property relevant to business operations, as well as the right to monitor the actual utilization of all corporate assets.
- Ensure that all employees understand their obligation to protect company information.
- Implement security practices and procedures that are consistent with Your Company policies and the value of the asset.
- Note variance from established security practice and for initiating corrective action.

Employees who fail to comply with the policies will be considered to be in violation of Your Company *Employee Standards of Conduct* and will be subject to appropriate corrective action.

## 3.10 Additional Hints

To have even the slightest hope of success, the policy must receive some level of visibility. Visibility takes a number of forms. The first, and probably most important form, will be management support. The issue of information security is not contained within the information systems organization. It is an enterprise-wide concern, and so any policy relating to the protection and security of organization information must come from the highest possible level within the enterprise. Begin early to develop strategies to gain management and employee support. Formulate a plan, in writing, on how to get senior management support. A written plan will foster a clear understanding of what you intend to do and how you plan to accomplish it. Your plan should identify key individuals or groups that might impact your success and should include a timetable for when essential activities or tasks will be accomplished. If the policy will be submitted to a formal committee for approval, begin early to solicit feedback from individual members of that group. Pay attention to individual concerns and work to reconcile any potential conflicts as the policy is developed. The idea is to provide individual decision-makers an opportunity to see and participate in the development of the policy before it is formally submitted to the approving-committee as a whole. It is much easier to sell a policy to those that helped create it.

As discussed in Chapter 9, a communication plan is necessary to take the message policy and all of its ramifications to the employees. This plan should include an employee awareness program. The program should include all existing employees and incoming new hires. If the organization desires to have contract personnel be compliant with the policies, then this must first be negotiated through the language of the contract. It is permissible to include contract personnel in the list of those who must comply with the policy; however, the actual compliance agreement must be included in the language of the purchase order and the contract.

## 3.11 Topic-Specific Policy Subjects to Consider

The ISO 17799 standard has identified a number of policies that every organization should consider. The following is a summary of those recommendations. Appendix A contains a Policy Baseline Checklist to assist you in your development process.

Remember that the ISO standards are really guidelines. That is, the listed topics should be considered, though not necessarily included, in your policy statement

### 3.11.1 Topic-Specific Policies

1. Security policy
    Information security policy
2. Security organization
    Information security infrastructure
    Security of third-party access
3. Assets classification and control
    Accountability for assets
    Information classification
4. Personnel security
    Security in job definition and resourcing
    User training
    Responding to incidents

5. Physical and environmental security
    Secure areas
    Equipment security
6. Computer and network management
    Operational procedures and responsibilities
    System planning and acceptance
    Protection from malicious software
    Housekeeping
    Network management
    Media handling and security
    Data and software exchange
7. System access control
    Business requirement for system access
    User access management
    User responsibilities
    Network access control
    Computer access control
    Application access control
    Monitoring system access and use
8. Systems development and maintenance
    Security requirements of systems
    Security in application systems
    Security in application system files
    Security in development and support environments
9. Business continuity planning
    Aspects of business continuity planning
10. Compliance
    Compliance with legal requirements
    Security reviews of IT systems
    System audit considerations

## 3.12 An Approach for Success

Effective policy statement is not an oxymoron. If properly drafted, a policy statement can actually improve productivity rather than add to organizational overhead. The following is a ten-step approach to help improve the likelihood of having a successful policy implementation process.

1. *Review existing policies* — Before writing a new policy, review what already exists. It is easier to update an existing policy than it is to gain acceptance of a totally new concept.
2. *Make the business objectives or mission of the organization an active part of the policy* — There is a reason that policies are created, and that is to support the activities of the enterprise. To help gain acceptance, use the language in your organization's "Shared Beliefs" or "Corporate Vision" in the policy statement.

3. *Make policies look like policies* — Take the time to ensure that whatever is created looks like existing policies. All to often the message gets lost because the format is unfamiliar. Save your development team some grief and research the policy format of your organization.

4. *Watch out for grammar and spelling* — The worst thing that you can do is sending out a draft document that has not been edited for spelling and grammar. Show the user community that proper care has been taken; by looking out for the "little" things, the chances of success will be increased.

5. *Streamline the language* — Most advanced writing courses have the students explore all the elements of language, painting pictures through the use of prose. Although that may be effective in a class in writing fiction, it will not help in a policy document.

6. *100 Percent security is not attainable* — Be realistic in your policy implementation. The most secure computer system is one that is turned off, locked away, and unplugged. A computer in this condition is secure, but productivity is probably going to be impacted. Seek out an acceptable level of security.

7. *Remember the audience* — Whenever writing, remember who you are writing for. The majority of the readers will not be technical or security professionals. Ensure that the words are understandable.

8. *Sell the policy prior to introduction* — We discuss this point in a later section; for now, remember that senior management must be fully aware of the policy and understand how it applies to the organization *before* it is submitted for approval.

9. *Keep the message brief* — Long-winded or complicated policies lead to trouble. Keep the policy as simple as possible. This will permit a limited variation on interpretation; and because it is brief, there will be a better chance that someone will actually read the policy.

10. *Take the message to the people* — Be prepared to develop employee awareness programs for the implementation of the policy.

## 3.13 Additional Examples

### 3.13.1 Example 1 — Information Protection Policy for QXZ

Information is an essential asset of QXZ. All information created in support of the business process, whether it is computer generated, manually produced, or spoken, is the property of QXZ. To ensure that business objectives and customer confidence are maintained, all associates have a responsibility to protect information from unauthorized access, modification, disclosure, and destruction, whether accidental or intentional.

Senior management and the officers of QXZ are required to employ internal controls designed to safeguard company assets, including business information. It is a management obligation to ensure that all associates understand and comply with the QXZ security policies and standards as well as all applicable laws and regulations. Associate responsibilities for protecting QXZ information are detailed in the Information Protection Policies and Standards.

QXZ management has the responsibility to manage corporate information, personnel, and physical property relevant to business operations, as well as the right to monitor the actual utilization of all corporate assets. Associates who fail to comply with this policy will be considered to be in violation of the QXZ Code of Corporate Responsibility and will be subject to appropriate corrective action.

## Responsibilities

- Managers shall develop and administer an information protection program that appropriately classifies and protects corporate information under their control and makes employees aware of the importance of information and methods for its protection.
- The Corporation should provide the highest level of visibility and support for the philosophy of protection and also provide a focal point for solving information protection problems.
- Employees shall protect corporate information from unauthorized access, modification, duplication, destruction, or disclosure.
- Information providers shall authorize access to only those with a genuine business need.

## 3.13.2   Example 2 — Hospital Information Classification Policy

### Preamble

It is a long-standing value that information be shared subject to privacy and confidentiality requirements; this reflects the fact that information is a unique resource that increases rather that dissipates when it is used. Consistent with this principle, Hospital University along with Hospital Healthcare (hereafter referred to as "Hospital") seek to provide appropriate access to Hospital information among its employees, students, faculty, physicians, contractors, vendors, volunteers, and other agents (hereafter referred to as "Hospital staff"). Access to Hospital information, however, carries with it the responsibility to protect confidentiality and integrity. To enhance access to Hospital information, this policy sets forth rules for its handling and use.

### Purpose

To establish Hospital's policy for the use, protection, and preservation of all information, in any form, which is generated by, owned by, or otherwise in the possession of Hospital, including all administrative, clinical, and academic information ("Hospital Information").

### Information Access Policy Statement

Hospital Information is one of the most valuable assets of Hospital and must, therefore, be safeguarded by all agents representing Hospital. Unless otherwise stated in writing, all Hospital Information is considered confidential.

Hospital staff, as either information providers or information users, that intentionally and without proper authorization (1) access or disclose confidential Hospital Information or (2) modify or destroy Hospital Information, are in direct violation of the Hospital Information Access Policy. Such violations may lead to disciplinary action by Hospital up to and including dismissal from Hospital. Under certain circumstances, such violations may give rise to civil and/or criminal liability.

The Hospital University Information Access Review Board and the Hospital Healthcare Professional Services Committee maintain oversight responsibility for this policy. Comprising key information custodians or their delegates, these groups are charged with custody of Hospital Information. The Hospital University Information Technology Division and Hospital Healthcare Information Services provide access to information and implement security, as authorized by the Hospital University Information Access Review Board and the Hospital Healthcare Professional Services Committee. The Information Technology Policy Committee has authority to resolve conflicts and arbitrate disputes.

### Scope

This policy applies to:

- All information supporting the academic, business, clinical, and operational needs of Hospital.
- Information in all forms, including information-processing activities, computerized information, whether kept in mainframes, databases, servers, or personal and manually maintained files.
- All application, network, and operating system software used for computerized management of this information.
- Computerized information-processing activities related to Hospital University's research and instruction only where the Hospital University Information Access Review Board determines that such activities should specifically be covered by this policy.

### Definitions

*Access* — Access is permission, privilege, or ability to read, enter, update, manage, or administer access to Hospital information assets. Authorized by the custodian of the information, access is dependent upon the sensitivity of the information. "Sensitivity" is determined by legal responsibility of Hospital and the specific job responsibilities of the individual(s) for whom access is requested.

*Agent* — An agent is anyone empowered to act for Hospital.

### 3.13.3   Example 3 — Information Protection Policy for the UNION Family of Companies

Information is an essential asset of the UNION Family of Companies. All information created in support of the business process, whether it is computer-generated, manually produced, or spoken is the property of UNION. To ensure that business objectives and customer confidence are maintained, all employees have a responsibility to protect information from unauthorized access, modification, disclosure, and/or destruction, whether accidental or intentional,

Senior management and the Officers of the Company are required to employ internal controls designed to safeguard company assets, including business information. It is a management obligation to ensure that all employees understand and comply with the Company's security policies and standards as well as all applicable laws and regulations. Employee responsibilities for protecting Company information are detailed in the Information Protection Policies and Standards..

Company management has the responsibility to manage corporate information, personnel, and physical property relevant to business operations, as well as the right to monitor the actual utilization of all corporate assets. Employees who fail to comply with the policies will be considered to be in violation of the Company's Ethical Standards of Conduct and will be subject to appropriate corrective action.

## 3.14  Summary

In this section we determined that the policy is the cornerstone of the information security architecture of an organization. It is important to establish both internally and externally what the position of an organization on a particular topic might be.

We then looked at what a policy is and what it is not. We reviewed the definitions for policy, standard, guideline, and procedure.

We examined the key elements of a policy:

- Be easy to understand
- Be applicable
- Be doable
- Be enforceable
- Be phased in
- Be proactive
- Avoid absolutes
- Meet business objectives

We reviewed format and component considerations for the three basic types of policy: program policy, topic-specific policy, and application specific policy.

In addition, we examined actual policy statements and critiqued them based on the checklist. Some helpful hints and pitfalls to avoid were provided.

It bears repeating that information is a unique enough asset to warrant a written statement regarding its protection. Policies, standards, guidelines, and procedures form the basis of good controls, and good controls make good business sense. Implementing proper controls, documenting them in writing, and communicating them to all affected individuals and entities can provide an organization with real cost benefit by avoiding public criticism and saving time in the event an investigation and subsequent disciplinary process is necessary.

Most importantly, only a written policy can be convincing in courts of law, customer contracts, vendor relations, acquisitions, and public relations.

# Chapter 4

# Mission Statement

A well-written and properly endorsed mission statement or charter will allow you to focus on the areas that require control. The mission statement will also educate employees about the overall direction of your assignment. By stating your mission, you will be laying the groundwork for the success, acceptance, and incorporation of a corporate information protection program.

Most organizations view mission statements or charters as enabling acts. That is, they establish the scope of responsibility for each department or individual. Most organizations have a procedures and methods division within the financial staff. The job of the procedures and methods division is to generate the accounting practices and procedures that will ensure that the organization complies with the generally accepted accounting practices (GAAP) standard. Fortunately, the field of information and computer security finally has an equivalent. The Information Technology–Code of Practice Security Management (ISO 17799) has devloped Section 4 Organization Security to provide the key elements for a mission statement.

## 4.1 Background on Your Position

Before you can begin working on your mission statement, you will have to understand two important issues. The first issue concerns why you are here. This is not an open-ended question about your existence, but rather why your function needs to be part of the structure of your organization. Most people would rather be doing something else, something exciting and visible, anything but be the information systems security officer. The second issue is why management assigned the task in the first place. Management does not undertake establishing positions unless it is getting pressure from another source, such as senior management or open audit comments.

Before you begin to write your mission statement, you must first fully understand why you were selected to do the job and why management decided that this is the time in the life of the organization to create a mission statement. The answers you receive will allow you to create a mission statement with an appropriate focus.

To create an efficient and effective computer security program, it is best to begin the process at the corporate headquarters or main office and then solicit input from the divisions, groups, units, and subsidiaries and from certain identified individuals. By involving as many of the business units as possible, the level of resistance may be reduced.

Because of varying organizational methods (and because you want to ensure your job will not be eliminated), you must understand fully the organizational structure and the events that led to assigning you to the project. Once you have this information, you can create an outline of specific goals that will be used to meet the policy objectives. When the outline is completed, you will want senior management to approve the development of your mission statement. Only when the mission statement is completed and endorsed will the road to a computer security program paved.

## 4.2   Business Goals versus Security Goals

People who work in computer departments often focus on their immediate concerns and, in the process, lose sight of the goals of the organization. Every organization has an overall business objective. To make your computer security program constructive, you must seek out the business objectives of the organization and ensure that your security program meets and supports those goals.

As an employee in the department charged with the role of defining security controls, you must acknowledge that security is not the most important product of your organization. Any computer and information security objectives you develop must be adapted to meet the practical business conditions of your organization. Security controls that inhibit the business function of the organization will be quickly discarded. Poorly written procedures will not support the fiduciary responsibility of management to protect assets.

Because of the inherent difference between protecting information and promoting business, your job assignment may often appear to be in direct conflict with the objectives of the rest of the organization.

After all, the most secure computer system is one that is down. However, although the data is safe from unauthorized access, having the system down does not meet any business goals or justify its installation in the first place. So your goal is to ensure that when the computers are operational, only those employees with a legitimate need for access will be granted access, and they will be allowed access on a need-to-know basis. With proper controls in place, the organization will have maximum security with a minimum of impact, and the security will be cost-effective.

The business objectives of your organization are usually stated in readily available sources, such as:

- Annual reports to stockholders
- Organizational charts
- Strategic planning information
- Interviews with staff members
- Annual corporate budget proposals

The annual report is especially valuable to you as a security officer. This document contains the management report, in which the chief operating officer and chief financial officer attest that there are adequate controls in place to protect the organization from loss of assets and prevent the organization from being at risk. By using this information, you will learn the business objectives of the organization and gain senior management support in the development of adequate controls.

## 4.3 Computer Security Objectives

Before reviewing existing mission statements and then creating your own, you must explore the elements of a comprehensive information security program. Remember: computer security is just one part of the overall asset protection program of the organization. Although you will address the physical security of computers and you need to protect the considerable investment in computer hardware, you must realize that the computer only functions as the processor and storage device for information. The information, data, programs, applications, transactions, and systems are extremely valuable, and they must be protected as well as the hardware. If the data has been backed up, then the system can eventually be brought back up. However, if the data has not been backed up, nothing can bring the system back. So be sure to include controls on the assets as well as the hardware.

The following items are generally accepted standards for a comprehensive security program:

- Ensure the accuracy and integrity of data.
- Protect classified data.
- Protect against unauthorized access, modification, disclosure, or destruction of data.
- Ensure the ability of the organization to survive the loss of computing capacity (disaster recovery planning).
- Prevent employees from probing the security controls as they perform their assigned tasks.
- Ensure management support for the development and implementation of security policies and procedures.

- Protect management from charges of imprudence in the event of any compromise of the information or computer security controls of the organization.
- Protect against errors and omissions (which still account for 75 to 80 percent of losses).

## 4.4 Mission Statement Format

Most mission statements begin with a brief paragraph explaining the overall goals of the information or computer security program. This initial statement takes the concepts established in the policy statement (refer to *Computer Security Journal*, Volume VII, Number 2, "Policy Statement: The Cornerstone to All Procedures") and expands them into the goals to be addressed by your department. Your mission statement or charter should also reflect the style of your organization. As discussed, you need the background on management's impetus for establishing policies and procedures and on the overall business objectives to begin writing a mission statement.

After the section on goals, the mission statement should then list your responsibilities. The responsibilities are usually presented in active voice and provide the key elements of your job description. The effectiveness of the security program you develop and your effectiveness as an individual employee will be judged on the basis of the responsibilities you describe.

## 4.5 Allocation of Information Security Responsibilities (ISO 17799–4.1.3)

Responsibilities for the protection of individual assets for carrying out specific security processes should be clearly defined.

The information security policy (see Chapter 3) should provide general guidance on the allocation of security roles and responsibilities in the organization. This will need to be supplemented, where necessary, with more-detailed guidance for specific sites, systems, or services. Local responsibilities for individual physical and information assets and security processes, such as business continuity planning, should be clearly defined.

In many enterprises an information security manager will be appointed to take overall responsibility for the development and implementation of security and support identification of controls. (Examples of job descriptions for Corporate/Chief Information Officer or CIO, Information Security Manager, Security Administrator and Firewall Administrator are found in Appendix E).

However, responsibility for resourcing and implementing the controls will normally remain with individual managers. One common practice is to appoint an owner for each information asset who then becomes responsible for its day-to-day security (see Information Protection Policy in the Appendix to the ISO 17799).

Owners of information assets may delegate their security responsibilities to individuals within their business unit or department. Nevertheless, the owner remains ultimately responsible for the security of the asset and should be able to determine that any delegated responsibility has been discharged correctly.

# 4.6   Mission Statement Examples

## 4.6.1   Example 1 — Mission Statement for a Global Manufacturing Corporation

As operations and related information processing become more decentralized through the use of PCs, controls and procedures become more important. And as remote access, networks, and distributed information processing make possible still greater globalization and decentralization of computer-generated data, the potential for unauthorized access to company secret, confidential, and restricted information increases. To provide the corporation with the highest level of visibility and support for the philosophy of information security and to provide the groups, units, divisions, sections, staffs, and departments with a focal point for solving security problems, a Corporate Information Security Group has been established and will report to the Director of Security.

---

**Example 1 — Mission Statement for a Global Manufacturing Corporation**

---

Corporate Information Security Group responsibilities include:

- Keep information and computer security policies and procedures current.
- Answer all inquiries on compliance and interpretation of corporate policies.
- Review all computer and information audit comments and the associated responses, thereby providing independent review of audit comments and unit responses.
- Review the employee Security Awareness Program to ensure that it remains an effective tool for information security controls.
- Assist departments in developing recovery plans and oversee the testing of these plans.
- Review new computer and information security products and make recommendations on these products to ensure they meet minimum corporate requirements.
- Assist in the investigation and reporting of computer equipment thefts, intrusions, viruses, and breaches of information security.
- Assist local Information Security Officers in developing effective training programs for the Plant Security Officers in the areas of computer crime and investigation.
- Assist in the development of effective monitoring programs to ensure that corporate information is protected as required.
- Ensure that the systems moved into production mode are safe from errors and omissions.

---

*(continued)*

**Example 1 (continued)**

**Report of Management**

Company management is responsible for the fair presentation and consistency of all financial data included in this Annual Report in accordance with generally accepted accounting principles. Where necessary, the data reflects management's best estimates and judgments.

Management is also responsible for maintaining a system of internal accounting controls with the objectives of providing reasonable assurance that Company assets are safeguarded against material loss from unauthorized use or disposition and that authorized transactions are properly recorded to permit the preparation of accurate financial data. Cost-benefit judgments are an important consideration in this regard. The effectiveness of internal controls is maintained by (1) personnel selection and training; (2) division of responsibilities; (3) establishment and communication of policies; and (4) ongoing internal review programs and audits. Management believes that Company system of internal controls as of December 31, 1989, is effective and adequate to accomplish the above described objectives.

(signed) Chairman and Chief Executive Officer

(signed) Senior Vice President and Chief Financial Officer

(date)

The statement in Example 1 has a broad scope to accommodate all the sites, both foreign and domestic, of a large organization. Although this is an effective charter for a multinational corporation, it may not suit the needs of your company. The next examples narrow the scope of responsibility and may be more in line with your needs.

## 4.6.2    Example 2 — Mission Statement for a North American Manufacturing Company

An Information Security Administration Function (ISAF) shall be developed to establish standards, procedures, and guidelines as deemed necessary to ensure the security of information throughout the company. The "owners" of information (as defined later) will be required to take prudent security measures, with the assistance of the ISAF, to protect information from unauthorized modification, destruction, or disclosure, whether accidental or intentional.

This mission statement says that the role of the ISAF is to develop written documents to ensure the security of company information. Beyond that, the specific duties of the ISAF are vague. This mission statement lacks the concrete identification of activities that can be completed by the ISAF. The tone of the language used for the Responsibilities (Example 2) could also

**Example 2 — Responsibilities: Data Security Goals**

- ■ Develop a uniform protection policy.
- ■ Have a data classification system to aid business managers in evaluating their data assets.
- ■ Identify owners for all data sets.
- ■ Have operators of the off-site data storage facility function as data custodians.
- ■ Install and administer an access control package with a minimal use of passwords.
- ■ Educate all users on the importance and use of security measures.

be more action-oriented. For example, "Have a data classification system..." could be improved by stating, "Implement a data classification system...."

A brief note about the term *security*: security is one of those words that everyone interprets differently. In this book, security is synonymous with protecting company assets, both physical and intellectual. Protection is an active process that motivates employees to safeguard the assets of the organization.

## 4.6.3   *Example 3 — Mission Statement for a Corporate Data Processing Department*

The Information Systems Security Officer (ISSO) has been established to ensure that corporate data is protected from unauthorized modification, disclosure, and destruction and to ensure that the corporation has security measures to carry out its responsibilities as defined by law and the courts.

While the goals listed in Example 2 are certainly admirable, there are no corresponding statements that define how the ISSO will implement these goals. More concrete recommendations are necessary for developing the security program of this company.

## 4.6.4   *Example 4 — Mission Statement for the Corporate Information Security Administration*

Example 4 shows an aggressive mission statement, but it may also be unrealistic. The CISA will assume the responsibility for security measures throughout the corporation. Unless there is adequate staff, the objectives are far too broad for a typical computer security department to undertake. If you develop a detailed mission statement like this one, make certain that you are not the only person assigned to work on computer security.

## 4.6.5   *Example 5 — Mission Statement for a Medium-Sized Manufacturing Company*

While the mission statement shown in Example 5 is longer than is typical, it is thorough. Management responsibilities are defined from the start, and these

## Example 4 — Mission Statement for the Corporate Information Security Administration

Contribute to the Corporate Information Security Program by performing the following tasks:

- Implement and coordinate the Corporate Information Security Policy and Program.
- Design and implement a Corporate Security Awareness Program.
- Design a strategy for detecting actual security risks.
- Prepare companywide policies.

Assist management in performing its security responsibilities by performing the following tasks:

- Assess proposed access controls.
- Prepare and publish guidelines and standards.
- Assist areas in the development and enforcement of internal security procedures.
- Ensure that criteria for sensitive and critical information are current and appropriate to the needs of the corporation.
- Train the area coordinators in maintaining the enforcing guidelines and standards.
- Participate in the application development cycle.
- Advise on contingency planning and disaster recovery plans.

Prepare and monitor management processes to prevent and handle perceived information access violations by performing the following tasks:

- Perform reviews of all information security access control systems.
- Ensure that appropriate information security requirements are being enforced.
- Approve all events in which established information safeguards are overridden and ensure that each override is documented.
- Ensure that security violations are reported to the appropriate manager.
- Contribute to the annual audit report on information security and access.

Recommend allocation of resources and technology enhancements to meet information security objectives by performing the following tasks:

- Select and administer all information security access control systems.
- Review existing and proposed hardware and software for security considerations and make recommendations, as appropriate.
- Delegate limited administrative authority to other individuals or groups, if appropriate.
- Execute a risk assessment of sensitive data and the cost of protecting it.

## Example 5 — Mission Statement for a Medium-Sized Manufacturing Company

**Introduction**

This document defines the scope and direction for the information security function. The duties and responsibilities set forth will serve as the charter for the group.

## Example 5 — Mission Statement for a Medium-Sized Manufacturing Company (continued)

### Responsibilities of Management

To fulfill present and future business commitments, steps must be taken to ensure the accuracy, privacy, and security of our computers, commmunication networks, electronically processed data, and manual data. The responsibility for safeguarding corporate information rests with all employees, but it is the coordinated effort of management and information security that will:

Minimize the probability of security breaches.

Minimize the damage if such a breach occurs.

Ensure the company's ability to recover from damage with minimal disruption of service.

It is a basic management responsibility to protect resources necessary to conduct business. Management is responsible for identifying and protecting hardware, software, and data resources under its control. This task is accomplished by implementing security policies and practicing security procedures commensurate with the value of the asset to the company.

### Responsibilities of Information Security Management

*Mission*

To provide a secure environment for the information assets of the company.

*Strategies*

- Monitor and audit adherence to security policies and procedures on a daily basis.
- Maintain an ongoing and corporatewide security awareness program relating to information asset protection.
- Act as a catalyst to make security a part of each employee's daily activities.
- Ensure that the company has adequate protection for its business information assets and the most cost-effective tools to eliminate security breaches.
- Maintain an ongoing security audit process to review security exposures of breaches in a timely manner.

*Key Responsibilities*

- Establish and enforce the following general data security rules in conjunction with management:
- Information shall be created and maintained in a secure environment.
- Practices shall be in place to prevent unauthorized modification, destruction, or disclosure of information, whether accidental or intentional.
- Safeguards shall be implemented to ensure the integrity and accuracy of vital company information.
- The cost of information security shall be commensurate with the value of the information to the company, the company's customers, and potential intruders.
- Formulate an overall security plan for the corporation.
- Review company information security practices regularly, considering technological, environmental, and statutory requirements and trends. Keep abreast of new security developments that could affect the company.

*(continued)*

**Example 5 — Mission Statement for a Medium-Sized Manufacturing Company (continued)**

- Perform reviews and act as a consultant in matters affecting information security.
- Provide support to all employees as they fulfill security-related responsibilities.
- Perform security administrator duties in areas where direct responsibility for information security has been assigned.
- Conduct periodic risk analysis inspections of data processing facilities and software systems to identify security exposures and report the findings to the respective management.
- Develop, maintain, and implement policies, procedures, and guidelines to assure information security.
- Assist plant security to develop, maintain, and implement policies, procedures, and guidelines to assure the physical protection of information assets.
- Provide information security awareness training to all company personnel.
- Coordinate the installation and maintenance of security software on systems for which direct responsibility has been assigned. Monitor the installation and maintenance of security software on all company hardware that is under the control of remote-site security administrators.

set the tone for what is expected from each segment of the company — management, employees, and security. Nevertheless, the section on strategies does not need to be shared by the company as a whole and probably should be an internal departmental function.

## 4.6.6    *Example 6 — Mission Statement for an Information Security Department*

The mission statement in Example 6 is strong, with the exception of item 5. Taking on the role of facilitator for the company business resumption plan should not be an add-on responsibility for the ISO. Business resumption planning (BRP) is a full-time job. In fact, BRP is an entire industry separate from computer and information security activities. Your role in a company BRP should only be the part that relates directly to data processing. A more appropriate responsibility statement would be: "Assist the departments and other business units in developing local business resumption plans and act as observer while these plans are being tested."

Your mission statement should spell out the goals that you believe can be accomplished. You have the opportunity to determine the direction your job will take, so be sure the responsibilities are attainable. Do not write a mission statement that assumes that you will have a staff of security personnel at your disposal. In the real world, the information security function is often a one- or two-employee operation, and security is just one of the assigned responsibilities. Be realistic about what you can accomplish and be certain to include educational responsibilities. For example, an appropriate item might state: "Attend workshops, seminars, and conferences annually to remain current on new developments in security technology."

**Example 6 — Mission Statement for the Information Security Department**

**Charter**

The mission of the Information Security Department (ISD) is to direct and support the company and affiliated organizations in the protection of their information assets from intentional or unintentional disclosure, modification, destruction, or denial through the implementation of appropriate information security and business resumption planning policies, procedures, and guidelines.

**Responsibilities**

The IDS shall be responsible for the development and administration of information security control plans, including the following tasks:

1. Develop information security policies, procedures, and guidelines in compliance with established company policies and generally accepted data processing controls.
2. Implement a data classification system and a management assessment program to be completed annually.
3. Develop and maintain a companywide information security awareness and education program.
4. Develop and maintain an overall access control program for mainframes, minicomputers, and microcomputers.
5. Select, implement, test, and maintain an appropriate business resumption plan for each company location responsible for processing critical systems and applications.
6. Ensure that information security requirements are incorporated in new applications by participating in the systems design and development process.
7. Investigate and evaluate emerging information security technologies and services and coordinate implementation of appropriate hardware, software, and services within company operating groups.
8. Coordinate the distribution of company security information and provide technical assistance to operating organizations as required.
9. Implement other information security responsibilities as deemed appropriate.

## 4.7 Support for the Mission Statement

Before publication, the mission statement must receive management approval. Although the format of the mission statement does not really affect how it will be received, it is extremely important to have the statement approved at the highest possible level of management.

The following examples show typical approval levels of mission statements for established organizations.

- *General Motors Corporation* — Chairman
- *Kmart Corporation* — Chairman of the Executive and Finance Committee
- *Capital Holding Corporation* — Chairman of the Board and Chief Financial Officer
- *AT&T New Jersey* — Chairman of the Board
- *Miller Freeman Publications* — Member, Board of Directors

It is important to note that in the preceding examples no data processing personnel approved the mission statement when published. Although an effective security program can be established and flourish with only data processing approval, the overall acceptance and support will be greatly reduced and your task will take much longer to succeed.

## 4.8   Key Roles in Organizations

This section describes some of the different roles within an organization and the responsibilities associated with each job. This section will provide the groundwork for identifying the management levels within your organization. The specific roles within your organization may vary, but you can find corresponding positions in your organization for each of the following key management functions.

- *Chief Executive Officer (CEO)* — A member of an organization who has authority over all other members in determining the conduct and direction the organization will take. The CEO is elected as a director by the shareholders and appointed CEO by the board. The CEO is responsible to the shareholders of the company for the successful conduct of the company.
- *Chief Financial Officer (CFO)* — Along with the CEO, the CFO is responsible for maintaining a system of internal controls designed to provide reasonable assurance that the books and records reflect the transactions of the organization and that its established policies and procedures are carefully followed. Perhaps the most important feature in the system of control is that it is continually reviewed for effectiveness and is augmented by written policies and guidelines, the careful selection and training of qualified personnel, and a strong program of internal control. The CEO and CFO must sign a statement regarding management's responsibility for the company financial statements. This statement, sometimes called *Report of Managment* or *Report of Management's Responsibility for Financial Statements*, attests that the organization has adequate controls to protect vital assets. The audit staff reports provide the information for this critical function.
- *Senior Management* — The senior manager of a business unit, such as the director of accounts payable, is responsible for specifying and implementing the operational controls for his or her work area. In addition, this individual is considered the owner of the information assets for the department he or she oversees. Senior management is responsible for ensuring that controls are in place to safeguard the department data, including who may read and update files. Senior management may delegate the responsibility for the day-to-day approval process for access to the data, programs, and transactions to another employee within the department. However, because the senior manager and the delegate are responsible for the routine reconciliation

of the department activities, their positions should not include the ability to originate data or transactions.

- *Director of Management Information Systems (DMIS)* — The DMIS is the highest level of management within the organization charged with responsibility for the operation of the computer systems (not including microcomputers). This individual is responsible for ensuring that systems programmers, application programmers, system operators, and scheduling, tape library, and other related personnel are conducting their daily activities in accordance with established policies and procedures. The DMIS is also responsible for the actions of the system security administrator and any privileged users.

- *Information Security Officer (ISO)* — The ISO is responsible for developing the computer and information security policy to be adopted by senior management. The ISO is also responsible for advising on protective measures (including standards and procedures), measuring performance, and reporting to management. The ISO may surpervise the system security administrator(s).

- *System Security Administrator (SSA)* — The SSA is responsible for creating and maintaining access control records. The SSA acts as surrogate for the system manager and the application and data owners. The SSA enrolls new users and grants access. The SSA works under the supervision of the director of information services or the ISO and is subject to review by internal auditors.

If you are not clear where you fit into your corporate organization, you should obtain current organization charts and find out who your ultimate boss is. In most instances, data processing falls under the responsibility of the financial staff. However, recently in companies such as IBM, Electronic Data Systems, BP America, Shell, and Aetna, the information security officer reports to the head of security. Knowing where you report in an organization will help you develop a mission statement that will support the business goals of your organization.

## 4.9   Business Objectives

Most computer security policies and procedures are based on the recognition that the organization is inextricably linked to computer systems. Without automated information processing, the corporate world would be unable to design new products, manufacture existing products, sell the products, or even collect money for the product or services rendered. Without the ability to access information in a timely and efficient manner, businesses would cease to function within days or even hours. As a result, management must understand that corporate information is vulnerable to errors, omissions, and unauthorized access, as well as modification, disclosure, and destruction.

As a member of the corporate team, computer security must present its goals and objectives in the format and language of the organization. In addition to the policy statement and mission statement, a five-year plan should be developed. Most organizations establish such plans to determine the overall direction. Like other departments of the corporation, computer security should establish its own short-term and long-term objectives. Once developed, the information security five-year plan should be reviewed annually and modified as necessary. During the annual review, you can list goals that have been completed, determine the status of ongoing projects, and prepare new updated, long-term objectives.

The business plan should support the goals established in the mission statement. Start with short-term goals that you are fairly sure you will be able to complete. Remember, nothing succeeds like success. When management sees that you are accomplishing your stated objectives, support for the security program will be easier to obtain.

## 4.10 Review

The mission statement should ensure that the security of the information and communication processing resources of the corporation are sufficient to reduce risk to a level acceptable to the management of the corporation. The following list identifies elements to consider when developing a mission statement.

- To recommend policies, standards, and procedures that foster the protection of information and information-processing resources.
- To assist units and divisions in the selection and implementation of the protective measures required in their areas responsibility.
- To evaluate new technology and recommend security strategies to protect it.
- To identify areas of potential risk in the protection of corporate computer and information assets and to alert management once those areas have been identified.
- To provide training for security control requirements during all phases of application and system development.
- To develop programs to increase security awareness at all levels of the corporation.
- To develop a liaison between the corporate security and audit staffs to ensure that security efforts are coordinated and resources are conserved by preventing duplication of effort.
- To coordinate and assist in the development of business resumption plans for all data centers supporting critical business functions.
- To work with the local ISSO to ensure that corporate-mandated programs are cost-effective and operationally effective.
- To act as a consultant to all areas on the security of information and computer systems.
- To monitor changes in laws and regulations as well as changes in technology and corporate goals to determine the impact of these changes on corporate security requirements.

Review Example 7 for ideas on what to include in your mission statement.

## Example 7 — Mission Statement for an Information Protection Group

**Mission Statement**
- To provide the Corporation with the highest level of visibility and support for the philosophy of protection and to provide this organizations with a focal point for solving information protection problems.

**Information Protection Group Responsibilities**
1. Keep information protection policies and practices current.
2. Prepare, publish, and maintain ISO guidelines and standards for information protection.
3. Answer all inquiries on compliance and interpretation of corporate policies and ISO practices.
4. Develop, implement, and maintain the Corporate Information Protection Awareness Program.
5. Assist the Corporate Organization Information Protection Coordinators (OIPCs) to develop, implement, and maintain their local information protection programs.
6. Develop, implement, and maintain standard risk assessment tools for use in determining critical corporate resources.
7. Ensure the criteria for determining sensitive information and critical applications and systems are current and appropriate to the needs of the corporation.
8. Coordinate the development, testing, and maintenance of a data center Business Continuity Plan (BCP).
9. Assist OIPCs in the development of their organization BCPs.
10. Review new system access and information protection products and make recommendations on these products to ensure they meet minimum corporate requirements.
11. Provide account administration across all platforms.
12. Provide consulting support for all application development projects.
13. Act as audit liaison for all information and computer security-related matters.
14. Assist in the investigation and reporting of computer thefts, intrusions, viruses, and breaches of information protection controls.
15. Assist in the development of effective monitoring programs to ensure that corporate information is protected as required.

# Chapter 5

# Standards

The are many existing sources for supporting standards. The banking industry has many that have been established by regulations and requirements from the federal government. The health-care industry also has standards that are required. We will explore where to find industry-specific standards and how to make them apply to your organization.

Standards for each phase or section of an information security handbook need to be developed. Almost everyone in the enterprise recognizes the need for standards. However, developing them, adhering to them, and monitoring them is a logistical problem.

Two things are necessary to achieve success with standards:

1. There must be a commitment to the standards by all personnel.
2. The standards must be:
   a. Reasonable
   b. Flexible
   c. Current

These two necessities are interdependent.

Commitment must start with senior management and then move throughout the enterprise. If line management does not get the proper message from senior management, then the standards have no chance of surviving. On the other hand, if the employees see their management is committed to the standards, there is a better chance that the employees will be committed. It is very much a two-way street, and therefore standards must be:

- Practical
- Applicable
- Up-to-date
- Reviewed regularly

## 5.1   Where Does a Standard Go?

Policies, standards, and procedures fit into a hierarchy.

- A *policy* states a goal in general terms.
- *Standards* define what is to be accomplished in specific terms.
- *Procedures* tell how to meet the standards.

Exhibit 1 also illustrates the hierarchy of policies, standards, and procedures. It shows the standards and procedures that result from a specific policy.

---

**Exhibit 1   Standards**

---

Examine the following:
- *Policy:* It is the policy to process insurance claims as quickly as possible.
- *Standard:* Each claim must be processed within six working days of receipt.
- *Procedure:*

    *Day 1* — Set up a file for correspondence, receipts, etc.
    *Day 2* — Verify data.
    *Day 3* — Adjudicate the claim.
    *Day 4* — Enter data into the system.
    *Day 5* — Print check.
    *Day 6* — Mail check.

---

## 5.2   What Is a Standard?

Policies, because they are written at a broad level, require a support structure to be meaningful and effective. Policies alone will not offer the user community the guidance necessary to implement policy and meet the objectives of the enterprise. Standards provide this support and guidance. They are the mandatory activities, actions, rules, or regulations designed to provide policies with the reinforcement required to be effective. They are often expensive to administer and, therefore, should be used judiciously (see Exhibit 2).

---

**Exhibit 2   Standard Format**

---

Complete the following outline for a typical enterprise task (getting an access account, establishing an e-mail account, logging onto the system):
- *Policy* —
- *Standard* —
- *Procedure* —

    Step 1
    Step 2
    Step 3
    Step 4

---

### 5.2.1  Examples of Standards

Overall responsibility for ensuring the satisfactory implementation of information security is that of the chief executive of a division or the executive responsible for an equivalent unit. To permit that responsibility to be discharged, roles and responsibilities must be defined.

Managers must:

- Be aware of legislative and regulatory requirements, risks, protective measures, and practices that are relevant to their area of responsibility.
- Ensure that they and their staff are familiar with these and their corresponding duties and obligations.
- Appoint appropriate information and system owners.
- Ensure that agreed-upon protective measures and practices are in place and operating effectively and efficiently.
- Report incidents that violate protective measures or threaten to cause an unacceptable risk.
- Investigate these occurrences.

To have standards, it will be necessary to have a subject to tie them to. As you can see in the Exhibit 3, there is an opening paragraph of the mission statement that describes what is to be discussed. Exhibits 4 through 6 are some of the standards that support the mission statement. We often see this kind of format in mission statements and job descriptions. In job descriptions the section that itemizes *required* skills can be viewed as standards. *Preferred* skills can be viewed as guidelines. *Remember, a guideline is not mandatory.* The example for user authorization (Exhibit 6) contains some points that are guidelines and others that are standards. For example, the first item regarding Logins and Passwords contains the word "should," which implies some leeway; a guideline. However, the last item uses the word "must" and is definitely a standard. It is important to be consistent.

## 5.3  International Standards

The two standards BS 7799 and ISO 17799 are very similar. The key difference between the two is that ISO 17799 has two non-action sections before its list of standards.

Section 1 in ISO 17799 sets the scope:

> This standard gives recommendations for information security management for use by those who are responsible for initiating, implementing or maintaining security in their organization. It is intended to provide a common basis for developing organizational security standards and effective security management practice and to provide confidence in inter-organizational dealings. Recommendations from this standard should be selected and used in accordance with applicable laws and regulations.

**Exhibit 3   Mission Statement**

### Information Protection Group
### Mission Statement

To provide the Corporation with the highest level of visibility and support for the philosophy of protection and to provide Company organizations with a focal point for solving information protection problems.

#### Information Protection Group Responsibilities

1.  Keep information protection policies and practices current.
2.  Prepare, publish, and maintain guidelines and standards for information protection.
3.  Answer all inquiries on compliance and interpretation of corporate policies and practices.
4.  Develop, implement, and maintain the Corporate Information Protection Awareness Program.
5.  Assist the Organization Information Protection Coordinators (OIPC) to develop, implement, and maintain its local information protection programs.
6.  Develop, implement, and maintain standard risk assessment tool for use in determining critical corporate resources.
7.  Ensure the criteria for determining sensitive information and critical applications and systems are current and appropriate to the needs of the corporation.
8.  Coordinate the development, testing, and maintenance of a Business Continuity Plan (BCP).
9.  Assist OIPCs in the development of the organization BCPs.
10. Review new system access and information protection products and make recommendations on these products to ensure they meet minimum corporate requirements.
11. Provide consulting support for all application development projects.
12. Act as audit liaison for all information and computer security–related matters.
13. Assist in the investigation and reporting of computer thefts, intrusions, viruses, and breeches of information protection controls.
14. Assist in the development of effective monitoring programs to ensure that corporate information is protected as required.

As we can see in Section 1, although this document is titled a "standard," it is really a strong guideline. So use 17799 as a road map, understanding that there are alternative routes that you can take to get to the same destination. Section 2 sets terms and definitions:

- *Information Security* — Preservation of confidentiality, integrity, and availability of information.
- *Confidentiality* — Ensuring that information is accessible only to those authorized to have access.
- *Integrity* — Safeguarding the accuracy and completeness of information and processing methods.
- *Availability* — Ensuring that authorized users have access to information and associated assets as required.

**Exhibit 4   Job Description**

Chief Information Officer (CIO)

**CIO Mission:** To provide technology vision and leadership for developing and implementing Information Technology (IT) initiatives that create and maintain leadership for the enterprise in a constantly changing and intensely competitive marketplace.

**Reporting Relationship:** To a senior functional executive (President, EVP, CFO) or CEO. This is a key management position for the organization responsible for IT policy and alignment of IT strategy with business objectives.

**Responsibilities:**
- Sponsor collaborative business technology planning processes.
- Coordinate new and existing application development initiatives between IT and business units.
- Ensure IT infrastructure and architecture continue to meet enterprise business needs.
- Certify "make versus buy" decisions relative to outsourcing to in-house provisioning of IT services, skills, and products.
- Establish strategic relationships with key IT suppliers and consultants.
- Provide enabling technologies to make it easier for customers and suppliers to conduct business with the enterprise as well as to increase revenue and profitability.
- Interact with internal and external clients to ensure continuous customer satisfaction.
- Provide training for all IT personnel and users to ensure productive use of existing and new systems.

**Skills Required:**
- Strong business orientation, broad experience in the IT sector and related activities (i.e., consulting and vendor activities).
- Demonstrated ability to bring the benefits of IT to solve business issues while effectively managing costs and risks.
- Skill at identifying and evaluating new technological developments and gauging their appropriateness for the enterprise.
- Ability to communicate with and understand the needs of nontechnical internal clients.
- Exceptional organizational skills to ensure proper management of central IS resources and applications and coordinate business unit initiatives and resources.
- Ability to conceptualize, launch, and deliver multiple IT projects on time and within budget.
- Ability to blend with the existing management team by being an effective listener, team builder, and an articulate advocate of the IT vision.

**Personal Qualities:**
Superb leadership, communication, and interpersonal skills; and ability to function in a collaborative and collegial environment; sensitivity to others; high integrity and intelligence; excellent judgment; a conceptual thinker strategically as well as pragmatically; and an ability to generate trust and build alliances with co-workers.

**Exhibit 5　Information Classification**

---

**Introduction:**
Information, wherever it is handled or stored (for example, in computers, file cabinets, desktops, fax machines, voice mail) needs to be protected from unauthorized access, modification, disclosure, and destruction. All information is *not* created equal. Consequently, segmentation or classification of information into categories is necessary to help identify a framework for evaluating the relative value of the information and the appropriate controls required to preserve its value to the company.

Three basic classifications of information have been established. Organizations may define additional subclassifications as necessary to complete their framework for evaluating and preserving information under their control.

When information does require protection, the protection must be consistent. Often, strict access controls are applied to data stored in the mainframe computers but not applied to office workstations. Whether in a mainframe, client server, workstation, file cabinet, desk drawer, wastebasket, or in the mail, information should be subject to appropriate and consistent protection.

The definitions and responsibilities described below represent the minimum level of detail necessary for all organizations across the company. Each organization may decide that additional detail is necessary to adequately implement information classification within the organization.

| | |
|---|---|
| **Corporate Policy:** | All information must be classified by the **owner** into one of three classifications: **Confidential**, **Internal Use**, or **Public**. (From: Company Policy on Information Management) |
| **Internal Use Definition:** | Classify information as internal use when the information is intended for use by employees when conducting company business. |
| **Examples:** | Some examples of internal use information are:<br>■ Operational business information/reports;<br>■ Non-company information which is subject to a nondisclosure agreement with another company;<br>■ Company phone book;<br>■ Corporate policies, standards, and procedures; and<br>■ Internal company announcements. |
| **Public Definition:** | Classify information as public if the information has been made available for public distribution through authorized company channels. Public information is not sensitive in context or content, and requires no special protection. |

---

**Exhibit 5   Information Classification   (continued)**

---

**Examples:**          The following are examples of public information:
■ Corporate Annual Report
■ Information specifically generated for public consumption, such as public service bulletins, marketing brochures, and advertisements

**Declassification:**

Classified information normally declines in sensitivity with the passage of time. Downgrading should be as automatic as possible. If the information owner knows the date that the information should be reclassified, then it might be labeled as *Confidential until (date)*. There should be an established review process for all information classified as confidential, and reclassified when it no longer meets the criteria established for such information.

Part of an effective information classification program is to destroy documents when they are no longer required. Placing restrictions on copying classified documents will ensure that the documents and data sets are controlled and logged regarding the number of copies created and to whom those copies were assigned. To assist in this process, it may be convenient to create an information handling matrix.

---

**Exhibit 6   User Authorization Example**

---

■ Log-ins and passwords: No log-in/user should be created without a password.
■ All database applications must have database-level security implemented with every user having his or her own database account. Application security is then optional. Sharing accounts is prohibited.
■ If users' application logins are the same as their Sybase database logins, then users can access databases directly through isql or some other interface. Application designers should be aware of this danger when designing protection schemes: restrictions at the database level are much more secure than restrictions that are only enforced at the application level.
■ Database-level restrictions are not sufficiently secure to allow users to access the database directly, if they allow individuals access to data for which the application owners did not grant access permission via the normal interface of the application. In those cases, database passwords should be different from application passwords (so that users do not know their database passwords).
■ Passwords must be changed every 30 days.

---

■ *Risk assessment* — Assessment of threats to, impacts on, and vulnerabilities of information and information processing facilities and the likelihood of their occurrence. (This process is also known as risk

> analysis and CRC Press offers a top-selling book on the subject: *Information Security Risk Analysis*.)
> ■ *Risk management* — Process of identifying, controlling and minimizing, or eliminating security risks that may affect information systems, for an acceptable cost.

See Exhibit 7 for a summary of controls.

ISO 17799 and BS 7799 are copyrighted documents that will require you to contact the organizations and purchase a complete copy of the documents. What is presented here is just an overview of what is in the complete set of standards. As an example, the unabridged version of ISO 17799, Section 8 — Computer and Network Management, has approximately 170 standard recommendations. When developing your supporting standards, remember Section 2 recommends performing a risk analysis to ensure that controls are needed.

## 5.4  Summary

In this chapter we discussed the standard. In the introduction we examined where it fits in the scheme of written documents and found that it is needed to provide a policy with direction. It was strongly recommended that standards not be made part of the policy. This was mainly due to the process required to get policies modified and approved.

On the other hand, it is quite permissible to have policies found in a standards manual. When developing a standards manual, it will be necessary to have an overview (topic-specific or application/system policy) provide the introduction to the topic and then have supporting standards. This might look something like Exhibit 8.

This is a fairly straightforward overview and standards. The underscored item indicates that it is optional and therefore we would call it a guideline. It would be necessary to create standards for other kinds of systems, such as Macs and laptops.

We discussed where the standard fit in the process of documentation for employee use and why policies were not enough. We reviewed what a standard is and examined examples of standards and how they can work in your enterprise. Finally, we discussed the ISO 17799 International Standard for information security and how it is actually a guideline document.

To assist you in understanding what might be necessary in developing a security manual, Appendix A has a Policy Baseline Checklist that identifies 71 key elements to be considered when developing your information security documentation.

In Chapter 6 we discuss a number of procedure types, the pros and cons of each style, and examples of each.

**Exhibit 7    Controls Found in ISO 17799 Summarized from the International Organization for Standardization**

**Section 3    Security Policy**
    *3.1    Information Security Policy*
        *Objective:* To provide management direction and support for information security.
        3.1.1    Information Security policy document
                 A written policy document should be available to all employees responsible for information security.

**Section 4    Security Organization**
    *4.1    Information security infrastructure*
        *Objective:* To manage information security within the organization.
        4.1.1    Management information security forum
        4.1.2    Information security coordination
        4.1.3    Allocation of information security responsibilities
        4.1.4    Authorization process for IT facilities
        4.1.5    Specialist information security advice
        4.1.6    Cooperation between organizations
        4.1.7    Independent review of information security
    *4.2    Security of third-party access*
        *Objective:* To maintain the security of organizational IT facilities and information assets by third parties.
        4.2.1    Identification of risks from third-party connections
        4.2.2    Security conditions in third-party contracts

**Section 5    Assets Classification and Control**
    *5.1    Accountability for assets*
        *Objective:* To maintain appropriate protection of organizational assets.
        5.1.1    Inventory of assets
    *5.2    Information classification*
        *Objective:* To ensure that information assets receive an appropriate level of protection.
        5.2.1    Classification standards
        5.2.2    Classification labeling

**Section 6    Personnel Security**
    *6.1    Security in job definition and resourcing*
        *Objectives:* To reduce the risks of human error, theft, fraud, or misuse of facilities.
        6.1.1    Security in job descriptions
        6.1.2    Recruitment screening
        6.1.3    Confidentiality agreement

*(continued)*

**Exhibit 7    Controls Found in ISO 17799 Summarized from the International Organization for Standardization (continued)**

6.2   *User training*
Objective: To ensure that users are aware of information security threats and concerns, and are equipped to support organizational security policy in the course of their normal work.
6.2.1      Information security education and training

6.3   *Responding to incidents*
Objective: To minimize the damage from security incidents and malfunctions and to monitor and learn from such incidents.
6.3.1      Reporting security incidents
6.3.2      Reporting security weaknesses
6.3.3      Reporting of software malfunctions
6.3.4      Disciplinary process

**Section 7     Physical and Environmental Security**
7.1   *Secure areas*
Objectives: To prevent unauthorized access, damage, and interference to IT services.
7.1.1      Clear desk policy
7.1.2      Removal of property

7.2   *Equipment inventory*
Objective: To prevent loss, damage, or compromise of assets and interruption to business activities.
7.2.1      Equipment siting and protection
7.2.2      Power supply
7.2.3      Cabling security
7.2.4      Equipment maintenance
7.2.5      Security of equipment off-premises
7.2.6      Secure disposal of equipment

**Section 8     Computer and Network Management**
8.1   *Operational procedures and responsibilities*
Objective: To ensure the correct and secure operation of computer and network facilities.
8.1.1      Documented operating procedures
8.1.2      Incident management procedure
8.1.3      Segregation of duties
8.1.4      Separation of development and operational facilities
8.1.6      External facilities management

8.2   *System planning and acceptance*
Objective: To minimize the risk of system failure.
8.2.1      Capacity planning
8.2.2      System acceptance
8.2.3      Fallback planning
8.2.4      Operational change control

**Exhibit 7    Controls Found in ISO 17799 Summarized from the International Organization for Standardization (continued)**

**8.3    *Protection from malicious software***
*Objective:* To safeguard the integrity of software and data.
8.3.1      Virus control

**8.4    *Housekeeping***
*Objective:* To maintain the integrity and availability of IT services.
8.4.1      Data back-up
8.4.2      Operator logs
8.4.3      Fault logging
8.4.4      Environmental monitoring

**8.5    *Network management***
*Objective:* To ensure the safeguarding of information in networks and the protection of the supporting infrastructure.
8.5.1      Network security controls

**8.6    *Media handling and security***
*Objective:* To prevent damage to assets and interruptions to business activities.
8.6.1      Management of removable computer media
8.6.2      Data handling procedures
8.6.3      Security of system documentation
8.6.4      Disposal of media

**8.7    *Data and software exchange***
*Objective:* To prevent loss, modification, or misuse of data.
8.7.1      Data and software exchange agreements
8.7.2      Security of media in transit
8.7.3      EDI security
8.7.4      Security of electronic mail
8.7.5      Security of electronic office systems

**Section 9    System Access Control**
**9.1    *Business requirements for system access***
*Objectives:* To control access to business information.
9.1.1      Documented access control policy

**9.2    *User access management***
*Objective:* To prevent unauthorized computer access.
9.2.1      User registration
9.2.2      Privilege management
9.2.3      User password management
9.2.4      Review of user access rights

**9.3    *User responsibilities***
*Objective:* To prevent unauthorized user access.
9.3.1      Password use
9.3.2      Unattended user equipment

*(continued)*

**Exhibit 7    Controls Found in ISO 17799 Summarized from the International Organization for Standardization (continued)**

| | | |
|---|---|---|
| *9.4* | *Network access control* | |
| | *Objective:* Protection of networked services. | |
| | 9.4.1 | Limited services |
| | 9.4.2 | Enforced path |
| | 9.4.3 | User authentication |
| | 9.4.4 | Node authentication |
| | 9.4.5 | Remote diagnostics port protection |
| | 9.4.6 | Segregation in networks |
| | 9.4.7 | Network connection control |
| | 9.4.8 | Network routing control |
| | 9.4.9 | Security of network services |
| *9.5* | *Computer access control* | |
| | *Objective:* To prevent unauthorized computer access. | |
| | 9.5.1 | Automatic terminal identification |
| | 9.5.2 | Terminal logon procedures |
| | 9.5.3 | User identifiers |
| | 9.5.4 | Password management system |
| | 9.5.5 | Duress alarm to safeguard users |
| | 9.5.6 | Terminal time-out |
| | 9.5.7 | Limitation of connection time |
| *9.6* | *Application access control* | |
| | *Objective:* To prevent unauthorized access to information held in computer systems. | |
| | 9.6.1 | Information access restriction |
| | 9.6.2 | Use of system utilities |
| | 9.6.3 | Access control to program source libraries |
| | 9.6.4 | Sensitive system isolation |
| *9.7* | *Monitoring system access and use* | |
| | *Objective:* To detect unauthorized activities. | |
| | 9.7.1 | Event logging |
| | 9.7.2 | Monitoring system use |
| | 9.7.3 | Clock synchronization |
| **Section 10** | **Systems Development and Maintenance** | |
| *10.1* | *Security requirements of systems* | |
| | *Objective:* To ensure that security is built into IT systems. | |
| | 10.1.1 | Security requirements analysis and specification |
| *10.2* | *Security in application systems* | |
| | *Objective:* To prevent loss, modification, or misuse of user data in application systems. | |
| | 10.2.1 | Input data validation |
| | 10.2.2 | Internal processing validation |
| | 10.2.3 | Data encryption |
| | 10.2.4 | Message authentication |

**Exhibit 7    Controls Found in ISO 17799 Summarized from the International Organization for Standardization (continued)**

|  |  |
|---|---|
| **10.3** | ***Security of application system files*** |

*Objective:* To ensure that IT projects and support activities are conducted in a secure manner.

10.3.1    Control of operational software

10.3.2    Protection of system test data

**10.4    *Security in development and support environments***

*Objective:* To maintain the security of application system software and data.

10.4.1    Change control procedure

10.4.2    Technical review of operating system changes

10.4.3    Restrictions on changes to software packages

**Section 11    Business Continuity Planning**

**11.1    *Aspects of business continuity planning***

*Objective:* To have plans available to counteract interruptions to business activities.

11.1.1    Business continuity planning process

11.1.2    Business continuity planning framework

11.1.3    Testing business continuity plans

11.1.4    Updating business continuity plans

**Section 12    Compliance**

**12.1    *Compliance with legal requirements***

*Objective:* To avoid breaches of any statuary, criminal, or civil obligations and of any security requirements.

12.1.1    Control of proprietary software coping

12.1.2    Safeguarding of organizational records

12.1.3    Data protection

12.1.4    Prevention of misuse of IT facilities

**12.2    *Security review of IT systems***

*Objective:* To ensure compliance of systems with organizational security policies and procedures.

12.2.1    Compliance with security policy

12.2.2    Technical compliance checking

**12.3    *System audit considerations***

*Objective:* To minimize interference to and from the system audit process.

12.3.1    System audit controls

12.3.2    Protection of system audit tools

**Exhibit 8   Overview — Recommended Minimum Computer Workstation Standards**

Please check with your College or Department technical staff before purchasing any computer or peripheral equipment to ensure compatibility and support.

The following represents the recommended minimum system configurations for computer systems purchased by Enormous State University. These standards were developed by the Minimum Workstation Site License Subcommittee (MWSSLS).

Standards
- Intel FCPGA PIII 733 or Celeron 633 MHz Processor with compatible chipset, USB port with connector
- Two 16C550 UART serial ports, one enhanced parallel port, and USB
- NT compliant, DMI compliant, Plug & Play
- 512 Pipeline Burst cache
- 128 MB SDRAM expandable to 512 MB (At least (2) additional slots available)
- 256 MB SDRAM recommend for Oracle, SPSS, SAS, or Multimedia
- 1.44 MB floppy disk drive (TEAC)
- DVD CD-ROM drive (Pioneer and Toshiba are recommended brands)
- 64-bit AGP video card with 16 MB vram, 1024 × 768 resolution at 70 Hz NI, 16-bit color with RAMDAC (possible brands: nVidia or ATI)
- 3COM Jumperless (software configurable) 10/100Base-T PCI Network card (Model: 3C905B)
- 15 GB or greater hard disk drive (recommended brands: IBM and Seagate) with ATA66 plus controller
- ATX lockable case w/250 UL, CSA power supply desktop, or medium tower lockable case with 230-Watt power supply
- SVGA 17-inch non-interlaced color monitor with a minimum of .26 dot pitch or lower, 1024 × 768 @ 72 Hz, Plug & Play, Energy Star, Speakers should be built-in (recommended brands are Sony, NEC, or Iiyama)
- External speakers (if not built into monitor) [recommended brand is Altec-Lansing]
- Two-button PS/2 mouse
- MS Windows 98 SE (CD version)/2000 CD (SP 1) or Windows NT operating system (v4.0) (CD with tutorial SP 4 or 6a)
- 104-key enhanced keyboard
- PCI-integrated sound card with 100 percent Sound Blaster compliance
- 100 MB Internal ZIP Drive or Imation LS-120 floppy drive or tape backup unit [optional]
- Adaptec PCI 19160 ultrawide SCSI host adapter and cable [optional — needed to attach external drives]
- CD-ROM burner (recommended brands: Plextor, Yamaha, and HP) [optional]
- Warranty: Three-year in-house parts service on repairs (ESU technicians must be able to troubleshoot and exchange parts)
- No toll charge for telephone support
- Next working day on-site support

Approximate price of this configuration is $1620.00.

# Chapter 6

---

# Writing Procedures

---

Procedures are as unique as the organization. There is no generally accepted standard for the proper way to write a procedure. What will determine how your procedures look will be how they currently look or what will work best to provide the target audiences with what they need. This means that it may be necessary to use a number of different styles. In this section, we examine what some of those procedure styles look like and how they are used.

## 6.1 Definitions

### 6.1.1 Policy

A policy is a high-level statement of enterprise beliefs, goals, and objectives and the general means for their attainment for a specified subject area.

### 6.1.2 Standards

Standards are mandatory activities, actions, rules, or regulations designed to provide policies with the support structure and specific direction they require to be meaningful and effective. They are often expensive to administer and, therefore, should be used judiciously.

### 6.1.3 Guidelines

Guidelines are more general statements that are designed to achieve the objective of the policy by providing a framework within which to implement procedures. Whereas standards are mandatory, guidelines are recommendations.

### *6.1.4   Procedures*

Procedures spell out the specific step of how the policy and the supporting standards and guidelines will actually be implemented. They are a description of tasks that must be completed in a specific order.

## 6.2   Writing Commandments

The following ten commandments should be followed (see Exhibit 1).

*Write to the audience.* Procedures are created and implemented with the sole purpose of being read and used by the user community. Always keep the audience for these procedures in mind when writing. Before any procedure can be written, it will be necessary to know who the audience is and what its level of knowledge of the subject at hand is. Every department has its own language; therefore, the procedures must be addressed to each in the terms that each is used to. If you write procedures using the wrong "language," the procedure may as well be written in Sanskrit. The intended audience will not be able to understand it, or will find it difficult to follow.

*Organize the material.* The procedures must be written in a logical and flowing manner so that the reader can understand the meaning. If the text is not properly planned, the possibility is great that the intended audience will not clearly understand what is expected. The procedure must be broken up into easily digestible bits of information. Do not expect the user to read a long and involved passage and then successfully execute the appropriate processes.

*Read and edit the materials.* Do not just run the spell checker and assume that the editing is complete. Before handing over the material to the editor, proofread what has been written and see if it makes sense to you. If you are unable to understand what you have written, then it will be impossible for others to understand.

*Find subject experts.* The first step in any procedure development process is either to know the subject or to find people who do and use their knowledge

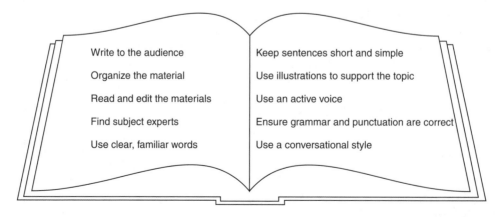

| | |
|---|---|
| Write to the audience | Keep sentences short and simple |
| Organize the material | Use illustrations to support the topic |
| Read and edit the materials | Use an active voice |
| Find subject experts | Ensure grammar and punctuation are correct |
| Use clear, familiar words | Use a conversational style |

**Exhibit 1   Writing's Important Keys**

to write the procedure. Subject experts may not understand the procedure-writing process, so it may be necessary for you to sit with them and take notes on how the process works and then write the procedure. Make sure that one of the editors is the subject expert. However, the subject expert should not be the person to test the procedure. Experts know the topic so well that they might assume information that is not present in the procedure.

*Use clear, familiar words.* The intended audience of the procedure will not be pleased if confronted with a document filled with words, expressions, and acronyms that are unfamiliar. It will be important to have a definition section in some procedures. This should be done up front and provide the reader with whatever is necessary to complete the process at hand.

Do not use big words; remember the reading and comprehension level of the intended audience (see Exhibit 2). Multiple syllables may be imprecise and use of the various "ese" languages should be avoided (finnancialese, auditese, legalese, securityese, computerese, etc.).

**Exhibit 2   Sample of Proper Words to Use in Writing Policies and Procedures**

| Words to Avoid | Familiar Words |
| --- | --- |
| accordingly | so |
| applicable | apply to |
| compensate | pay |
| foregoing | this |
| furthermore | also |
| in order to | to |
| in the near future | soon |
| subsequently | after |

Make sure to define all acronyms. There is nothing more irritating than to be reading a text that contains a number of *TLAs* (a TLA is a Three Letter Acronym for three-letter acronyms). The user will lose interest and comprehension if there are undefined terms in the text.

*Keep sentences short and simple.* Remember the KISS (Keep It Simple Sweetie) principle. Long sentences increase the level of frustration of the user and decrease the level of understanding. An appropriate average sentence length for procedures is between 10 and 15 words. Unless you are a writer of the caliber of a James Joyce, it would be wise to keep the sentences to the 15-word maximum level.

*Use illustrations to support the topic.* "A picture is worth a thousand words" may be a cliché, but it is true. Whenever applicable, break up the text with a graphic that depicts what is being discussed. These graphics can be pictures, charts (flow, pie, bar, etc.), tables, or diagrams. These will help the user visualize the subject and can provide the material necessary for a clear understanding of the process.

Illustrations include the use of screen prints. This will help users if they are interacting with a computer system. By providing a picture of the screen, users will be able to visualize what the process looks like and what is expected as a response.

*Use an active voice.* In the active voice, the sentences stress what has to occur. It will identify who is responsible for what action. For example, a *passive voice* might read as follows: "All tape drives are to be cleaned by the tape operators." An *active voice* might read as follows: "The tape operators are responsible for cleaning the tape drives on each shift." The active voice identifies who is responsible, and for what.

*Ensure grammar and punctuation are correct.* The number-one deadly sin is not taking care of this key element. Too many times materials have been sent out for content review and the text is filled with errors of grammar and punctuation. It is hard enough to get a critique of the subject. By presenting reviewers with error-filled material, they will correct the form and forget to comment on the substance. If this is not your strong suit, find someone who can do these edits.

*Use a conversational style.* This does not mean that the text should be full of slang and idioms; it should just be presented in an informal style. Most people communicate better when they are speaking than when they are writing. It could be that many individuals write to impress the reader as opposed to writing to express an idea. One very easy way around this problem is to write as if you are talking to the intended audience. However, if you have a tendency to speak like William F. Buckley, Jr., then you might want to have someone else review the material. Although a conversational style is preferred, this form does not relieve you of the responsibility of being precise.

## 6.3   Key Elements in Procedure Writing

There are four key purposes for writing a procedure.

1. The first is fulfill some need. If a task or process has to be performed in a specific manner, then there is a definite need for a procedure.
2. Once the need has been established, it will be necessary to identify the target audience.
3. Describe the task that the procedure will cover. It will be necessary to have opening remarks that present the scope of what the procedure is attempting to accomplish.
4. The intent of the procedure should also be made known to the user.

## 6.4   Procedure Checklist

Not every procedure will require all of the elements found in this procedure development checklist. Some may even require additional steps. As with any checklist, this is only a series of thought starters. The list that will be used by you may have additional items, or fewer.

1. *Title* — Establish what the topic of the procedure is going to be. Try to avoid being cute with your choice of words. Remember that you are writing for a business environment.
2. *Intent* — Discuss what the procedure is attempting to accomplish in general terms.
3. *Scope* — Briefly describe the process that the procedure is going to cover (e.g., Implementing a UNIX userid request).
4. *Responsibilities* — Identify who is to perform what steps in the procedure. Use job functions rather than individual names.
5. *Sequence of events* — It is very important for the user to understand the timing and conditions for performing the tasks identified in the procedure. Some tasks are not executed at a specific time, but must be performed when a specific condition is met.
6. *Approvals* — Identify any necessary approvals and when these approvals must be met. Approvals will be obtained prior to the execution of the procedure process.
7. *Prerequisites* — List any pre-conditions that must be met before starting the procedure process.
8. *Definitions* — Remember the audience. It will be beneficial to include a discussion of any terms and acronyms that are included in the body of the procedure.
9. *Equipment required* — Identify all equipment, tools, documents, and anything else the individual executing the procedure will need to perform the tasks.
10. *Warnings* — Some tasks, if operated in an improper sequence, could cause severe damage to the enterprise. Identify those key tasks and review the importance of understanding exactly when the task is to be executed and under what set of circumstances.
11. *Precautions* — Identify all steps to be taken to avoid problems or dangers (e.g., "Unplug before performing maintenance.")
12. *Procedure body* — This lists the actual steps to be performed in the execution of the procedure.

## 6.5 Getting Started

Now that you understand what the "do's and don'ts" of procedure writing are all about, we must now get down to the actual task. A procedure is the step-by-step process that an employee will use to complete a specific task. To write a procedure, then, it will be necessary to have a strong understanding of the task at hand. Very few of us have a sufficient level of knowledge for every subject. Therefore, it will be necessary for us to seek out subject matter experts (SMEs) to help in the development of procedures.

- The SMEs are usually those employees who handle a specific set of tasks daily, and it will be their knowledge that must be turned into a procedure. Many organizations have requested that the SMEs write the procedures themselves. This method has met with limited success. What is currently recommended is that the organization hire documentation experts to interview the SMEs and then write the procedures.

- Our employees are generally overworked now. Asking them to perform a task that most do not want to do will cause lengthy delays in completing the process. By conducting an interview (not to last longer that 90 minutes) and having the documentation expert write the draft document, it may be possible actually to complete the procedure development process on time.

- Once the draft is completed, it should be given to the SME and the SME backup for review and critique. Allow this process to take five to ten workdays. Once the comments are incorporated, send the procedures out for a final review and include the supervisor of the SME. After the procedures are returned, make any final adjustments and then publish them. Ensure that the SME reviews the procedures at least annually for changes.

## 6.6   Procedure Styles

There are perhaps as many as six different styles of procedures. Any one of them may meet the needs of your organization.

1. Headline
2. Caption
3. Matrix
4. Narrative
5. Flowchart
6. Playscript

Of these six, Narrative and Headline should be used very seldom. Others (especially Caption and Playscript) should be used very often. The choice of layout will depend upon the subject matter to be presented and the individuals using the material. Each has its advantages and disadvantages. We will examine six of the most popular forms of procedures and will identify the positive side to each as well as any shortcomings.

The following general guidelines should be applied no matter what layout is used.

- Ensure that every subject has a summary.
- Use a summary (topic policy) to introduce the topic to the reader and outline the scope and objectives of the procedure.
- Present policy and/or background information such as why a procedure is to be carried out and who is responsible for carrying it out.
- Use brief paragraphs.
- Keep your words and sentences brief and simple, as well as paragraphs.
- Keep subjects brief.

- Do only one procedure per procedure.
- Write only to the audience concerned.
- Know to whom you are writing and use them as a focus group.
- Cross-reference only when necessary (cross-referencing will increase the need to monitor other sources to keep the procedures current).
- Include detail (the inclusion of detail does not contradict the requirement to be brief).
- Be aware that one of the most consistent problems with procedures is the tendency to leave out details.

## *6.6.1 Headline*

A headline style is a title line placed above the text. It is usually printed in bold and briefly summarizes or suggests the content of the text that follows (like a newspaper). See Exhibit 3 for samples of various sorts of headlines.

**Exhibit 3    Example of Headline Style**

**P&PME PROCESS**

**0. Project Initiation**
- 0.1.    Conduct project definition and confirmation meeting with customer
- 0.2.    Develop documentation
- 0.3.    Present findings and obtain approval of SOW
- 0.4.    Develop Engagement Agreement
- 0.5.    Develop Non-Disclosure Agreement

**1. Pre-Site Visit to Outline Expectations and Security Requirements**
- 1.1.    Determine project ownership
- 1.2.    Determine client's expectations
- 1.3.    Define project scope
  - 1.3.1.    Scope statement
  - 1.3.2.    Scope verification
  - 1.3.3.    Scope change control
- 1.4.    Define project approach
  - 1.4.1.    Define project milestones
  - 1.4.2.    Define project schedule
  - 1.4.3.    Define project deliverables
- 1.5.    Define project organization
- 1.6.    Define project constraints
- 1.7.    Define project assumptions
- 1.8.    Define project risks
- 1.9.    Define quantifiable project success criteria
- 1.10.   Develop and submit Project Charter
- 1.11.   Obtain client approval of Project Charter

**2. Facilitated Site Visit to Gather Data**
- 2.1.    Identify existing security policy and procedure documentation
- 2.2.    Determine existing security policy hierarchy/definitions

*(continued)*

**Exhibit 3   Example of Headline Style (continued)**

2.3.   Identify existing corporate policy development/maintenance process
2.4.   Evaluate organizational security culture
2.5.   Determine Requirements
 2.5.1.   Regulatory
 2.5.2.   Legal requirements
 2.5.3.   Contractual
 2.5.4.   Business
2.6.   Identify policy responsibilities
 2.6.1.   Development
 2.6.2.   Review
 2.6.3.   Approval
 2.6.4.   Communication
 2.6.5.   Implementation
 2.6.6.   Compliance Monitoring
 2.6.7.   Exception Approval
 2.6.8.   Maintenance
 2.6.9.   Awareness
2.7.   Collect documentation
 2.7.1.   Incident reports
 2.7.2.   Risk assessments
 2.7.3.   Audit reports
 2.7.4.   Organization charts
 2.7.5.   Security awareness materials
3.   **Planning for the Development of Policies and Procedures Documentation**
3.1.   Analyze existing policies against identified policy requirements
3.2.   Conduct analysis of existing policies against leading practices (e.g., BS 7799)
3.3.   Document and prioritize policy shortfalls and identify policy needs
3.4.   Present interim findings to client
3.5.   Obtain client approval of findings
3.6.   Develop required documentation
4.   **Documentation Review by Client**
4.1.   Provide draft policy and procedure documentation to the client for review
4.2.   Establish review process
 4.2.1.   Establish Review Panel composition
 4.2.2.   Validate review responsibilities
 4.2.3.   Validate review schedule
4.3.   Assist client with review sessions
4.4.   Coordinate with client to keep review on schedule
4.5.   Address comments received from client reviewers
5.   **Formal Presentation of Engagement Deliverables**
5.1.   Prepare final deliverable by updating draft deliverable to incorporate validated reviewer comments
5.2.   Obtain client sign-off and approval

Pros:

- The procedure is divided into organized blocks of data.

Cons:

- The procedure is meant to be read from beginning to end.
- The headline is used to grab the reader's eye and not as a means of retrieval.

## *6.6.2    Caption*

Captions are key words that appear in the left margin of the page and that highlight or describe the blocks of text opposite them. See Exhibit 4 for examples of captions.

Pros:

- Simple layout
- Easy to read
- Easy to retrieve information
- Can be used for almost any subject
- Can be mixed with other styles

Cons:

- Writers tend to overuse
- Should not be used for describing sequenced actions
- Sometimes difficult to organize material into meaningful order

This style is used best for descriptive text that answers all writing questions: who, what, when, where, why. Examples of subject matter that lends itself to caption best include:

- Policy statements
- Responsibility statements
- Descriptions of forms, reports, or equipment

**Exhibit 4    Example of Caption Style**

**Hiring Responsibilities**

| | |
|---|---|
| Systems: | The Supervisor is responsible for: |
| | ■ Recommending a candidate |
| | ■ Obtaining approval to hire from the manager |
| | ■ Notifying Human Resources |
| Human Resources: | The Hiring Officer is responsible for: |
| | ■ Making the job offer, in accordance with company policy |
| | ■ Induction and orientation interviews |

### 6.6.3    Matrix

A matrix is a chart that lists related constants and variables (or independent and dependent variables) on horizontal and vertical axes. At the intersection of lines drawn from each axis may be found such information as:

- Relationship between constants and variables
- Actions to be performed depending on variables or conditions

Pros:

- Data is presented in a simple and logical order.
- Repetitive information is eliminated.
- A one-page matrix may replace many pages of text.
- Retrieval time and reading time are saved.

Cons:

- Maintaining data can be time-consuming.
- Initial setup can also take time.

Exhibit 5 shows an example of a matrix.

### 6.6.4    Narrative

Narrative procedure style presents information in paragraph format. It presents the process in a conversational or narrative form. This method does not present the user with easy-to-follow steps; rather, it requires the user to read the entire paragraph to find out what is expected. This method is recommended for such items as policy statements, company philosophy, or background material.

Exhibit 6 shows an example of the narrative form of procedure writing. Note how all of the information that the user will need is presented. The discussion flows through a logical progression of the steps to be followed.

Pros:

- Written in the manner people speak
- Very thorough

Cons:

- Too difficult to use
- Reader cannot retrieve information quickly

The narrative style lets users know how to do something by telling them a story. For some, this is the method that is easiest to understand. However, for most, the narrative style is too long.

**Exhibit 5  Example of Matrix Style**

| | Confidential | Internal Use | Public |
|---|---|---|---|
| *Labeling* of documents | Document should identify owner and be marked "CONFIDENTIAL" on cover or title page | No special requirements | Document may be marked "PUBLIC" on cover or title page |
| *Duplication* of documents | Information owner to determine permissions | Duplication for business purposes only | No special requirements |
| *Mailing* of documents | No classification marking on external envelope; "CONFIDENTIAL" marking on cover sheet; confirmation of receipt at discretion of information owner | Mailing requirements determined by information owner | No special requirements |
| *Disposal* of documents | Owner Observed physical destruction beyond ability to recover | Controlled physical destruction | No special requirements |
| *Storage* of documents | Locked up when not in use | Master copy secured against destruction | Master copy secured against destruction |
| *Read* access to documents | Owner establishes user access rules; generally highly restricted | Owner establishes user access rules, generally widely available | No special requirements; generally available within and outside company |
| *Review* of document classification level | Information owner to establish specific review date (not to exceed one year) | Information owner to review at least annually | No special requirements |

**Exhibit 6  Example of Narrative Style**

**TOKEN CARDS**
*Intent:*
Secure remote access. To identify and authenticate an authorized system user using a SecurID that requires a memorized personal identification number (PIN) and something that is unique to the user who possesses the SecurID token.

*Scope:*
The following procedures provide direction on the proper use of the SecurID and procedures for remote log-ins.

*Responsibilities:*
Management:
ISSO keeps track of when cards are scheduled to expire and will notify you and arrange for a replacement card in advance so that your access privileges will not be interrupted. Access control remains in the hands of management.

Users:
■ Are responsible for the safekeeping and protection of their SecurID card
■ Are responsible for ensuring that their SecurID card is not used by any other individual
■ Are responsible for immediately informing (the appropriate institutional personnel) when a card is lost or misplaced so that it can be de-activated

*Sequence of Events:*
1. Application for SecurID
2. First-time use and PIN change procedure
3. Log-on procedure
4. Next code procedure
5. Activating a replacement SecurID card

*Approvals:*
■ Approval of immediate supervisor for SecurID
■ Approval of ISSO for SecurID

*Prerequisites:*
■ Get approval to use a SecurID
■ Get procedure for access
■ Load software on workstation
■ Must have SecurID card available for remote log-ins

*Request for SecurID*
Requestor        ■ Complete template for SecurID
                 ■ Forward to Supervisor for approval
Supervisor       ■ Approve template for SecurID and forward to IP account administration

**Exhibit 6   Example of Narrative Style (continued)**

| | |
|---|---|
| IP Account | ■ Process SecurID request |
| Administration | ■ Provide requestor with SecurID Card |
| | ■ Associated software for remote system access |
| Requestor | ■ Load necessary software for remote access |
| | ■ Activate SecurID card |

*Definitions:*

*Access* A specific type of interaction between a subject and an object that results in the flow of information from one to the other. The capability and opportunity to gain knowledge of, or to alter information or materials, including the ability and means to communicate with (i.e., input or receive output) or otherwise make use of any information, resource, or component in a computer system.

*Access Control* The process of limiting access to the resources of a system to only authorized persons, programs, processes, or other systems. Synonymous with controlled access and limited access. Requires that access to information resources be controlled by or for the target system. In the context of network security, access control is the ability to limit and control the access to host systems and applications via communications links. To achieve this control, each entity trying to gain access must first be identified, or authenticated, so that access rights can be tailored to the individual.

*Authenticate/Authentication* The process to verify the identity of a user, device, or other entity in a computer system, often as a prerequisite to allowing access to resources in a system. A process used to verify that the origin of transmitted data is correctly identified, with assurance that the identity is not false. To establish the validity of a claimed identity.

*Authenticated User* A user who has accessed the Company system with a valid identifier and authentication combination.

*Authorization* The privileges and permissions granted to an individual by a designated official to access or use a program, process, information, or system. These privileges are based on the individual's approval and need-to-know.

*Authorized Person* A person who has the need-to-know sensitive information in the performance of official duties and who has been granted authorized access at the required level. The responsibility for determining whether a prospective recipient is an authorized person rests with the person who has possession, knowledge, or control of the sensitive information involved, and not with the prospective recipient.

*Cardcode* The cardcode is the six-digit number displayed on a SecurID card.

*Computer Security* Technological and managerial procedures applied to the Company systems to ensure the availability, integrity, and confidentiality of information managed by the Company.

*Confidentiality* The condition when designated information collected for approved purposes is not disseminated beyond a community of authorized personnel. It is distinguished from secrecy, which results from the intentional concealment or withholding of information. Confidentiality refers to: (1) how data will be maintained and used by the organization that collected it; (2) what further uses will be made of it; and (3) when individuals will be required to consent to such uses. It includes the protection of data from passive attacks and requires that the information (in the Company system or transmitted) be accessible only for reading by authorized parties. Access can include printing, displaying, and other forms of disclosure, including simply revealing the existence of an object.

*(continued)*

**Exhibit 6   Example of Narrative Style (continued)**

*Data* A representation of facts, concepts, information, or instructions suitable for communication, interpretation, or processing. It is used as a plural noun meaning "facts or information" as in: These data are described fully in the appendix, or as a singular mass noun meaning "information" as in: The data is entered into the computer. [Random House Webster's College Dictionary, 1994]

*Data Integrity* The state that exists when computerized data are the same as those that are in the source documents and have not been exposed to accidental or malicious alterations or destruction. It requires that the Company systems assets and transmitted information be capable of modification only by authorized parties. Modification includes writing, changing, changing status, deleting, creating, and the delaying or replaying of transmitted messages. See also: Integrity.

*Denial of Service* The prevention of authorized access to resources or the delaying of time-critical operations. Refers to the inability of the Company system or any essential part to perform its designated mission, either by loss of or by degradation of operational capability.

*Discretionary Access Control (DAC)* A means of restricting access to objects based on the identity of subjects and/or groups to which they belong or on the possession of an authorization granting access to those objects. The controls are discretionary in the sense that a subject with certain access permission is capable of passing that permission (perhaps indirectly) onto any other subject.

*Information Security* The protection of information systems against unauthorized access to or modification of information, whether in storage, processing, or transit, and against the denial of service to authorized users or the provision of service to unauthorized users, including those measures necessary to detect, document, and counter such threats.

*Information Systems Security (INFOSEC)* The protection of information assets from unauthorized access to or modification of information, whether in storage, processing, or transit, and against the denial of service to authorized users or the provision of service to unauthorized users, including those measures necessary to detect, document, and counter such threats. INFOSEC reflects the concept of the totality of the Company system security.

*Identification* The process that enables recognition of an entity by a system, generally by the use of unique machine-readable user names.

*Information System Security Officer (ISSO)* The person responsible to the DAA for ensuring that security is provided for and implemented throughout the life cycle of a Company system from the beginning of the system concept development phase through its design, development, operations, maintenance, and disposal.

*Integrity* A sub-goal of computer security which ensures that (1) data is a proper representation of information; (2) data retains its original level of accuracy; 3) data remains in a sound, unimpaired, or perfect condition; (3) the Company systems perform correct processing operations; and (4) the computerized data faithfully represents that in the source documents and has not been exposed to accidental or malicious alteration or destruction.

*Need-to-Know* A determination by the owner of sensitive information that a prospective recipient has a requirement for access to, knowledge of, or possession of the information in order to perform tasks or services essential to carry out official duties.

## Exhibit 6   Example of Narrative Style (continued)

*Network* A communications medium and all components attached to that medium whose responsibility is the transference of information. Such components may include The Company systems, packet switches, telecommunications controllers, key distribution centers, and technical control devices.

*Network Security* Protection of networks and their services from unauthorized modification, destruction, or disclosure, and the provision of assurance that the network performs its critical functions correctly and there are no harmful side effects.

*Passcode* The passcode is your PIN followed by your cardcode with no spaces. For example, if the number displayed on your card (your cardcode) is 444678 and your PIN is 1234, then your passcode is 1234444678.

*Password* A protected and private character string used to authenticate the Company systems user.

*PIN* The PIN is your personal identification number. It is initially set to a four-digit number.

*Security Dynamics [SecurID]* A network access security system developed by Security Dynamics, Inc. (SDI). SecurID sits between the incoming modem and the remote access server that provides access to the network; when a dial-in client calls in to the network, the user must first enter the correct SecurID information before connecting to the remote access server. The SecurID card is a credit-card-sized token that lets authorized users access protected computer systems. It consists of a microprocessor that calculates and displays a cardcode. The cardcode is, in essence, your password. The cardcode changes unpredictably at specified intervals, typically between 30 and 60 seconds.

*Security Dynamics [ACE/Server]* Security Dynamics ACE/Server is a system of server and client software and SecurID cards. Once enabled, SecurID authentication is used for the following protocols: IP, IPX, NetBEUI, LLC, and ARA.

*Security Policy* The set of laws, rules, directives, and practices that regulate how an organization manages, protects, and distributes controlled information.

### *Equipment Required:*
- ACE/Server
- SecurID

### *Warnings:*
The SecurID card is rugged enough to withstand reasonably adverse conditions. However, the card is an electronic device and should be handled with care.

- DO NOT immerse the card in water or get it wet.
- DO NOT let it be exposed to temperature extremes (temperatures colder than –5°F or hotter than 120°F, nor to sustained temperatures above 90°F).
- DO NOT subject it to excessive (i.e., dangerous to people) electric or electromagnetic activity, including such radiation as microwaves, x-rays, or electrostatic shock.
- DO NOT drop it on a hard surface, bend, or otherwise stress it excessively. In particular, do not carry it in a pants pocket or put it in a wallet carried in a back pocket. The cardcode display area of the card is an LCD (liquid crystal display) screen and is made of glass that can be damaged by too much pressure, such as when sitting down.

*(continued)*

**Exhibit 6   Example of Narrative Style (continued)**

■ DO NOT write on or stick anything to the card.
■ DO NOT use a pen or any other sharp object to press the PIN keys on the card. This will permanently damage the card.

***Precautions:***
The SecurID card is a sophisticated microprocessor and is costly to replace. You are responsible for the card issued to you.
■ DO NOT lend your SecurID card to anyone else.
■ NEVER leave your SecurID card on your desk or next to your personal computer where it can be taken or used by someone else. When you are not using the card, put it back in its protective jacket. Carry it with you or lock it in your desk drawer or a filing cabinet for safekeeping.
■ Your SecurID card has a Personal Identification Number (PIN) associated with it. The PIN is confidential and should not be divulged or shared with anyone else. Treat your SecurID PIN like you treat the PIN for your credit and bank cards. Sharing a PIN is against the Company information security policy and may lead to disciplinary action.
■ Your PIN must be between four and six digits long. You cannot use alphabetic or special characters as part of your PIN. Longer PINs are more secure and therefore a six-digit PIN is recommended.
■ PINs may not start with a zero, but a zero may be used in any other position.
■ Pick a PIN that is easy for you to remember but hard from someone else to guess.
■ If you feel someone knows your PIN, contact your department Access Control Representative right away and your PIN will be reset for you.
■ DO NOT write down the PIN and, more importantly, do not write the PIN on the card.
■ If you forget your PIN, contact your department Access Control Representative and your PIN will be reset for you.
■ DO NOT use obvious, trivial, or predictable PINs. Examples of bad PINs include:
    Your birth date
    Your home/office telephone number or parts thereof
    Your Company or home street number or your office room number
    PINs using numbers in sequence such as 1234, 3456, 4321, etc.
    PINs using repetitive numbers

***Procedure Body:***
*First-Time Use and PIN Change Procedure*
The first time you use your SecurID card and whenever your Personal Identification Number (PIN) is reset, you must register your SecurID card on the system.
■ When you first access the system, the LOGON screen is displayed.
■ Enter your User ID and press the TAB key. Do not press the Enter key at this time.
■ Enter the Card Serial Number (see example below) printed on the back of your SecurID card, followed by a Forward slash "/" and the cardcode displayed on your SecurID LCD screen.
    *Example:*
    If the serial number of your card is 03103144 and the cardcode displayed on your card is 582984, enter 03103144/582984 in the passcode field.

**Exhibit 6   Example of Narrative Style (continued)**

- Do not enter any spaces between the card serial number, the forward slash, and the cardcode.
- Press the Enter key.
- The system displays the "ENTER NEW USER DEFINED PIN" screen.
- Choose a PIN (For more information refer to The Personal Identification Number (PIN) section.)
- Enter the PIN you have chosen.
- Press the Enter key.
- The system displays the "RETYPE TO CONFIRM:" screen.
- Reenter the PIN you have chosen to confirm that you have entered it correctly the first time.
- Press the Enter key.
- The system displays the log-on screen one more time.
- Proceed to the Log-on Procedure.

*Log-on Procedure*
- The system displays the log-on screen when you first access the system.
- Enter your User ID.
- Press the TAB key. Be careful not to start entering the cardcode before pressing the * key. Do not press the Enter key at this time.
- Enter your PIN into the SecurID card PIN pad and then press the Diamond Symbol to display the cardcode.
- Enter the six-digit cardcode displayed on your SecurID card LCD screen in the passcode field.
- Now press the Enter key.

If you enter the information incorrectly, the system will not approve your access. Try again. You have five chances to enter the correct information. If for some reason you are not able to enter the right information after ten attempts, your SecurID card will be suspended by the system. This is for security reasons. If this happens, contact your Access Control Representative immediately so that your card can be reactivated.

Once you enter a valid passcode, the system may display the "CARDCODE APPROVED" message.

The system now displays your Menu screen.

For security reasons, once accepted, a SecurID cardcode cannot be reused. If you log out and try to log in again before the cardcode changes, you will not succeed the second time. Wait until the cardcode changes before trying again.

*Next Code Procedure*
On occasion after you have entered your cardcode correctly, the system may ask you to enter the next cardcode that is displayed on the LCD screen of your SecurID card. This occurs either when your card has not been used for a few weeks or if you had several failed attempts prior to a successful log-in.

*(continued)*

**Exhibit 6   Example of Narrative Style (continued)**

1. When this happens, the system displays the "NEXT CODE" screen.
2. Wait until the next cardcode is displayed and then enters it.
3. Press the Enter key.
4. The system now displays your Menu screen.

*Activating a Replacement SecurID Card*
When your SecurID card expires or if you damage or lose your SecurID card, Computer Security Administration will issue a replacement card. The replacement card must be activated before it can be used to access the system(s) you are authorized for.

*Activating Your Replacement SecurID Card*
Your replacement card is reactivated automatically by the SecurID system. Follow the same procedure you use when logging in. The system will remember the PIN you used on your previous card.

## 6.6.5   Flowchart

Flowcharts are pictorial representations in which symbols are used to depict persons, places, actions, functions, or equipment. They give the user a diagram of the decision-making process and what is expected at each step.

Flowcharts are best used when providing the user with an overview of what the process is going to be. The flowchart will help users understand their portion of the procedure. They will be able to see where decisions are to be made and what direction to take based on the decision. It will be necessary to have a key to ensure that the user understands what the flowchart symbols mean.

The flowchart procedure style should be considered a supplement to the actual procedure text. This process of laying out the procedure in a flowchart is actually beneficial to the writer of the procedure. By developing a decision flow process, the procedure writer will have a better chance of developing a logical and correct procedure.

Pros:

■ It is easy to read.
■ Technical types are familiar with the style.

Cons:

■ Nontechnical types do not like flowcharts.

An example of a flowchart-type policy might include the narrative and then the actual flowchart, as shown in Exhibit 7.

**Exhibit 7  Example of Flowchart Style**

**Levels of ROOT Exposure**

An individual may obtain a ROOT (or systems administration) level account, depending upon the user's work assignment. Securing a ROOT account requires the approval of a level B Information Systems Manager, with subordinate approval as well.

If a user is part of the System Administration Staff, the user may be granted access via the System Administration or Root group, depending upon the platform being utilized. Users who are Department System Administrators may be granted department administrator access. Any user who is a Workgroup Administrator may be granted Workgroup Administrator access. Users who are project administrators may be granted access as necessary, depending upon the project. Any user-initiated root request will be denied root access.

***Definitions (Levels of Root Access):***
*System Administrator or Root Access*   Full access to all computer resources.
*Department System Administrator Access*   Full access to all computer resources available to the specific department.
*Workgroup Administrator Access*   Full access to all computer resources available to the specific workgroup.
*Project Administrator Access*   Access will be determined on a project-by-project basis and limited to only those areas necessary to satisfy the requirements of the project.

All user IDs with any ROOT level access will be added to the audit log functions and Security will be notified to monitor all ROOT access IDs.

Any violations or abuses of a ROOT level access must be reported to Security Management (e-mail notification or security incident form) and to the MIS Department (security incident form).

## 6.6.6   Playscript

For anyone who has ever been in a play or has had the opportunity to read a play in a literature class, this style will be familiar. The process identifies each of the main participants, the actual commands to be entered, and any direction needed to complete the process. Exhibit 8 gives an example of this.

The playscript identifies each individual involved in the procedure. Each step involved in the procedure is described in detail and when each step is to be executed. The playscript is easy to understand and the language used eliminates unnecessary words (adjectives and adverbs). Keep the sentences to the point; remember that you are writing procedure, not the great American novel. A typical statement might be "sign and date forms" or "forward form 1040A to supervisor."

**Exhibit 8   Example of Playscript Style**

---

**Submitting Papers for Public**

Employees:

I. Shall submit to their manager

    A.  Information about the conference, journal, magazine, etc. where the information will be submitted for potential presentation.

    B.  The submission guidelines of the conference, journal, magazine, etc. where the information will be presented.

    C.  An abstract of the presentation, article, or white paper that will be published or presented.

    D.  A writing and research timeline.

The Manager will then:

5.  Approve the presentation, white paper, or article.

6.  Not approve the presentation, white paper, or article. → Stop.

The Employee will then:

1.  Submit the abstract to conference.

2.  Begin writing white paper or article.

3.  Begin any required research.

4.  Provide brief updates to manager when each part of timeline is completed.

5.  Ensure presentation, white paper, or article complies with the Information Protection policy.

6.  If submitting to a conference, receive presentation acceptance. If declined → Stop

7.  Submit final paper or presentation to manager for final approval.

Manager will then:

1.  Give final approval

2.  Decline → Stop

Employee:

1.  Submit article or white paper to journal or magazine, etc.

2.  Receive acceptance from magazine or journal or they decline. → Stop

3.  Give presentation at conference.

Stop

---

    In the playscript style it is best to describe only one function in any one step. As part of the definition section of the procedure, define the key participants in the procedure and use a form of shorthand to call out that participant. For example, instead of having to identify the Corporate Information Officer, use CIO. For the Manager of Information Systems, Operation, and Quality Assurance, you may want to shorten this title to Manager. The key here is to keep it simple, but eliminate any confusion.

    Another variation on the playscript style of procedure writing is the *tree style* (see Exhibit 9). This uses the same basic layout as the playscript, but it allows the user to drill down to each of the steps identified.

## Exhibit 9  Example of Tree Style

**Employee Standards of Conduct**

*Intent:*   The intent is to define standard procedures for employee conduct.

*Scope:*   The procedure will outline acceptable and unacceptable behavior for all employees of the Company.

*Responsibilities:*   It is the responsibility of management to ensure a just and fair environment for all employees. It is the responsibility of the employee to avoid conflicts of interest, report misconduct, and follow all standards of conduct.

*Sequence of Events:*   A grievance, misconduct, or question regarding a conflict-of-interest situation must arise.

*Approvals:*   The termination of an employee must have final approval from senior management.

*Prerequisites:*   None

*Definitions:*
> *Employee:*   Any person compensated for services rendered by The Company.
> *General Auditor:*   Person who is responsible for advising in and investigating all reported misconduct and violations of standards of conduct.
> *Immediate Family Member:*   As defined by the Internal Revenue Code of the United States.
> *Insider Information:*   Nonpublic information.

*[Equipment Required:]*
- Information Protection policy
- Conflict of Interest policy

*Warnings:*   None

*Precautions:*   None

**Procedure Body:**
***Standards of Conduct***
*Employees*
1. Shall act in an ethical manner, and shall avoid actions that have the appearance of being unethical
2. Shall abide by applicable laws, regulations, and professional standards
3. Shall avoid conflict of interest situations (see Conflict of Interest policy for more information)
4. Shall meet individual performance expectations
5. Shall abide by company and organizational policies and practices

*(continued)*

**Exhibit 9    Example of Tree Style (continued)**

6. Shall accurately and honestly record and report corporate information; employees shall also maintain the confidentiality of corporate information (see Information Protection policy)
7. Shall treat co-workers and others with dignity and respect

| Employees | Manager | General Auditor |
|---|---|---|
| 1. Are expected to use intelligence, common sense, and good judgment in applying these standards of conduct. | | |
| 2. When in doubt shall direct questions relating to the standards of conduct to their managers. | | |
| 3. Those who observe conduct that does not appear consistent with these standards of conduct should discuss the matter with their managers. However, employees who feel uncomfortable reporting to their managers, or who are not satisfied with the action taken, rather than letting the matter drop, should seek the counsel of the General Auditor. | 1. Take reports of Standard of Conduct violations, or suspected violations, from employees. | |
| Employees who feel that they have been the subject of a violation of the standards of conduct should immediately report the matter to their manager or to the Vice President of Human Resources. | 2. Report fraudulent activity to the General Auditor, in the Risk Management Office. | |
| | 3. Investigate all complaints in as discreet a fashion as possible. | Take reports of fraudulent activity from Managers. |
| | 4. Take action where appropriate, once the investigation is complete. | Investigate all complaints in as discreet a fashion as possible. |
| | 5. Provide appropriate feedback to those who report misconduct. | Take action where appropriate, once investigation is complete |
| | | Provide appropriate feedback to those who report misconduct. |

---

**Exhibit 9   Example of Tree Style (continued)**

---

*Vice President of Human Resources*
1. Take reports of possible standards of conduct violations from employees.
2. Investigate all complaints in as discreet a fashion as possible.
3. Take action where appropriate, once investigation is complete
4. Provide appropriate feedback to those who report misconduct.

*The Corporation*
1. Will not retaliate against any employee who reports suspected misconduct.
2. Shall provide or select legal counsel and indemnify any employee who becomes involved in a legal matter arising out of employment with the Company, if, in the opinion of the General Counsel, the employee was acting in good faith, within the scope of the job responsibilities, and legal counsel or indemnification is not otherwise available to the employee.

---

## 6.7   Creating a Procedure

After the SME has been interviewed, write the procedure and then send it to both the SME and the SME backup. Have them review and edit the procedure. Take the edits and incorporate them into the procedure and then publish the procedure. There is no need for additional rounds of reviews. When writing the procedure, remember the following:

- Establish a small, knowledgeable initial review panel.
- Do not create all the procedures by yourself. Seek out personnel in areas affected by the controls and gain their expertise and assistance in this process.
- Be certain that the procedures resemble the procedures currently being used in your organization.
- Try to get on the agenda of the IS Steering Committee to present your program and solicit the support of the committee.
- Whenever possible, accept and implement the comments created by the reviewers. At the very least, contact the reviewer and explain why the comments could not be included.
- If there appears to be a conflict, set up a meeting, at the respondent's location if possible, to resolve the problem.
- Be persistent. You are going to have to keep after the reviewers to get their responses.

## 6.8   Summary

When writing procedures, it is best to keep the language as simple as possible. Attempt to stay away from flowery phrases and multi-syllable words. Keep the sentences short and the terms crisp. Identify what each role is in the procedure and find the style that best meets the needs of your organization.

In this chapter we have reviewed the definitions of policy, procedure, standard, and guideline. The writing "Ten Commandments" were discussed. We then examined the procedure key elements:

- Identify the procedure need.
- Identify the target audience.
- Establish the scope of the procedure.
- Describe the intent of the procedure.

We then examined a procedure twelve-point checklist and the six styles of procedures:

1. Headline
2. Caption
3. Matrix
4. Narrative
5. Flowchart
6. Playscript

# Chapter 7

# Information Classification

This chapter is devoted to addressing a specific topic, information classification, and what the policies for this topic might look like. Included in the text is a formal discussion on each of the classifications and examples of existing policy statements. We critique these policies and establish the framework for the development of such a policy for any organization. We examine what constitutes confidential information, employee responsibilities, an example of an information handling matrix, and an information classification methodology.

## 7.1  Introduction

Information is an asset and the property of the organization. All employees are to protect information from unauthorized access, modification, disclosure, and destruction. Before employees can be expected to protect information, they must first understand their responsibility. An information classification policy and methodology will provide them with the help they need.

There are four essential aspects of information classification: (1) information classification from a legal standpoint, (2) responsibility for care and control of information, (3) integrity of the information, and (4) the criticality of the information and systems processing the information. Examples of how the classification process fits into the application and system development life cycle are presented to assist you in the development of your own information classification process.

## 7.2  Why Classify Information

Organizations classify information to establish the appropriate levels of protection for those resources. Because resources are limited, it will be necessary

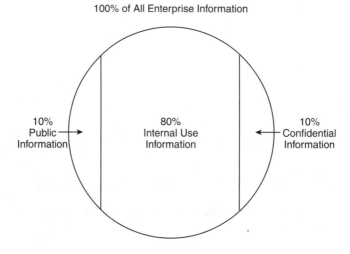

**Exhibit 1    Information Classification Breakdown**

to prioritize and identify what really needs protection. One of the reasons to classify information is to ensure that scarce resources be allocated where they will do the most good. All information is created equally, but not all information is of equal value (Exhibit 1).

The old concept in computer security was that everything is closed until it is opened. However, after nearly 20 years of working with companies in establishing information classification systems, I have found that nearly 90 percent of all enterprise information needs to be accessed by employees or is available through public forums. Because resources are limited, the concept that all information is open until it requires closing is perhaps a better way of protecting information.

Most organizations do not have information that is all of the same value. Therefore, it is necessary at least to develop an initial high-level attempt at classification. This should be done, if for no other reason than to ensure that budgeted resources are not misused in protecting or not protecting information assets. Before employees can protect information assets, they must first have a mechanism in place that allows them to establish the value of the information. An information classification system and a scoring methodology that relies on common sense and a knowledge of the corporate culture and market sensitivity can be a significant advantage in most organizations.

## 7.3    What Is Information Classification?

An information classification process is a business decision process. When developing a system for your organization, it will be necessary to limit the role of the security professionals and the computer technicians. The project to develop an information classification system is one in which the business side of the enterprise must take an active role.

**Exhibit 2 Fortune 500 Managers Rate Information Importance**

|  | Deloitte & Touche | Ernst & Young |
|---|---|---|
| Availability | 1 | 2 |
| Confidentiality | 3 | 3 |
| Integrity | 2 | 1 |

In a recent pair of surveys (Exhibit 2), the Big Four accounting firms of Ernst & Young and Deloitte & Touche interviewed Fortune 500 managers and asked them to rank in importance to them information availability, confidentiality, and integrity. As can be seen from the results, the managers responded that information needed to be available when they needed to have access to it. Implementing access control packages that rendered access difficult or overly restrictive is a detriment to the business process. Additionally, other managers felt that the information must reflect the real world. That is, controls should be in place to ensure that the information was correct. Preventing or controlling access to information that was incorrect was of little value to the enterprise.

## 7.4 Establish a Team

Because the establishment of an information classification system and policy is a business function, it will be necessary to create a team for this project. It is recommended that there be two teams: a core group made up of three to five members and a support team. The support team should consist of members from each of the major user departments or groups. The core group will be responsible for actually drafting the information classification policy. This will be accomplished after interviewing each of the user departments and determining their needs.

The support team will be used for two vital elements in this process. It will review and critique the information classification policy and it will assist in the sale of the policy to management. To be effective, the policy will have to be accepted by all members of management. To be accepted, it will be necessary to sell this product to each of the managers based on each individual needs and business objectives. Using the support team members, you will be able to determine what each manager is expecting. Once the draft policy has been reviewed by the support team (probably twice) and its comments addressed, it is strongly recommended that a meeting with key management personnel be set up.

These meetings should be in the individual manager's office and should have one or two representatives from the core group and the support team member from the policy development team. The objective of this session is to explain quickly what the policy is about, how it will assist the managers in meeting their mission, and then to answer any questions that they might have. Input from personnel from that manager's organization will assist in the acceptance of the information classification policy.

## 7.5 Developing the Policy

The first cut at the development process is to examine information from two perspectives:

1. *Sensitivity* — The need for confidentiality, integrity, and controlled usage; and
2. *Availability* — Information that is there when it is needed.

It may be necessary to examine examples of different kinds of information found within the organization. Each of the support team members should be prepared to discuss examples of the kinds of information used within the organization. It will be necessary to have examples from all of the organizations — information examples from human resources, engineering, financial, budget, legal, information systems, administrative records.

As a team, examine each of the examples of corporate information and apply them to a scoring table like the one shown in Exhibit 3. Using the information gained from this process, the team should be able to establish classification categories and criteria for confidentiality, integrity, and availability that:

- Are based on the impact to the business or mission
- Can be clearly and consistently interpreted by managers and employees
- Will result in different protective actions for each category

If the difference between two types of information is not important to the organization from a confidentiality or availability perspective, then do not include it. Make the language and the categories as simple as possible. When developing a category system, try the categories out on different groups of managers and solicit their input. It may be beneficial to conduct two or three brainstorming sessions to test out the category possibilities.

**Exhibit 3   Priority Matrix: Unauthorized Disclosure**

| Priority | Impact to the Organization | | |
|---|---|---|---|
| | *Low* | *Medium* | *High* |
| Low | 1 | 4 | 7 |
| Medium | 2 | 5 | 8 |
| High | 3 | 6 | 9 |

## 7.6 Resist the Urge to Add Categories

Keep the number of information classification categories to as few as possible. If two possible categories do not require substantially different treatment, then combine them. The more categories that are available, the greater the chance for confusion among managers and employees. Normally, three or four categories should be sufficient to meet the needs of your organization.

Additionally, avoid the impulse to classify everything the same. To simplify the classification process, some organizations have flirted with having everything classified as confidential. The problem with this concept is that confidential information requires special handling. This would violate the concept of placing controls only where they are actually needed. This method would require the organization to waste limited resources protecting assets that do not really require that level of control.

Another pitfall to avoid is to take the information classification categories developed by another enterprise and adopt them verbatim as your own. Use the information created by other organizations to assist in the creation of a unique set of categories and definitions for your organization.

## 7.7   What Constitutes Confidential Information

There are a number of ways to look at information that may be classified as confidential. We examine a number of statements relating to confidential information. The first is a general statement about sensitive information. For a general definition of what might constitute confidential information, it may be sufficient to define such information as:

> Information that if disclosed could violate the privacy of individuals, reduce the company's competitive advantage, or could cause damage to the organization

The Economic Espionage Act of 1996 (EEA) defines "trade secret" information to include "all forms and types of financial, business, scientific, technical, economic, or engineering information" regardless of "how stored, complied, or memorialized." The EEA has a two-edged sword: while it is illegal for someone to steal trade secret information, the act requires that the owner must take reasonable measures to keep the information secret, and it must be shown that the information derives value from being kept secret.

There are a number of other information classification types that you may have heard about over the years. Let's take just a minute to review one of them — copyright.

### 7.7.1   *Copyright*

At regular intervals, employees will create new work in the form of application programs, transactions, systems, Web sites, and so forth. To protect the organization from loss of created material, enterprise policies on copyright ownership must be implemented and all employees must be reminded of these policies on a regular basis.

Unlike other forms of intellectual property protection, the basis for copyright occurs at the creation of an original work. Although copyrights are granted by government copyright offices, every original work has an inherent right to a copyright and is protected by that right even if the work is not published or registered.

All original works of authorship created by employees for a company are the property of the company and are protected by the copyright law. The copyright also applies to consultants doing work for your organization while under a purchase order or other contractual agreement. Unless there is an agreement to the contrary, any work created by a contractor under contract to an organization is owned by the organization, not the contractor.

The types of work that qualify for copyright protection include:

- All types of written works
- Computer databases and software programs (including source code, object code, and micro code)
- Output (including customized screens and printouts)
- Photographs, charts, blueprints, technical drawings, and flowcharts
- Sound recordings

A copyright does not protect:

- Ideas, inventions, processes, and three-dimensional designs (these are covered by patent law); and
- Brands, products, or slogans (covered by trademark law).

For confidential information, if the organization takes adequate steps (operates in good faith) to keep confidential information secret both internally and externally, then if there is a breach, the organization can seek relief through the courts. For trade secret and competitive advantage information, there may be criminal penalties for individuals as well as organizations as well as civil penalties (see Exhibit 4).

Information Classification protects the intellectual assets.

**Exhibit 4   Typical Organization Confidential Information**

## 7.8   Classification Examples

In Exhibits 5 through 9, we examine attributes and examples of different classification categories. We will also present examples of organization information classification definitions.

**Exhibit 5   Example 1**

---

**Information Classification**

**Policy:**        Security classifications should be used to indicate the need and priorities for security protection.

**Objective:**   To ensure that information assets receive an appropriate level of protection.

**Statement:**  Information has varying degrees of sensitivity and criticality. Some items may require an additional level of security protection or special handling. A security classification system should be used to define an appropriate set of security protection levels, and to communicate the need for special handling measures to users.

---

**Exhibit 6   Example 2**

---

**Classification Requirements**

Classified data is information developed by the organization with some effort and some expense or investment that provides the organization with a competitive advantage in its relevant industry and that the organization wishes to protect from disclosure.

Although defining information protection is a difficult task, four elements serve as the basis for a classification scheme:

■ The information must be of some value to the organization and its competitors so that it provides some demonstrable competitive advantage.
■ The information must be the result of some minimal expense or investment by the organization.
■ The information is somewhat unique in that it is not generally known in the industry or to the public or may not be readily ascertained.
■ The information must be maintained as a relative secret, both within and outside the organization, with reasonable precautions against disclosure of the information. Access to such information could only result from disregarding established standards or from using illegal means.

**Top Secret (Secret, Highly Confidential)**
Attributes:

■ Provides the organization with a very significant competitive edge
■ Is of such a nature that unauthorized disclosure would cause severe damage to the organization
■ Shows specific business strategies and major directions
■ Is essential to the technical or financial success of a product

---

*(continued)*

**Exhibit 6     Example 2 (continued)**

Examples:
- Specific operating plans, marketing strategies
- Specific descriptions of unique parts or materials, technology intent statements, new technologies and research
- Specific business strategies and major directions

**Confidential (Sensitive, Personal, Privileged)**

Attributes:
- Provides the organization with a significant competitive edge
- Is of such a nature that unauthorized disclosure would cause damage to the organization
- Shows operational direction over extended periods of time
- Is extremely important to the technical or financial success of a product

Examples:
- Consolidated revenue, cost, profit, or other financial results
- Operating plans, marketing strategies
- Descriptions of unique parts or materials, technology intent statements, new technological studies and research
- Market requirements, technologies, product plans, revenues

**Restricted (Internal Use)**

Attributes:
- All business-related information requiring baseline security protection, but failing to meet the specified criteria for higher classification
- Information that is intended for use by employees when conducting company business

Examples:
- Business information
- Organization policies, standards, procedures
- Internal organization announcements

**Public (Unclassified)**

Attributes:
- Information that, due to its content and context, requires no special protection, or
- Information that has been made available to the public distribution through authorized company channels

Examples:
- Online public information, Web site information
- Internal correspondences, memoranda, and documentation that do not merit special controls
- Public corporate announcements

**Exhibit 7   Example 3**

---

### Information Classification

**Introduction**

Information, wherever it is handled or stored (for example, in computers, file cabinets, desktops, fax machines, voice mail), needs to be protected from unauthorized access, modification, disclosure, and destruction. All information is *not* created equal. Consequently, segmentation or classification of information into categories is necessary to help identify a framework for evaluating the information's relative value of the information and the appropriate controls required to preserve its value to the company.

Three basic classifications of information have been established by the corporation (see below). Business units may define additional subclassifications as necessary to complete their framework for evaluating and preserving information under their control.

When information does require protection, the protection must be consistent. Often strict access controls are applied to data stored in the mainframe computers but not applied to office workstations. Whether in a mainframe, client/server, workstation, file cabinet, desk drawer, wastebasket, or in the mail, information should be subject to appropriate and consistent protection.

The definitions and responsibilities described below represent the minimum level of detail necessary for all organizations across the company. Each organization may decide that additional detail is necessary to adequately implement information classification within its organization.

**Corporate Policy:**

All information must be classified by the *owner* into one of three classifications: **Confidential, Internal Use**, or **Public**.

(From Company Policy on Information Management)

**Confidential**

Definition:

Information that, if disclosed, could:

■ Violate the privacy of individuals,

■ Reduce the competitive advantage of the company, or

■ Cause damage to the company.

**Examples:**

Some examples of **Confidential** information are:

■ Personnel records (including name, address, phone, salary, performance rating, social security number, date of birth, marital status, career path, number of dependents, etc.)

■ Customer information (including name, address, phone number, energy consumption, credit history, social security number, etc.)

---

*(continued)*

**Exhibit 7    Example 3 (continued)**

■ Shareholder information (including name, address, phone number, number of shares held, social security number, etc.)

■ Vendor information (name, address, product pricing specific to the company, etc.)

■ Health insurance records (including medical, prescription, and psychological records)

■ Specific operating plans, marketing plans, or strategies

■ Consolidated revenue, cost, profit, or other financial results that are not public record

■ Descriptions of unique parts or materials, technology intent statements, or new technologies and research that are not public record

■ Specific business strategies and directions

■ Major changes in the company management structure

■ Information that requires special skill or training to interpret and employ correctly, such as design or specification files

If any of these items can be found freely and openly in public records, the company obligation to protect them from disclosure is waived.

**Internal Use**
**Definition:**
Classify information as **Internal Use** when the information is intended for use by employees when conducting company business.

**Examples:**
Some examples of **Internal Use** information are:

■ Operational business information/reports

■ Non-company information that is subject to a nondisclosure agreement with another company

■ Company phone book

■ Corporate policies, standards, and procedures

■ Internal company announcements

**Public**
**Definition:**
Classify information as **Public** if the information has been made available for public distribution through authorized company channels. **Public** information is not sensitive in context or content, and requires no special protection.

**Examples:**
The following are examples of **Public** information:

■ Corporate Annual Report

■ Information specifically generated for public consumption such as public service bulletins, marketing brochures, and advertisements

## Exhibit 8   Example 4

**Information Management**
1.   **General**
  A.   Corporate information includes electronically generated, printed, filmed, typed, or stored.
  B.   Information is a corporate asset and is the property of the Corporation.
2.   **Information Retention**
  A.   Each organization shall retain information necessary to the conduct of business.
  B.   Each organizational unit shall establish and administer a records management schedule in compliance with applicable laws and regulations, and professional standards and practices, and be compatible with Corporate goals and expectations.
3.   **Information Protection**
  A.   Information must be protected according to its sensitivity, criticality, and value, regardless of the media on which it is stored, the manual or automated systems that process it, or the methods by which it is distributed.
  B.   Employees are responsible for protecting corporate information from unauthorized access, modification, destruction, or disclosure, whether accidental or intentional. To facilitate the protection of corporate information, employee responsibilities have been established at three levels: Owner, Custodian, and User.
    1.   *Owner:* Company management of the organizational unit where the information is created, or management of the organizational unit that is the primary user of the information. Owners are responsible to:
      a.   Identify the classification level of all corporate information within their organizational unit,
      b.   Define appropriate safeguards to ensure the confidentiality, integrity, and availability of the information resource,
      c.   Monitor safeguards to ensure they are properly implemented,
      d.   Authorize access to those who have a business need for the information, and
      e.   Remove access from those who no longer have a business need for the information.
    2.   *Custodian:* Employees designated by the owner to be responsible for maintaining the safeguards established by the owner.
    3.   *User:* Employees authorized by the owner to access information and use the safeguards established by the owner.
  C.   Each Vice President shall appoint an Organization Information Protection Coordinator who will administer an information protection program that appropriately classifies and protects corporate information under the Vice President's control and makes employees aware of the importance of information and methods for its protection.

*(continued)*

**Exhibit 8    Example 4 (continued)**

---

4.    **Information Classification.** To ensure the proper protection of corporate information, the owner shall use a formal review process to classify information into one of the following classifications:

   A.    *Public:* Information that has been made available for public distribution through authorized company channels. (Refer to Communication Policy for more information.)

   B.    *Confidential:* Information that, if disclosed, could violate the privacy of individuals, reduce competitive advantage of the the company, or could cause significant damage to the company.

   C.    *Internal Use:* Information that is intended for use by all employees when conducting company business. Most information used in the company would be classified as internal use.

---

## 7.9   Declassification or Reclassification of Information

Classified information normally declines in sensitivity with the passage of time. Downgrading should be as automatic as possible. If the information owner knows the date that the information should be reclassified, then it might be labeled as: *Confidential until (date).* There should be an established review process for all information classified as confidential, and reclassified when it no longer meets the criteria established for such information.

   Part of an effective information classification program is to destroy documents when they are no longer required. Placing restrictions on copying classified documents will ensure that the documents and data sets are controlled and logged regarding the number of copies created and to whom those copies were assigned. To assist in this process, it may be convenient to create an information handling matrix (see Exhibit 10).

### 7.9.1   Protection Requirements

Data must be protected according to its classification to reduce risks to a minimum acceptable level. Protection must be provided and planned according to the how the data is transmitted, stored, and processed. Protection mechanisms must be specified for the multiple functions. Exhibit 11 indicates the minimum data protection mechanisms for each classification of data and activity related to the data.

## 7.10 Information Classification Methodology

The final element in an effective information classification process is to provide management and employees with a method with which to evaluate information and provide them with an indication of where the information should be classified. To accomplish this, it may be necessary to create an information classification worksheet (Exhibit 12). These worksheets can be used by the business units to determine what classification of information they have within their organization.

**Exhibit 9  Information Classification Matrix**

**A. Classification Definitions and Examples**

Four classification categories exist within Sprocket Inc. The three most sensitive categories (Internal Use Only, Restricted, and Highly Restricted) are collectively referred to as proprietary classifications.

| Public<br>*"Would Not" is the key word discriminator* | Internal Use Only<br>*"Might" is the key word discriminator* | Restricted<br>*"Could" is the key word discriminator* | Highly Restricted<br>*"Would" is the key word discriminator* |
|---|---|---|---|
| 1. Considered to have value but there is no risk of unauthorized disclosure. | 1. Might provide a business advantage over those who do not have access to the same data. | 1. Provides a competitive advantage. | 1. Provides a significant competitive advantage. |
| 2. It would not provide a business or competitive advantage and is routinely made available to interested members of the general public. | 2. Might be useful to a competitor. | 2. Disclosure/loss could cause moderate damage to the company or an individual. | 2. Disclosure/loss would cause severe damage to operations. |
| 3. This type of data is available to the public with no special restrictions. | 3. Not easily identifiable by inspection of a product. | 3. Relates to or describes an important part of the operational direction of the company over time. | 3. Relates to or describes a long-term strategy or critical business plans. |
| 4. Data officially released for widespread public disclosure. | 4. Not generally known outside the company or available from public sources. | 4. Important technical or financial aspect of a product line or a business unit. | 4. Disclosure would cause regulatory or contractual liability. |
| | 5. Generally available internally. | 5. Disclosure/loss could cause a loss of customer or shareholder confidence. | 5. Disclosure would cause severe damage to our reputation or the public image. |
| | 6. Little competitive interest. | 6. Disclosure/loss could cause a temporary drop in stock value. | 6. Disclosure/loss would cause a severe loss of market share or the ability to be the first to market. |

*(continued)*

**Exhibit 9   Information Classification Matrix (continued)**

| | | |
|---|---|---|
| 7. Intended for use within Sprocket Inc., not to be shared outside the company without proper management approval. | 7. A likelihood that somebody could seek to acquire this data.<br><br>8. Proprietary data generated in the course of business, for which inadvertent access or disclosure adversely impacts the company, its employees, or its customers. | 7. Disclosure/loss would cause a loss of an important customer, shareholder, business partner, or the ability to patent.<br><br>8. Disclosure/loss would cause a long-term or severe drop in stock value.<br><br>9. Strong likelihood somebody is seeking to acquire this data.<br><br>10. Proprietary data, whose disclosure would have legal, regulatory, or financial repercussions or would severely alter public perception. |
| *Examples:* Corporate intranet home site,<br><br>*Unstructured Data Examples:* Company newsletter, telephone directories, employee handouts, training manuals<br>*Configuration Data Examples:* User ID format | *Examples:* Purchase plans, employee records, user IDs<br><br>*Unstructured Data Examples:* Most operational communications, customer information, marketing and sales plans, customer social security numbers, business unit strategies, and other intellectual property; and information that must be safeguarded against insider trading. | *Structured Data Examples:* User ID passwords, employee medical claim information, credit card numbers<br><br>*Unstructured Data Examples:* Financial information prior to public disclosure; business, marketing and sales plans; internal legal materials; customer/intermediary relationship information; employee social security numbers; research and development information; leasing contracts |

*Examples:* Press releases, public marketing materials, financial planning tools, and employment advertising

Configuration Data Examples:
Access Control Lists

Configuration Data Examples:
Security logs

## B. Information Types and Examples

To help determine the best access controls to place around information based upon the classification, it is important to know where and how the information is stored and transmitted, and who controls access to the information. There are three types of information that are used to associate with these characteristics. It is important to understand that information type can change during its life cycle. For example, structured information becomes unstructured as soon as end users move it to their client PC, or transmit it via an e-mail attachment to someone else. Because of the ease with which the end user can compromise security by improperly storing or transmitting the data, it is vital that information end users know and understand the security implications and the role they have in protecting the information.

| Type | Definition | Examples |
|---|---|---|
| Structured Information or Data | Data that is stored and modified within one database that has a defined schema. Some characteristics of structured data include the following:<br><br>■ Each data item can normally be accessed only through front-end applications, and end users do not select where structured data is stored.<br>■ Data is usually viewed on a screen and is modified with a front-end program.<br>■ Structured data typically cannot be downloaded to other systems, or printed, via any method other than through the front-end application.<br><br>■ Many users can typically access structured data at the same time. Data can be most easily controlled and monitored. | Data stored in SQL databases, mainframe regions, DB2 databases, software code, etc.<br><br>Data electronically controlled and stored in a central location that is not modifiable and/or printable by anyone other than a small group of authorized persons through a front-end application that has security controls.<br><br>Examples may include telephone directories, employee HR records, BWG accounting data, marketing plans, nonreleased financial data, user IDs/passwords, etc. |

*(continued)*

**Exhibit 9  Information Classification Matrix (continued)**

**C. Information Protection Roles**

Each member of the project development team has information protection roles. End users also have responsibilities for ensuring the security of the information that they process and to which they have access. Using role-based management principles is an effective method for appropriately securing and protecting information based upon classification.

| Role | Definition | Responsibilities | Examples |
|---|---|---|---|
| Information asset owner (business/ process owner) | The information asset owner for a specific data item is a management position within the business area facing the greatest negative impact from disclosure/loss of that information. The information asset owner is ultimately responsible for ensuring that the appropriate protection requirements for the information assets are defined and implemented. | The information owner responsibilities include, but are not limited to, the following:<br>■ Assign initial information classification and periodically review the classification to ensure it still meets the business needs.<br>■ Ensure security controls are in place, commensurate with the classification.<br>■ Review and ensure currency of the access rights associated with information assets they own.<br>■ Determine security requirements, access criteria, and backup requirements for the information assets they own.<br>■ Report suspected security breaches to Corporate Security.<br>■ Perform or delegate, if desired, the following:<br>Approval authority for access requests from other business units or assign a delegate in the same business unit as the executive or manager owner<br>Backup and recovery duties or assign to the Information Custodian<br>Approval of the disclosure of information<br>Act on notifications received concerning security violations against their information assets.<br>■ Determine information availability requirements.<br>■ Assess information risks. | Information owners are typically department heads, product managers, or division managers who own an accounting distribution. They are accountable for ensuring the information is created, gathered, maintained, but they do not necessarily deal with the day-to-day handling of the information. |

**Exhibit 10  Information Handling Procedures Matrix**

Different classifications and types of information must be protected according to where the information is stored, transmitted, or processed and specifically how the information is accessed. The varying locations where information is accessed and transmitted are considered risk zones.

| Type of Access and Risk Zones | Internal Use Only | Restricted | Highly Restricted |
|---|---|---|---|
| **General Access Rules** <br> All Risk Zones | ■ Information asset owners must control access to information based on business need <br><br> ■ Do not have to label the "Internal Use Only" nature of the document if distributed only inside Sprocket Inc. <br><br> ■ Must label documents as "Proprietary" if distributed outside of Sprocket Inc. <br><br> ■ Must be encrypted if transmitted over the Internet <br><br> ■ User authentication to prevent unauthorized access | ■ Must be labeled "Restricted" <br><br> ■ Must be password protected if on the intranet <br><br> ■ Must be encrypted if transmitted over the Internet <br><br> ■ Structured electronic information must be stored on a controlled network server, not on a workstation or laptop <br><br> ■ Unstructured information must be stored only on authorized systems | ■ Must be labeled "Highly Restricted" <br><br> ■ A list of receipts must be kept, identifying individuals who possess hard or electronic copies of unstructured information <br><br> ■ Must be encrypted when electronically stored or transmitted <br><br> ■ Cannot be placed on the Sprocket Inc. intranet until access controls approved by BWG Security Program Manager <br><br> ■ Structured information must be stored encrypted on a secured network server, not on a workstation or laptop <br><br> ■ Unstructured information must be stored encrypted only on authorized systems |

*(continued)*

**Exhibit 10  Information Handling Procedures Matrix (continued)**

| | | | |
|---|---|---|---|
| **Computer-Based Access to or from Secure Corporate Networks/Systems** Risk Zones: CNP, CNB | ■ Encrypted via Web browser | ■ Password access control<br>■ Encrypted using a method approved by Corporate Security | ■ Password access control<br>■ Encrypted using a method approved by Corporate Security<br>■ Label information on screens or documents as "Highly Restricted" |
| **Computer-Based Access to or from High Risk Corporate Networks/Systems** Risk Zones: CND, CNU, CNT | ■ Encrypted via Web browser<br>■ Encrypted using a method approved by Corporate Security | ■ Password access control<br>■ Encrypted using a method approved by Corporate Security | ■ Password access control<br>■ Encrypted using a method approved by Corporate Security<br>■ Label information on screens or documents as "Highly Restricted" |
| **Computer-Based Access to or from Secure Extranets** Risk Zones: PEC, VNC | ■ Encrypted via Web browser<br>■ Encrypted using a method approved by Corporate Security<br>■ Require each extranet partner representative to sign a nondisclosure agreement | ■ Encryption using a method approved by Corporate Security<br>■ Require each extranet partner representative to sign a nondisclosure agreement<br>■ Strong authentication (e.g., token-based access control) | ■ Encryption using a method approved by Corporate Security<br>■ Require each extranet partner representative to sign a nondisclosure agreement<br>■ Strong authentication (e.g., token-based access control)<br>■ Place notice or label on data "Highly Restricted" |
| **Computer-Based Access to or from High Risk Extranets** Risk Zones: PEU, PEP, VNU, VNP | ■ Encrypted via Web browser<br>■ Encryption using a method approved by Corporate Security | ■ Encryption using a method approved by Corporate Security<br>■ Require each extranet partner representative to sign a nondisclosure agreement | ■ Encryption using a method approved by Corporate Security<br>■ Require each extranet partner representative to sign a nondisclosure agreement |

**Computer-Based Access to or from the Internet**

Risk Zones: PIU, PIE, VNU

| | | |
|---|---|---|
| ■ Require each extranet partner representative to sign a nondisclosure agreement | ■ Strong authentication (e.g., token-based access control) | ■ Strong authentication (e.g., token-based access control)<br>■ Place notice or label on data "Highly Restricted" |
| ■ Information sent over Internet must have encryption using a method approved by Corporate Security<br>■ Password for access<br>■ Require each extranet partner representative to sign a nondisclosure agreement | ■ Information sent over Internet must have encryption using a method approved by Corporate Security<br>■ Strong authentication (e.g., token-based access control)<br>■ Require each extranet partner representative to sign a nondisclosure agreement | ■ Information sent over Internet must have encryption using a method approved by Corporate Security<br>■ Strong authentication (e.g., token-based access control)<br>■ Require each extranet partner representative to sign a nondisclosure agreement.<br>■ Data cannot be permanently stored on Internet Web server; data must be stored independently from the Web server behind a corporate firewall<br>■ Information temporarily stored on Internet Web server must be encrypted with a method approved by Corporate Security |

**Computer-Based Access from Dial-up Networks (Vendors, Telecommuters)**

Risk Zones: DN, VNU

| | | |
|---|---|---|
| ■ Password for access<br>■ Vendor access according to terms of contract<br>■ Require each extranet partner representative to sign a nondisclosure agreement | ■ Password for access<br>■ Vendor access according to terms of contract<br>■ Require each extranet partner representative to sign a nondisclosure agreement | ■ Strong authentication (e.g., token-based access control)<br>■ Vendor access according to terms of contract<br>■ Require each extranet partner representative to sign a nondisclosure agreement |

*(continued)*

**Exhibit 10   Information Handling Procedures Matrix (continued)**

- Other non-BWG employees — not permitted
- Other non-BWG employees — not permitted
- Other non-BWG employees — not permitted
- BWG employee — approval from management and and securID cards

**Risk zone definitions:**

| Abbr. | Risk Zone | Definition |
|---|---|---|
| DN | Dial-up network | Unsecure |
| PIU | Public Internet | Unsecure |
| PIE | Public Internet | Encrypted |
| PEU | Partner extranet | Unknown security level; typically part of the business application system and process |
| PEP | Partner extranet | Protected but uncertified; typically part of the business application system and process |
| PEC | Partner extranet | Certified security; typically part of the business application system and process |
| VNU | Vendor network | Unknown security level; typically supports business processing |
| VNP | Vendor network | Protected but uncertified; typically supports business processing |
| VNC | Vendor network | Certified security; typically supports business processing |
| CND | Corporate network | Public/DMZ |
| CNU | Corporate network | All WAN users behind the public firewalls |
| CNP | Corporate network | Production systems |
| CNT | Corporate network | Testing/lab systems |
| CNB | Corporate network | Backoffice/administration systems |

**Exhibit 11  Minimum Data Protection Mechanisms**

| Function | Internal Use Only | Restricted | Highly Restricted |
|---|---|---|---|
| Marking for use within corporate facilities | No restriction | ■ Every page marked "Restricted"<br>■ Every page marked with page number (page ___ of ___)<br>■ Hard-copy draft and final documents must be marked with information owner | ■ Every page marked "Highly Restricted"<br>■ Every page numbered (page ___ of ___)<br>■ Every copy numbered (copy ___ of ___)<br>■ Hard-copy draft and final documents must be marked with information owner<br>■ All hard-copy documents must have a cover page that includes the information owner's name, department, and phone number<br>■ Include "Legend" on hard-copy documents stating restrictions<br>■ Recipient of copy must sign and return-receipt to information owner<br>■ Reviewed annually by Information Owner to ensure marking is still appropriate |
| Marking for sharing with extended enterprise | ■ Every page marked "Proprietary"<br>■ Electronic information must be identifiable as "Proprietary" | ■ Every page marked "Restricted"<br>■ Management approval to distribute | ■ Every page marked "Highly Restricted"<br>■ Electronic information must be identifiable as "Highly Restricted" |

*(continued)*

**Exhibit 11  Minimum Data Protection Mechanisms (continued)**

| Function | Internal Use Only | Restricted | Highly Restricted |
| --- | --- | --- | --- |
| | ■ Management approval to distribute<br>■ Electronic information must be identifiable as "Restricted" | ■ Include "Legend" on hard-copy documents stating restrictions (i.e., for use only by "group, organization, etc.")<br>■ Distribution to named person; distribution to "group" prohibited<br>Electronic information must be password-protected<br>Electronic information must be encrypted according to corporate standards<br>■ Every page marked with page number (page ___ of ___) | ■ Management approval to distribute<br>■ Include "Legend" on hard-copy documents stating restrictions (i.e., for use only by "group, organization, etc.")<br>■ Distribution to named person; distribution to "group" prohibited<br>■ Information owner must maintain a list of those who have access or who possess a hard copy<br>■ Electronic information must be encrypted according to corporate standards<br>■ Every page marked with page number (page ___ of ___)<br>■ Every copy numbered (copy ___ of ___)<br>■ Recipient of copy must sign and return-receipt to information owner<br>■ Electronic information must be password-protected<br>■ Cannot be placed on a non-Sprocket Inc. intranet |

| Storage within corporate facilities (media, procedures, facilities) | Storage off corporate premises (media, procedures, facilities) |
|---|---|
| ■ Lock in desk or cabinet accessible only by authorized persons when not in use; if this is not possible, store in secured media library<br>■ Accessible only by persons with a business need-to-know | ■ Sprocket Inc.-appointed delegate must use reasonable care and Sprocket Inc.-approved controls |
| ■ Lock in desk or cabinet accessible only by authorized persons when not in use; if this is not possible, store in secured media library<br>■ Protected when stored electronically by using a screen saver with password, and encrypted file or drive<br>■ Information must not be stored on end-user PC (client) hard drives unless controls are used to prevent unauthorized use of the PC<br>■ Hard-copy and electronic media must be stored in a locked office, secured filing cabinet, or locked desk drawer accessible only by authorized persons | ■ Information must be under the control of a Sprocket Inc.-appointed delegate at all times<br>■ Information must not be left unattended in automobiles, in homes, hotel rooms, or other publicly accessible places<br>■ Information stored electronically must be password-protected |
| ■ Lock in desk or cabinet accessible only by authorized persons when not in use; if this is not possible, store in secured media library<br>■ Protected when stored electronically by using a screen saver with password, and encrypted file or drive<br>■ Information must not be stored on end-user PC (client) hard drives unless controls are used to prevent unauthorized use of the PC<br>■ Hard-copy and electronic media must be stored in a locked office, secured filing cabinet, or locked desk drawer accessible only by authorized persons | ■ Locked when unattended<br>■ Information must be under the control of a Sprocket Inc.-appointed delegate at all times<br>■ Information must not be left unattended in automobiles, in homes, hotel rooms, or other publicly accessible places |

*(continued)*

**Exhibit 11  Minimum Data Protection Mechanisms (continued)**

| Function | Internal Use Only | Restricted | Highly Restricted |
|---|---|---|---|
| Mailing/shipping within corporate facilities | ■ Routing envelope/container with no special markings | ■ Information stored electronically must be encrypted if technically possible<br><br>■ Sealed opaque envelope/container marked "Restricted"<br><br>■ Include delivery instructions<br><br>■ Place information in envelope labeled "Confidential" within the opaque mailing *Note:* Do not mark "Confidential" on exterior package labels sent through the U.S. mail; the label must be on the interior envelope<br><br>■ Must be business need<br><br>■ Must be authorized by information owner | ■ Protected when stored electronically – screen saver with password and encrypted file or drive<br><br>■ Sealed opaque envelope/container marked "Highly Restricted"<br><br>■ Registered mail<br><br>■ Place information in envelope labeled "Confidential" within the opaque mailing *Note:* Do not mark "Confidential" on exterior package labels sent through the U.S. mail; the label must be on the interior envelope.<br><br>■ Sender must confirm receipt of package from recipient within five working days<br><br>■ Information must be sent to a named individual, not just to an office, title, or location<br><br>■ Include delivery instructions<br><br>■ Recipient of copy must sign and return-receipt to information owner |

| Mailing/shipping to the extended enterprise or external | | | |
|---|---|---|---|
| | ■ Routing envelope/container with no special markings<br>■ For technical data, software or computer programs sent outside the United States, check with Legal Department for export regulations<br>■ Must be business need<br>■ Must be authorized by information owner<br>■ Must not send customer information unless the consent of the party described by the information is obtained | ■ Sealed opaque envelope/container marked "Restricted"<br>■ Include delivery instructions<br>■ Place information in envelope labeled "Restricted" within the opaque mailing<br>*Note:* Do not mark "Confidential" on exterior<br>package labels sent through the U.S. mail; the label must be on the interior envelope<br>■ Must be business need<br>■ Must be authorized by information owner<br>■ For technical data, software, or computer programs sent outside the United States, check with Legal Department for export regulations<br>■ Contact Corporate Security to send outside the United States<br>■ Must not send customer information unless the consent of the party described by the information is obtained<br>■ Lost or disclosed information must be reported to Corporate Security immediately | ■ Sealed opaque envelope/container marked "Highly Restricted"<br>■ Registered mail<br>■ Place information in envelope labeled "Highly Restricted" within the opaque mailing<br>*Note:* Do not mark<br>"Confidential" on exterior<br>package labels sent through the U.S. mail; the label must be on the interior envelope<br>■ Sender must confirm receipt of package from recipient within five working days<br>■ For technical data, software, or computer programs sent outside the United States, check with Legal Department for export regulations<br>■ Contact Corporate Security to send outside the United States<br>■ Must be business need<br>■ Must not send customer information unless the consent of the party described by the information is obtained<br>■ Must be authorized by information owner |

*(continued)*

**Exhibit 11    Minimum Data Protection Mechanisms (continued)**

| Function | Internal Use Only | Restricted | Highly Restricted |
|---|---|---|---|
| Facsimile transmittal within corporate facilities | ▪ Remove immediately from fax machine<br>▪ Protect to prevent unauthorized disclosure | ▪ Remove immediately from fax machine<br>▪ Protect to prevent unauthorized disclosure<br>▪ Requires notification and verification of receipt | ▪ Must have prior written authorization by the originating department officer-level management<br>▪ Lost or disclosed information must be reported to Corporate Security immediately<br>▪ Remove immediately from fax machine<br>▪ Protect to prevent unauthorized disclosure<br>▪ Requires notification and verification of receipt<br>▪ Ensure fax machine is monitored by authorized recipient before sending |
| Facsimile transmittal over outside lines | ▪ Remove immediately from fax machine<br>▪ Protect to prevent unauthorized disclosure<br>▪ Attach corporate-approved fax cover/transmittal sheet | ▪ Remove immediately from fax machine<br>▪ Protect to prevent unauthorized disclosure<br>▪ Attach corporate-approved fax cover/transmittal sheet<br>▪ Requires notification and verification of receipt<br>▪ Verify correct fax number prior to transmittal<br>▪ Notify recipient time and date for transmittal | ▪ Remove immediately from fax machine<br>▪ Protect to prevent unauthorized disclosure<br>▪ Attach corporate-approved fax cover/transmittal sheet<br>▪ Requires notification and verification of receipt<br>▪ Verify correct fax number prior to transmittal<br>▪ Notify recipient time and date for transmittal |

| Transport method | | | |
|---|---|---|---|
| *(Fax, continued)* | ■ Ensure receiving equipment does not retain fax image | ■ Ensure receiving equipment does not retain fax image | ■ Ensure receiving equipment does not retain fax image<br>■ Use end-to-end encryption<br>■ Ensure fax machine is monitored by authorized recipient before sending |
| E-mail within corporate network | ■ No special requirements | ■ Must use an encryption method approved by Corporate Security<br>■ Used in a controlled location where access is limited to personnel with a business need<br>■ Set sensitivity to "Confidential" using message option | ■ Must use an encryption method approved by Corporate Security<br>■ Use in a controlled location where access is limited to personnel with a business need<br>■ Must be reasonably sure the source and destination are who/what they claim to be<br>■ Set sensitivity to "Confidential" using message option |
| E-mail through outside networks | ■ Must use an encryption method approved by Corporate Security<br>■ Set sensitivity to "Confidential" using message option<br>■ Direct recipient not to forward to anyone | ■ Use a secure link or encrypt the information using a method approved by Corporate Security<br>■ Must be reasonably sure the source and destination are who/what they claim to be<br>■ Use in a controlled location where access is limited to personnel with a business need<br>■ Cannot allow unattended access to the information | ■ Use a secure link and encrypt the information using a method approved by Corporate Security<br>■ Must positively ensure the source and destination are who/what they claim to be<br>■ Use in a controlled location where access is limited to personnel with a business need<br>■ Cannot allow unattended access to the information |

*(continued)*

**Exhibit 11   Minimum Data Protection Mechanisms (continued)**

| Function | Internal Use Only | Restricted | Highly Restricted |
|---|---|---|---|
| | | ■ Lost or disclosed information must be reported to Corporate Security immediately<br>■ Contact Corporate Security to send outside the United States<br>■ Set sensitivity to "Confidential" using message option<br>■ Direct recipient not to forward to anyone | ■ Lost or disclosed information must be reported to Corporate Security immediately<br>■ Contact Corporate Security to send outside the United States<br>■ Set sensitivity to "Confidential" using message option<br>■ Direct recipient not to forward to anyone |
| Electronic file transfer (FTP) within corporate network (via automated or manual processes) | ■ No special requirements | ■ Use in a controlled location where access is limited to personnel with a business need | ■ Use in a controlled location where access is limited to personnel with a business need<br>■ Information must be encrypted<br>■ Must be reasonably sure the source and destination are who/what they claim to be |
| Electronic file transfer (FTP) through outside networks | ■ Must occur using firewall proxy accounts<br>■ Scan for viruses | ■ Must occur using firewall proxy accounts<br>■ Scan for viruses<br>■ Use a secure link or encrypt the information using a method approved by Corporate Security<br>■ Must be reasonably sure the source and destination are who/what they claim to be | ■ Must occur using firewall proxy accounts<br>■ Scan for viruses<br>■ Use a secure link and encrypt the information using a method approved by Corporate Security method<br>■ Must positively ensure the source and destination are who/what they claim to be |

| Electronic transaction processing | |
|---|---|
| ■ Use a secure link or encrypt the information using a method approved by Corporate Security | ■ Use in a controlled location where access is limited to personnel with a business need<br>■ Cannot allow unattended access to the information<br>■ Lost or disclosed information must be reported to Corporate Security immediately<br>■ Contact Corporate Security to send outside the United States<br>■ Define roles approved by information owners to obtain appropriate access rights<br>■ Use a secure link or encrypt the information using a method approved by Corporate Security<br>■ Use in a controlled location where access is limited to personnel with a business need<br>■ Cannot allow unattended access to information being processed within an active customer transaction (e.g., require reauthentication to transaction following a minimum time of inactivity)<br>■ Lost or disclosed information must be reported to Corporate Security immediately | ■ Use in a controlled location where access is limited to personnel with a business need<br>■ Cannot allow unattended access to the information<br>■ Lost or disclosed information must be reported to Corporate Security immediately<br>■ Contact Corporate Security to send outside the United States<br>■ Define roles approved by information owners to obtain appropriate access rights<br>■ Use a secure link or encrypt the information using a method approved by Corporate Security<br>■ Use in a controlled location where access is limited to personnel with a business need<br>■ Cannot allow unattended access to information being processed within an active customer transaction (e.g., require reauthentication to transaction following a minimum time of inactivity)<br>■ Lost or disclosed information must be reported to Corporate Security immediately |

*(continued)*

**Exhibit 11   Minimum Data Protection Mechanisms (continued)**

| Function | Internal Use Only | Restricted | Highly Restricted |
|---|---|---|---|
| Logging of access within corporate facilities or systems | ■ Record user ID, date, and time structured information accessed<br>■ Retain logs offline according to Sprocket Inc. record retention policies | ■ Contact Corporate Security to send outside the United States<br>■ Record user ID, date, and time structured information accessed<br>■ Log failed access attempts for structured data<br>■ Review weekly by information custodian<br>■ Review operator logs for errors, corrective actions<br>■ Fault logging for user-reported problems<br>■ Audit trails record exceptions and other security-relevant events<br>■ Computer and communications clocks synchronized to ensure log accuracy<br>■ Retain logs offline according to Sprocket Inc. record retention policies. | ■ Contact Corporate Security to send outside the United States<br>■ Record user ID, date, and time structured information accessed<br>■ Log failed access attempts for structured data<br>■ Review daily by information custodian<br>■ Record of reason for access<br>■ Operator logs for errors, corrective actions<br>■ Fault logging for user-reported problems<br>■ Audit trails record exceptions and other security-relevant events<br>■ Computer and communications clocks synchronized to ensure log accuracy<br>■ Retain logs offline according to Sprocket Inc. record retention policies |
| Logging of access from extended enterprise | ■ Business partner agreements must include requirements that they share log and audit trail data applicable to Sprocket Inc. business processing | ■ Business partner agreements must include requirements that they share log and audit trail data applicable to Sprocket Inc. business processing | ■ Business partner agreements must include requirements that they share log and audit trail data applicable to Sprocket Inc. business processing |

Destruction/ disposal within corporate premises

- When applicable, in accordance with Records Management or the contractual agreement with other company information handling requirements

---

- Record user ID, date, and time structured information was accessed
- Log failed access attempts for structured data
- Review weekly by information custodian
- Review operator logs for errors, corrective actions
- Fault logging for user-reported problems
- Audit trails record exceptions and other security-relevant events
- Computer and communications clocks synchronized to ensure log accuracy
- Copy audit logs to a separate server dedicated to log accumulation, preferably in a secured area with access limited to only authorized individuals with a need to access such logs
- When applicable, in accordance with Records Management or the contractual agreement with other company information handling requirements

---

- Record user ID, date, and time accessed
- Log failed access attempts for structured data
- Review daily by information custodian
- Record reason for access
- Review operator logs for errors, corrective actions
- Fault logging for user-reported problems
- Audit trails record exceptions and other security-relevant events
- Computer and communications clocks synchronized to ensure log accuracy
- Copy audit logs to a separate server dedicated to log accumulation, preferably in a secured area with access limited to only authorized individuals with a need to access such logs
- When applicable, in accordance with Records Management or the contractual agreement with other company information handling requirements

*(continued)*

**Exhibit 11  Minimum Data Protection Mechanisms (continued)**

| Function | Internal Use Only | Restricted | Highly Restricted |
|---|---|---|---|
| | ■ No special requirements; dispose of in trash | ■ Cross-shred or burn using corporate methods hard-copy information to prevent reconstruction and readability of the data<br>■ Tapes, diskettes, and hard drives must be degaussed, completely overwritten, or destroyed<br>■ Data on defective or damaged magnetic media must be overwritten before sending to vendor for repair | ■ Cross-shred or burn using corporate methods hard-copy information to prevent reconstruction and readability of the data<br>■ Tapes, diskettes, and hard drives must be degaussed, completely overwritten, or destroyed<br>■ Data on defective or damaged magnetic media must be overwritten before sending to vendor for repair<br>■ In copy areas, place papers in security trash bins<br>■ Information owner must be notified |
| Destruction/disposal off site | ■ Shred hard-copy information to prevent reconstruction and readability of the data<br>■ Use a method that prevents reconstruction of the data | ■ Cross-shred or burn using corporate method hard-copy information to prevent reconstruction of the data<br>■ Must be accomplished in a manner to render the information unreadable<br>■ Tapes, diskettes, and hard drives must be degaussed, completely overwritten, or destroyed by burning using a corporate method | ■ Cross-shred hard-copy information to prevent reconstruction of the data<br>■ Must be accomplished in a manner to render the information unreadable<br>■ Tapes, diskettes, and hard drives must be degaussed, completely overwritten, or destroyed by burning using a corporate method |

- Microfiche must be finely shredded
- Use a disposal vendor approved by Corporate Security
- In copy areas, place papers in security trash bins
- Ensure contracts with disposal services cover liability issues related to the service's mishandling or misplacement of the disposed information by the service
- Information owner must be notified when information is sent off-site for destruction
- Must be backed up regularly
- Local (laptop) drives must be backed up to diskettes or server directories
- Must be stored at least five miles from the site where the original copies reside
- Must be transported by authorized personnel or a courier service
- During transportation care must be taken to safeguard electronic media from loss, damage, or destruction from both human and environmental threats

- Microfiche must be finely shredded
- Use a disposal vendor approved by Corporate Security
- In copy areas, place papers in security trash bins
- Ensure contracts with disposal services cover liability issues related to the service's mishandling or misplacement of the disposed information by the service
- Must be backed up regularly
- Local (laptop) drives must be backed up to diskettes or server directories
- Must be stored at least five miles from the site where the original copies reside
- Must be transported by authorized personnel or a courier service
- During transportation care must be taken to safeguard electronic media from loss, damage, or destruction from both human and environmental threats

Backup and recovery

- Must be backed up regularly
- Local (laptop) drives must be backed up to diskettes or server directories
- Secure backup media in a fireproof locked desk, cabinet, or office
- Retained at least three generations of backup data
- Test backup data regularly to ensure reliability

*(continued)*

**Exhibit 11   Minimum Data Protection Mechanisms (continued)**

| Function | Internal Use Only | Restricted | Highly Restricted |
|---|---|---|---|
|  | ■ Identify retention periods and permanent archive requirements<br>■ Off-site backup storage facilities must be inspected at least annually to ensure adequate controls | ■ Sprocket Inc. facilities backups must be stored in a fireproof vault or safe rated to protect against heat and fire and accessible only by authorized persons<br>■ Backup archives must be stored off site in a location that will preclude it from suffering the same effects of a natural or human disaster<br>■ Backup media must be accessible only by authorized persons<br>■ Retain at least three generations of backup data<br>■ Test backup data regularly to ensure reliability<br>■ Identify retention periods and permanent archive requirements<br>■ Off-site backup storage facilities must be inspected at least annually to ensure adequate controls | ■ Sprocket Inc. facilities backups must be stored in a fireproof vault or safe rated to protect against heat and fire and accessible only by authorized persons<br>■ Backup archives must be stored off site in a location that will preclude it from suffering the same effects of a natural or human disaster<br>■ Backup media must be accessible only by authorized persons<br>■ Retain at least three generations of backup data<br>■ Test backup data regularly to ensure reliability<br>■ Identify retention periods and permanent archive requirements<br>■ Off-site backup storage facilities must be inspected at least annually to ensure adequate controls |
| Documentation for hardware, operating system, utility software, applications code | ■ Document all security within the application<br>■ Implement appropriate operating systems security | ■ Document all security within the application<br>■ Not accessible by information users or user managers | ■ Document all security within the application<br>■ Not accessible by information users or user managers |

| | | | |
|---|---|---|---|
| **Audit and systems logs** | ■ Protect from being modified | ■ Protected as appropriate for this level<br>■ Implement appropriate operating systems security<br>■ Protect from being modified<br>■ Accessible only by information custodians | ■ Protected as appropriate for this level<br>■ Implement appropriate operating systems security<br>■ Protect from being modified<br>■ Accessible only by information custodians |
| **Handling non-Sprocket Inc. information** | ■ Protect according to terms of contract or agreement with non-Sprocket Inc. entity<br>■ Contact Legal Department for specific details | ■ Protect according to terms of contract or agreement with non-Sprocket Inc. entity<br>■ Contact Legal Department for specific details | ■ Protect according to terms of contract or agreement with non-Sprocket Inc. entity<br>■ Contact Legal Department for specific details |
| **Declassify/reclassify authority** | ■ The authority to declassify or reclassify information belongs to the information owner/delegate | ■ The authority to declassify or reclassify information belongs to the information owner/delegate | ■ The authority to declassify or reclassify information belongs to the information owner/delegate |
| **Duplication and copying of information** | ■ Must be authorized by information owner or information delegate | ■ Must be authorized by information owner or information delegate | ■ Must be authorized by information owner or information delegate<br>■ Information owner or information delegate must maintain distribution record and number and label all copies of media containing the information as "Highly Restricted"<br>■ Recipients of authorized copies must ensure no further unauthorized copies are made |

*(continued)*

**Exhibit 11   Minimum Data Protection Mechanisms (continued)**

| Function | Internal Use Only | Restricted | Highly Restricted |
|---|---|---|---|
| Printing | ■ Information must be sent only to printers in controlled environments to which only authorized personnel demonstrating a need-to-know have access; if this cannot be accomplished, the printer must be attended by a person granted access to the information for the duration of the printing | ■ Information must be sent only to printers in controlled environments to which only authorized personnel demonstrating a need-to-know have access; if this cannot be accomplished, the printer must be attended by a person granted access to the information for the duration of the printing<br><br>■ Printers must be checked at the end of each business day for the presence of checks and other restricted documents<br><br>■ Information owners must control the number of copies printed | ■ Information must be sent only to printers in controlled environments to which only authorized personnel demonstrating a need-to-know have access; if this cannot be accomplished, the printer must be attended by a person granted access to the information for the duration of the printing<br><br>■ Printers must be checked at the end of each business day for the presence of checks and other highly restricted documents<br><br>■ Information owners must control the number of copies printed |
| Third-party access | ■ Access only to information required to fulfill business contracts<br><br>■ Security conditions must be documented in contracts; conditions must include:<br>  Requirements for protecting "Internal Use Only" data<br>  Nondisclosure requirements<br>  Copy and distribution restrictions | ■ Access only to information required to fulfill business contracts<br><br>■ Security conditions must be documented in contracts; conditions must include:<br>  Requirements for protecting "Restricted" data<br>  Nondisclosure requirements<br>  Copy and distribution restrictions | ■ Access only to information required to fulfill business contracts<br><br>■ Security conditions must be documented in contracts; conditions must include:<br>  Requirements for protecting "Highly Restricted" data<br>  Nondisclosure requirements<br>  Copy and distribution restrictions |

| | Column 1 | Column 2 | Column 3 |
|---|---|---|---|
| Notification responsibilities | ■ Before entering into contract, the following must occur: Background investigation Search for previous violations of Sprocket Inc. policies Review of third-party internal controls Evaluation of third-party business continuity plans Appropriate controls for third parties must be established<br>■ Violations must be reported immediately to Corporate Security | ■ Before entering into contract, the following must occur: Background investigation Search for previous violations of Sprocket Inc. policies Review of third-party internal controls Evaluation of third-party business continuity plans<br>■ Risk identification (analysis) must occur<br>■ Appropriate controls for third parties must be established<br>■ Violations must be reported immediately to Corporate Security | ■ Before entering into contract, the following must occur: Background investigation Search for previous violations of Sprocket Inc. policies Review of third-party internal controls Evaluation of third-party business continuity plans<br>■ Risk identification (analysis) must occur<br>■ Appropriate controls for third parties must be established<br>■ Violations must be reported immediately to Corporate Security |
| User training | ■ Persons fulfilling roles associated with the data must receive adequate security awareness training to ensure they understand the need for security<br>■ Persons fulfilling roles associated with the data must be told the data security requirements and controls necessary for "Internal Use Only" data prior to gaining access to the information or application | ■ Persons fulfilling roles associated with the data must receive adequate security awareness training to ensure they understand the need for security<br>■ Persons fulfilling roles associated with the data must be told the data security requirements and controls necessary for "Restricted" data prior to gaining access to the information or application | ■ Persons fulfilling roles associated with the data must receive adequate security awareness training to ensure they understand the need for security<br>■ Persons fulfilling roles associated with the data must be told the data security requirements and controls necessary for Highly "Restricted" data prior to gaining access to the information or application |

*(continued)*

**Exhibit 11   Minimum Data Protection Mechanisms (continued)**

| Function | Internal Use Only | Restricted | Highly Restricted |
|---|---|---|---|
| Legal requirements | ■ Software controls must be in place to prevent unauthorized and unlicensed copying and use<br>■ Records must be destroyed that have been retained beyond the statutory retention time<br>■ Roles/persons identified to keep inventory of the classification characteristics<br>■ Data must be protected from use or disclosure in any way incompatible with the intended purpose<br>■ Personal data must be accurate, kept current, and kept only as long as necessary for its intended purpose<br>■ Personal data must be protected from unauthorized access, alterations, disclosure, or destruction, and to prevent accidental loss or destruction | ■ Software controls must be in place to prevent unauthorized and unlicensed copying and use<br>■ Records must be destroyed that have been retained beyond the statutory retention time<br>■ Roles/persons identified to keep inventory of the classification characteristics<br>■ Data must be protected from use or disclosure in any way incompatible with the intended purpose<br>■ Personal data must be accurate, kept current, and kept only as long as necessary for its intended purpose<br>■ Personal data must be protected from unauthorized access, alterations, disclosure, or destruction, and to prevent accidental loss or destruction | ■ Software controls must be in place to prevent unauthorized and unlicensed copying and use<br>■ Records must be destroyed that have been retained beyond the statutory retention time<br>■ Roles/persons identified to keep inventory of the classification characteristics<br>■ Data must be protected from use or disclosure in any way incompatible with the intended purpose<br>■ Personal data must be accurate, kept current, and kept only as long as necessary for its intended purpose<br>■ Personal data must be protected from unauthorized access, alterations, disclosure, or destruction, and to prevent accidental loss or destruction |

**Exhibit 12 Sample Information Classification Worksheet**

**Information Classification Review Worksheet**

Organization: _____  Group _____

Review Performed _____  Date: _____

By/Phone: _____

*Classification (select one)*

| Information Name/Description | Storage Medium | *CONFIDENTIAL* If disclosed, could violate the privacy of individuals, reduce the company's competitive advantage, or could cause damage to the company | *RESTRICTED* Intended for use by a subset of employees when conducting company business (Usually regulatory requirement) | *INTERNAL USE* Intended for use by all employees when conducting company business | *PUBLIC* Made available for public distribution through authorized company channels |
|---|---|---|---|---|---|
| **Employee Records** | | | | | |
| 1 | | | | | |
| 2 | | | | | |
| 3 | | | | | |
| 4 | | | | | |
| 5 | | | | | |
| **Group Administration Records** | | | | | |
| 1 | | | | | |
| 2 | | | | | |
| 3 | | | | | |
| 4 | | | | | |
| 5 | | | | | |
| **Business Process Records** | | | | | |
| 1 | | | | | |
| 2 | | | | | |
| 3 | | | | | |
| 4 | | | | | |
| 5 | | | | | |

To complete this worksheet, the employee would fill in the information requested at the top of the sheet:

- *Organization* — The department designated as the information owner
- *Group* — The reporting group of the individual performing the information classification process
- *Review performed by/Phone* — The name and phone number of the individual performing the review
- *Date* — The date of the review
- *Information Name/Description* — An identifier and description of the information being reviewed

In the section for Information Name/Description, it will be necessary to enter the information type. For example:

- Employee Records
    Employee performance review records
    Timecards
    Employee discipline documents
    Pay records
    Medical records
- Group Administrative Records
    Monthly status reports
    Yearly status reports
    Yearly business objectives
- Business Process Records
    Purchasing contracts
    Quarterly financial reports
    Project management tasks, schedules
    Reference manuals
    Contract negotiations
- Operations Information
    Business partner information
    Asset allocation
    Trading activities
    Production formulas
    Production cost information
    Customer lists
- Distribution Records
    Distribution models
    Inventory records
    Parts supplies

Using the definitions, the person(s) performing the review would place a check in the appropriate column — only one check for each item being reviewed. This process would allow the user department to identify all of the various types of information found in the department and then be able to determine under which classification the information probably falls.

## 7.11 Authorization for Access

To establish a clear line of authority, some key concepts will have to be established. As discussed above, there are typically three categories of employee responsibilities. Depending on the specific information being accessed, an individual may fall into more than one category. For example, an employee with a desktop workstation becomes the owner, custodian, and user. To help better understand the concepts, the responsibilities of each category are listed below.

### 7.11.1  Owners

Minimally, the information owner is responsible for:

- Judging the value of the information resource and assigning the proper classification level
- Periodically reviewing the classification level to determine if the status should be changed
- Assessing and defining appropriate controls to assure that information created is properly safeguarded from unauthorized access, modification, disclosure, and destruction
- Communicating access and safeguard requirements to the information custodian and users
- Providing access to those individuals with a demonstrated business need for access
- Assessing the risk of loss of the information and assuring that adequate safeguards are in place to mitigate the risk to information integrity, confidentiality, and availability
- Monitoring safeguard requirements to ensure that information is being adequately protected
- Assuring a business continuity plan has been implemented and tested to protect information availability

### 7.11.2  Custodians

At a minimum, the custodian is responsible for:

- Providing proper safeguards for processing equipment, information storage, backup, and recovery
- Providing a secure processing environment that can adequately protect the integrity, confidentiality, and availability of information
- Administering access requests to information properly authorized by the owner

### 7.11.3  User

The user must:

- Use the information only for the purpose intended
- Maintain the integrity, confidentiality, and availability of information accessed

Being granted access to information does not imply or confer authority to grant other users access to that information. This is true whether the information is electronically held, printed, hard copy, manually prepared, copied, or transmitted.

## 7.12 Summary

Information classification drives the protection control requirements and this allows information to be protected to a level commensurate with its value to the organization. The cost of overprotection is eliminated and exceptions are minimized. With a policy and methodology, specifications are clear and accountability is established.

There are costs associated with implementing a classification system. The most identifiable costs include labeling classified information, implementing and monitoring controls and safeguards, and proper handling of confidential information.

Information, wherever it is handled or stored, needs to be protected from unauthorized access, modification, disclosure, and destruction. All information is not created equal. Consequently, segmentation or classification of information into categories is necessary to help identify a framework for evaluating the relative value of the information. By establishing this relative value, it will be possible to establish cost-effective controls that will preserve the information asset for the organization.

# *Chapter 8*

# Security Awareness Program

Development of security policies, standards, procedures, and guidelines is only the beginning of an effective information security program. A strong security architecture will be rendered less effective if there is no process in place to make certain that the employees are aware of their rights and responsibilities. All to often, security professionals implement the "perfect" security program, and then forget to include the personnel into the formula. To be as successful as possible, the information security professional must find a way to sell this product to the customers. An effective security awareness program could be the most cost-effective action management can take to protect its critical information assets.

Implementing an effective security awareness program will help all employees understand why they need to take information security seriously, what they will gain from its implementation, and how it will assist them in completing their assigned tasks. The process should begin at new employee orientation and continue annually for all employees at all levels of the organization.

## 8.1 Key Goals of an Information Security Program

For security professionals there are three key elements for any security program: *integrity, confidentiality,* and *availability*. Management is concerned that information reflects the real world and that it can have confidence in the information available to it so that management can make informed business decisions. One of the goals of an effective security program is to ensure that the information of an organization and its information-processing resources are properly protected.

The goal of confidentiality extends beyond just keeping the bad guys out; it also ensures that those with a business need have access to the resources they need to get their job done. Confidentiality ensures that controls and reporting mechanisms are in place to detect problems or possible intrusions with speed and accuracy.

In a recent roundtable discussion reported in the April 1999, *Information Security Magazine*, information security professionals Terri Curran of the Gillette Company, Harry DeMaio of Deloitte & Touche Services LLC, Dan Erwin of the Dow Chemical Company, and Kathleen Zarsky of Cigna Corporation discussed the changing perception of the security professional. These four well-respected members of the information security profession were able to present ideas that most of us in the business agree with.

Ms. Zarsky stated that in the past "unless management faces an audit — or the company has been embarrassed by breaches in security — it's very hard to convince them that security is worth the expense." As most of us have seen, management often views security as, at best, a necessary evil. However, with the move to E-commerce, management is looking to information security as a business enabler. This concept is beginning to make the rounds in recent security conferences around the world. David Lynas of Sheerwood Associates conducts conference sessions to train security professionals to turn away from the traditional role of saying "NO!" and to the more effective process of being part of the business.

An effective information security program must review the business objectives and the mission of the organization and ensure that these goals are met. Meeting the business objectives of the organization and understanding the customers' needs are what the goal of a security program is all about. An awareness program will reinforce these goals and will make the information security program more acceptable to the employee base.

## 8.2   Key Elements of a Security Program

The starting point with any security program is the implementation of policies, standards, procedures, and guidelines. As important as the written word is in defining the goals and objectives of the program and the organization, the truth is that most employees will not have the time or desire to read these important documents. An awareness program will ensure that the messages identified as important will get to all of those who need it.

Having individuals responsible for the implementation of the security program is another key element. To be most effective, the enterprise will need to have leadership at a minimum to two levels. There is a strong need to identify a senior-level manager to assume the role of corporate information officer (CIO). In a supporting capacity, an information security coordinator responsible for the day-to-day implementation of the information security program and reporting to the CIO is the second key player in the overall security program. Because a security program is more than just directions from the IT organization, each business unit should have its own coordinator responsible for the implementation of the program within that business unit.

The ability to classify information assets according to their relative value to the organization is the third key element in an information security program. Knowing what information an organization has that is sensitive will allow the informed implementation of controls and will allow the business units to use their limited resources where they will provide the most value. Understanding classification levels, employee responsibilities (owner, custodian, user), intellectual property requirements (copyright, trade secret, patent), and privacy rights is of critical importance. An effective awareness program will have to take this most confusing message to all employees and provide training material for all non-employees needing access to such resources.

The fourth key element is the implementation of the basic security concepts of separation of duties and rotation of assignments.

> *Separation of duties* — No single individual should have complete control of a business process or transaction from inception to completion. This control concept limits the error, opportunity, and temptation of personnel and can best be defined as segregating incompatible functions (accounts payable activities with disbursement). The activities of a process are split among several people. Mistakes made by one person tend to be caught by the next person in the chain, thereby increasing information integrity. Unauthorized activities will be limited because no one person can complete a process without the knowledge and support of another.
>
> *Rotation of assignments* — Individuals should periodically alternate various essential tasks involving business activities or transactions. There are always some assignments that can cause an organization to be at risk unless proper controls are in place. To ensure that desk procedures are being followed as well as to provide for staff backup on essential functions, individuals should be assigned to different tasks at regular intervals.

One of the often-heard concerns against rotation of assignments is that it reduces job efficiency. However, it has been proved that an employee's interest declines over time when doing the same job for extended periods. Additionally, employees sometimes develop shortcuts when they have been in a job too long. By rotating assignments, the organization can compare how the task was being done and where changes should be made.

The final element in an overall security program is an employee awareness program. Each of these elements will ensure that an organization meets its goals and objectives. The employee security awareness program will ensure that the program has a chance to succeed.

## 8.3   Security Awareness Program Goals

To be successful, a security awareness program must stress how security will support the business objectives of the enterprise. Selling a security program requires the identification of business needs and how the security program supports those objectives. Employees want to know how to get things accomplished and who to turn to for assistance. A strong awareness program will provide those important elements.

All personnel need to know and understand the management directives relating to the protection of information and information-processing resources. One of the key objectives of a security awareness program is to ensure that all personnel get this message. It must be presented to newly hired employees as well as to existing employees. The program must also work with the purchasing people to ensure that the message of security is presented to contract personnel. It is important to understand that contract personnel need to have this information, but it must be handled through their contract house. Work with purchasing and legal departments to establish the proper process.

All too often the security program fails because there is little or no follow-up. There is usually a big splash with great fanfare to kick off a new program. Unfortunately, this is where many programs end. Employees have learned that if they wait long enough, the new programs will die due to lack of interest or follow-up. It is very important to keep the message in front of the user community and to do this on a regular basis. To assist you in this process, there are a number of "days" that can be used in conjunction with your awareness program.

- May 10 — International Emergency Response Day
- September 8 — Computer Virus Awareness Day
- November 30 — International Computer Security Day

Keeping the message in front of the user community is not enough. The message must make the issues of security alive and important to all employees. It is important to find ways to tie the message in with the goals and objectives of each department. Every department has different objectives and different security needs. The awareness message needs to know and understand those concerns. We will discuss this in more detail presently.

Find ways to make the message important to the employees. When discussing controls, identify how they help protect the employee. When requiring employees to wear identification badges, many security programs tell the employees that this has been implemented to meet security objectives. What does this really mean? What the employees should be told is that the badges ensure that only authorized persons have access to the workplace. By doing this, the company is attempting to protect the employees. Find out how controls support or protect the assets (including the employees) will make the security program message more acceptable.

Finally, a security program is meant to reduce losses associated with intentional or accidental information disclosure, modification, destruction, and denial of service. This can be accomplished by raising the consciousness of all employees in ways that protect information and information-processing resources. By ensuring that these goals are met, the enterprise will be able to improve employee efficiency and productivity.

## 8.4   Identify Current Training Needs

To be successful, the awareness program should take into account the needs and current levels of training and understanding of the employees and management. There are five keys to establishing an effective awareness program. These include:

1. Assess current level of computer usage.
2. Determine what the managers and employees want to learn.
3. Examine the level of receptiveness to the security program.
4. Map out how to gain acceptance.
5. Identify possible allies.

To assess the current level of computer usage, it will be necessary to ask questions of the audience. Although sophisticated workstations may be found in employee work areas, their understanding of what these devices can do may be very limited. Ask questions about what the jobs are and how the tools available are used to support these tasks. It may come as a surprise to find the most-sophisticated computer is being used as a glorified 3270 terminal. Be an effective listener. Listen to what the users are saying and scale the awareness and training sessions to meet their needs. In the awareness field, one size or plan does not fit all.

Work with the managers and supervisors to understand what their needs are and how the program can help them. It will become necessary for you to understand the language of the business units and to interpret their needs. Once you have an understanding, then you will be able to modify the program to meet these special needs. No single awareness program will work for every business unit. There must be alterations and a willingness to accept suggestions from nonsecurity personal.

Identify the level of receptiveness to the security program. Find out what is accepted and what is meeting with resistance. Examine the areas of noncompliance and try to find ways to alter the program if at all possible. Do not change fundamental information security precepts just to gain unanimous acceptance; this is an unattainable goal. Make the program meet the greater good of the enterprise and then work with pockets of resistance to lessen the impact.

The best way to gain acceptance is to make your employee and manager partners in the security process. Never submit a new control or policy to management without sitting down with the managers individually and reviewing the objectives. This will require you to do your homework and to understand the business process in each department. It will be important to know the peak periods of activity in the department and what the managers' concerns are. When meeting with the managers, be sure to listen to their concerns and be prepared to ask for their suggestions on how to improve the program. Remember: the key here is to partner with your audience.

Finally, look for possible allies. Find out what managers support the objectives of the security program and those who have the respect of their peers. This means that it will be necessary to expand the area of support beyond physical security and the audit staff. Seek out business managers who have a vested interest in seeing this program succeed. Use their support to springboard the program to acceptance.

A key point in this entire process is never to refer to the security program or the awareness campaign as "my program." The enterprise has identified the need for security and you and your group are acting as the catalysts to move the program forward. When discussing the program with employees and managers, it will be beneficial to refer to it as their program or our program. Make them feel that they are key stakeholders in this process.

In a presentation used to introduce the security concept to the organization, it may be beneficial to say something like:

> Just as steps have been to taken to ensure the safety of the employees in the workplace, the organization is now asking that the employees work to protect the second most important enterprise asset — information. If the organization fails to protect its information from unauthorized access, modification, disclosure, and destruction, then the organization faces the prospect of loss of customer confidence, competitive advantage, and possibly jobs. All employees must accept the need and responsibility to protect our property and assets.

Involve the user community and accept its comments whenever possible. Make the information security the users' program. Use what they identify as important in the awareness program. By having them involved, then the program truly becomes theirs and they are more willing to accept and internalize the process.

## 8.5   Security Awareness Program Development

Different people do not need the same degree or type of information security awareness to do their jobs. An awareness program that distinguishes between groups of people, and presents only information that is relevant to that particular audience, will have the best results. Segmenting the audiences by job function, familiarity with systems, or some other category can improve the effectiveness of the security awareness and acceptance program. The purpose of segmenting audiences is to give the message the best possible chance of success. There are many ways in which to segment the user community; some of the more common methods are provided here.

■  *Level of Awareness* — Employees may be divided based on their current level of awareness of the information security objectives. One method of determining levels of awareness is to conduct a "walkabout." A walkabout is conducted after normal working hours and looks for certain key indicators. Look for just five key indicators:

1. Offices locked
2. Desks and cabinets locked
3. Workstations secured
4. Information secured
5. Recording media (diskettes, tapes, CDs, cassettes, etc.) secured

■ *Job category* — Personnel may be grouped according to job titles.
   Senior managers (including officers and directors)
   Middle management
   Line supervision
   Employees
   Others

■ *Specific job function* — Employees and personnel may be grouped according to job function.
   Service providers
   Information owners
   Users

■ *Information-processing knowledge* — As discussed above, not every employee has the same level of knowledge of how computers work. A security message for technical support personnel may be very different from that for data entry clerks. Senior management may have a very different level of computer skills than the office administrator.

■ *Technology, system, or application used* — To avoid "religious wars" it may be prudent to segment the audience based on the technology used. Mac and Intel-based systems users often have differing views, as do MVS users and UNIX users. The message may reach the audience faster if the technology used is considered.

Once the audience has been segmented, it will be necessary to establish the roles expected of the employees. These roles may include information owners, custodians of the data and systems, and general users. For all messages it will be necessary to employ the KISS process; that is, Keep It Simple Sweetie. Inform the audience, but try to stay away from commandments or directives. Discuss the goals and objectives using real-world scenarios. Whenever possible, avoid quoting policies, procedures, standards, or guidelines.

Policies and procedures are boring and if employees want more information, then they can access the documents on the organization intranet. If you feel that you must resort to this method, then you have missed the most important tenet of awareness, that is, to identify the business reason. Never tell employees that something is being implemented to "be in compliance with audit requirements." This is at best a cop-out and fails to explain in business terms why something is needed.

## 8.6   Methods Used to Convey the Awareness Message

How do people learn and where do people obtain their information? These are two very important questions to understand when developing an information security awareness program. Each of these is different. If we were implementing a training program, we would be able to select from three basic methods of training:

1. Buy a book and read about the subject.
2. Watch a video on the subject.
3. Ask someone to show you how.

For most employees the third method is best for training. They like the hands-on approach and want to have someone there to answer questions. With awareness the process is a little different. According to findings reported in *USA Today*, over 90 percent of Americans obtain their news from television or radio. To make an awareness program work, it will be necessary to tap into that model.

There are a number of different ways to get the message out to the user community. The key is to make the message stimulating to the senses of the audience. This can be accomplished by using posters, pictures, and videos. Because so many of our employees use the television as their primary source for gathering information, it is important to use videos to reinforce the message. The use of videos will serve several purposes.

With the advent of the news magazine format so popular in television today, our employees are already conditioned to accept the information presented as factual. This allows us to use the media to present them with the messages we consider important. Because they accept material presented in this format, the use of videos allows us to bring in an informed outsider to present the message. Many times our message fails because our audience knows the messenger. As a fellow worker, our credibility may be questioned. A video provides an expert on the subject.

There are a number of organizations that offer computer and information security videos. You might want to consider having a senior executive video-tape a message that can be run at the beginning of the other video. Costs for creating a quality in-house video can be prohibitive. A 20-minute video that is more than just "talking heads" can run $90,000 to $100,000.

An effective program will also take advantage of brochures, newsletters, or booklets. In all cases the effectiveness of the medium will depend on how well it is created and how succinct the message is. One major problem with newsletters is finding enough material to complete the pages each time you want to go to print. One way to present a quality newsletter is to look for vendors to provide such material. The Computer Security Institute offers a document titled *Frontline*. This newsletter is researched and written every quarter by the CSI editorial staff and provides the space for a column written by your organization to provide pertinent information for your organization. Once the materials are ready, CSI sends out either camera-ready or PDF format versions of the newsletter. The customer then is authorized to make unlimited copies of the newsletter.

As we discussed above, many organizations are requiring business units to name information protection coordinators. One of the tasks of these coordinators is to present awareness sessions for their organizations. An effective way of getting a consistent message out is to "train the trainers." Create a security awareness presentation and then bring in the coordinators to train them in presenting the corporate message to their user community. This will ensure that the message presented meets the needs of each organization and that they view the program as theirs.

It will be necessary to identify those employees will have not attended awareness training. By having some form of sign-in or other recording mechanism, the program will be assured of reaching most of the employees. By having the coordinator submit annual reports on the number of employees trained, the enterprise will have a degree of comfort in meeting its goals and objectives.

## 8.7 Presentation Key Elements

Although every organization has its own style and method of training, it might help to review some important issues when creating an awareness program. One very important item to keep in mind is that the topic of information security is very broad. Do not get overwhelmed with the prospect of providing information on every facet of information security in one meeting. The old adage of "How do you eat an elephant? One bite at a time" must be remembered.

Prioritize your message to the employees. Start small and build on the program. Remember: you are going to have many opportunities to present your messages. Identify where to begin, present the message, reinforce the message, and then build to the next objective. Keep the training sessions as brief as possible. It is normally recommended to keep these session to no more than 50 minutes. There are a number of reasons for under an hour: biology (you can only hold coffee for so long), attention spans, and productive work needs. Start with an attention-grabbing piece and then follow up with additional information.

Tailor the presentations to the vocabulary and skill set of the audience. Know who you are talking to and provide them with information they can understand. This will not be a formal doctoral presentation. The awareness session must take into account the audience and the culture of the organization. Understand the needs, knowledge, and jobs of the attendees. Stress the positive and business side of security: protecting the assets of the organization. Provide the audience with a reminder (booklet, brochure, or trinket) of the objectives of the program.

## 8.8 Typical Presentation Format

In any program that hopes to modify behavior, there are the three keys: tell them what you are going to say; say it; and then remind them of what you said. A typical agenda might look like the following.

Start with an introduction of the topic of what information security is about and how it will impact their business units and departments. Follow with a video that will reinforce the message and present the audience with an external expert supporting the corporate message. Discuss any methods that will be employed to monitor compliance to the program and provide them with the rationale for the compliance checking. Provide them with time for questions and ensure that every question either gets an answer or is recorded and the answer provided as soon as possible. Finally, give them some item that will reinforce the message.

## 8.9   When to Do Awareness

Any awareness program must be scheduled around the work patterns of the audience. Take into account busy periods for the various departments and make certain that the sessions do not impact the peak periods. The best times for having these sessions is in the morning on Tuesday, Wednesday, and Thursday. First thing Monday morning will impact those getting back and starting the week's work. Having the session on Friday afternoon will not be as productive as you would like. Scheduling anything right after lunch is always a worry. The physiological clock of humans is at its lowest productivity level right after lunch. If you turn out the lights to show a movie, the snoring may drown out the video. Also, schedule sessions during off-shift hours. Second and third-shift employees should have the opportunity to view the message during their work hours just as those on the day shift do.

## 8.10 The Information Security Message

The employees need to know that information is an important enterprise asset and is the property of the organization. All employees have a responsibility to ensure that this asset, like all others, must be protected and used to support management-approved business activities. To assist them in this process, employees must be made aware of the possible threats and what can be done to combat those threats. The scope of the program must be identified. Is the program dealing only with computer-held data, or does it reach to all information wherever it is resident? Make sure the employees know the total scope of the program. Enlist their support in protecting this asset. The mission and business of the enterprise may depend on it.

## 8.11 Information Security Self-Assessment

Each organization will have to develop a process in which to measure the compliance level of the information security program. As part of the awareness process, staff should be made aware of the compliance process. Included for you is an example of how an organization might evaluate the level of information security within a department or throughout the enterprise. See Appendix F for examples.

## 8.12 Conclusion

Information security is more than just polices, standards, procedures, and guidelines. It is more than audit comments and requirements. It is a cultural change for most employees. Before employees can be required to be compliant with a security program, they first must become aware of the program. Awareness is an ongoing program that employees must have contact with on at least an annual basis.

Information security awareness does not require huge cash outlays. It does require time and proper project management. Keep the message in front of the employees. Use different methods and means. Bring in outside speakers whenever possible and use videos to best advantage.

## Chapter 9

# Why Manage This Process as a Project?

Although a project is usually defined as a *one-time* effort that has a definite beginning and end and the implementation of security policies can be an *ongoing* effort, managing this process as a project will help keep the implementation team focused on the results to be achieved. Applying project management practices will also help with the assessment of those results to ensure they meet the needs of the organization.

Consideration should be given to such questions as: What is included within the area of concern or what is the scope? What should be done first? How much time will it take? Is there a deadline that will act as a constraint on how much can be accomplished? How should changing requirements be managed? How much will it cost? How relevant are the policies and procedures to the environment? Who should create them? How should they be reviewed? How should they be communicated? How can opportunities for improvement be maximized? How can the potential for resistance by staff be mitigated? When should external sources be considered for providing assistance?

Creating and implementing security policies and procedures begin with a thorough understanding of why your organization is concerned that these policies and procedures exist. Understanding the reasons the effort was undertaken will help you set goals and objectives when determining how the security needs of your organization will be met. Later, the results of your effort should be reviewed to ensure that they accomplished what was expected.

## 9.1 First Things First — Identify the Sponsor

A key factor in implementing policies and procedures successfully is to have commitment from senior-level management. The person with the means to commit resources to this effort should be identified as the project sponsor. This sponsor will be the final person responsible for all major implementation decisions. The absence of a sponsor of sufficient organizational prominence is a major risk to successful implementation of policies and procedures. Work completed without this sponsor may be subject to rework if the project team proceeds in a direction not supported by management. It is important that support be explicitly obvious. Clear management support will help obtain the cooperation and contributions needed from individuals who may not be direct members of the project team.

The project manager is the individual who leads the work effort and is responsible for the day-to-day planning, management, and control of the project. The successful completion of project deliverables on time, within budget, and to the specified quality standards is included in the project manager's responsibilities.

The project manager may be recruited from any area concerned with security, such as information security or internal auditing. This individual could also be recruited from outside the organization. Superior communication, organization, and team-building skills are among the traits that this individual should possess.

It is best to have only one project manager so that the management and control of project activities can be effectively coordinated. Managing the implementation of policies and procedures requires contributions and feedback from multiple sources. A project manager fulfills the role of the conductor in ensuring that these contributions are well integrated within the overall project.

Ensure that the project manager possesses a sufficient level of experience and skill to manage the challenges that can be encountered when policies are being implemented. Be conscious of the tendency toward resistance among staff when it comes to documenting business processes or practices that may be perceived as candidates for remediation. Review any previous studies or reports that address existing security policies, procedures, or findings. A good place to start is with your internal audit staff or other groups that might perform audit or compliance tracking functions. Determine whether any constraints might inhibit progress and document all assumptions that have been made. Measurable criteria should be established to assess the success of the policy and procedure implementation. If there are quality objectives, quantitative requirements, expected benefits, or cost objectives to consider, document them.

Once the sponsor and project manager have been identified, the project manager should talk with the sponsor to obtain an understanding of desired outcomes. Interviews are also an opportunity to identify other interested parties, or project stakeholders.

Initiatives to create or revise policies and procedures may be a response to any number of stimuli. Legal requirements, especially in publicly traded or financial organizations, may need to be addressed. An adverse event that has occurred or nearly occurred may prompt the effort. Sometimes the effort is begun to guard against a situation that has occurred at another organization.

A change in management can also spur a commitment to implement new or updated policies and procedures. Whatever the reason, the reason itself can be a good starting point for helping to define the overall objectives of this effort. Remember: it is extremely helpful to interview management to gain and document an understanding of their expectations. Clear, concise objectives that are documented and agreed upon by top-level management are a key success factor that should not be overlooked. Strive to obtain explicit confirmation, with a signature if possible, of the major objectives for the project to create and implement the policies and procedures you will be producing.

## 9.2   Defining the Scope of Work

Defining the scope of work draws boundaries on what is to be accomplished. A scope statement should be developed that clearly defines what is and what is not included within the area of work to be completed. For example, your approach to developing policies may be very different if the scope addresses issues from an enterprise perspective rather than at a more specific departmental position. Whether you are addressing an enterprise or departmental perspective, determine the high-level objectives that the policies and procedures are supposed to address and relate them to the business objectives of the organization. Relating your project to the business objectives of the enterprise helps address issues associated with competing demands for limited resources. You need to demonstrate that the activities associated with the implementation of security policies and procedures provide a positive contribution to the goals of your organization.

To help define objectives, consider the types of information security challenges your organization must face. These objectives, or project requirements, lay the foundation for the plan of activities that will be developed to address those requirements. Careful consideration should be given to defining project requirements, and they should always be documented. Requirements that are not documented are subject to ambiguity and misinterpretation. Developing a consistent understanding of the scope and requirements is extremely important in ensuring that the outcomes of your effort meet those requirements. If you are not sure of your organization requirements, you are not likely to develop policies to address those needs. A clear understanding of requirements will help direct effort toward achieving your goals. Clear requirements will guide your activities and provide a basis for future decisions as you define, organize, and implement the policies and procedures that are created.

Once requirements have been clearly defined, a high-level breakdown of project components or activities can be developed. This high-level breakdown, or work breakdown structure (WBS; Exhibit 1), is a deliverable-oriented grouping of elements that help organize and define the total scope of the project. The WBS may be grouped by type of policy or procedure and should also include other supporting elements such as the communications plan. It is a good visual aid for identifying the work that the project will undertake. Work not identified in the WBS is outside the scope of the project.

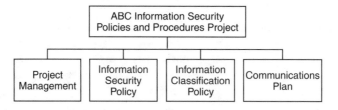

**Exhibit 1    High-Level Work Breakdown Structure**

After a high-level grouping of project deliverables has been defined, each high-level group should be further subdivided into more manageable components until enough detail is obtained to allow estimates of time, cost, and resource requirements to be assigned to each component. Although the sponsor and project manager can identify the high-level groups, the decomposition into subcomponents should be completed with the participation of other team members. See the Section 9.3 for more details.

Once high-level requirements are defined and agreed upon, a project kickoff meeting (see Exhibit 2) can be held to officially "begin" the project. This kickoff is a special meeting at which all stakeholders, project participants, and other interested parties are introduced to the project. It is very helpful in terms of obtaining cooperation and buy-in if the project sponsor delivers a statement that emphasizes the importance of the project as well as key expectations.

The kickoff should also include an outline of the proposed approach to achieving the defined project requirements and should provide an opportunity for participants to ask questions of and give feedback to the project team.

## 9.3   Time Management

Time management processes are designed to promote the timely completion of the policies and procedures project. These processes include identifying the various activities required to complete the project. These activities can then be sequenced to identify activity interdependencies. Once interdependencies are identified, then estimates can be determined to establish a project schedule. The project schedule will provide the basis for controlling the project activities.

To identify project activities, review the scope, high-level objectives, and constraints of the project. Then identify the appropriate lower-level steps and tasks to be accomplished. The WBS should be reviewed and adjusted to ensure that all necessary tasks are included and that any unnecessary work has been removed. A basic project management tenet is to ensure that the project is controlled so that it includes all the work required and only the work required to bring it to successful completion. The project manager can start this process, but other project participants should supplement it with their contributions. Brainstorming techniques may be used when decomposing the high-level elements of the WBS into its lower-level components (Exhibit 3). After each element has been broken down, review each one and gain consensus on the validity of its subcomponents.

**Exhibit 2  Sample Project Kickoff Meeting Agenda**

**Security Policies & Procedures Project**
Date
Time
Place

The purpose of this meeting is to begin the Security Policies and Procedures Project.
- *Invitees:* Sponsor, Project Manager, Project Team Members, other stakeholders
- *Desired Outcomes:*
  1. Establish working relationships and lines of communication
  2. Establish and review project scope and objectives
  3. Review project approach
  4. Establish responsibilities
  5. Identify and document issues to be addressed
  6. Identify next steps

| Agenda Items | Who |
| --- | --- |
| Introduction | Project Manager |
| Review agenda | Project Manager |
| Project briefing — the purpose of this project | Sponsor |
| Project scope and objectives | Project Manager |
| Project approach | Team |
| Responsibilities | Team |
| Issues | All |
| Next steps | Project Manager |

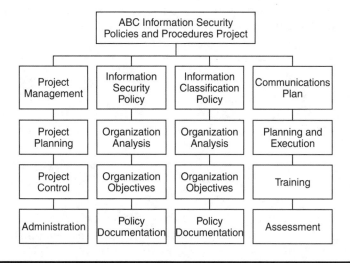

**Exhibit 3  Sample Work Breakdown Structure Organized by Policy Type**

Each element should be decomposed to a level sufficient to later support an estimate of required time, cost, and resources to complete. The WBS is intended to organize and define the scope of the project and is not meant to demonstrate the sequence of work to be performed. Sequencing is performed later, after all the activities have been identified and defined. The sequencing activity will support the development of a schedule.

After decomposition, a list of all project activities to be performed can be developed based on the refined WBS. This list should include descriptions to ensure that the individuals assigned to complete the work understand what is to be delivered. After all activities are identified, they should be analyzed to identify interdependencies. Activities must be sequenced appropriately to develop a realistic schedule. Be sure to include activities that are administrative in nature, such as planning and conducting meetings and completing status reports. These activities may be grouped together, but careful consideration to this area will help prevent an overly optimistic estimate. Exhibit 4 displays a sample of a decomposed WBS.

Estimates for time to complete or effort can be developed after all activities and their interdependencies have been identified. Effort estimates will be influenced by the project manager's prior experience, ability to make judgments based on limited information, and knowledge of the subject matter. The estimating process should include the project team members; estimates developed by obtaining consensus from the team will probably be more accurate. Producing and reviewing estimates with the participation of the people who will do the work will also support team building and will build confidence for the estimates produced.

A bottom-up estimate for the overall project can be produced by allocating effort estimates to each lowest-level component and aggregating them up to obtain an initial estimate for the total project. Effort estimates for each WBS component together with the identified activities to be performed and their interdependencies will allow the project manager to develop the project schedule. Be sure to record all assumptions and issues identified.

Before beginning the estimating process, review the following questions:

- Who should be involved?
- What units of measure should be used: hours, days, weeks? The unit determined should be appropriate to the level of detail used to define the activities and ideally should be consistent across the entire project.
- How will contingencies be applied?

Two possible approaches to use are consensus-based and weighted-average estimating. A consensus-based estimate is an estimate that is developed by the people who are involved in an activity. The estimates produced will vary based on the differing viewpoints and experiences of the people on the team. Participants are asked to produce estimates and then to explain the reasoning behind the estimates. The estimates can be discussed in reference to these explanations and, eventually, agreement can be reached for a single estimate.

**Exhibit 4   Sample Decomposed WBS**

1.    **Project Planning, Scheduling, and Budgeting**
      1.1    Project Kickoff
      1.2    Establish Project Sponsor
      1.3    Identify Benefits and Costs
      1.4    Develop Business Case
      1.5    Establish Objectives
      1.6    Define Project Scope
      1.7    Define Project Approach
      1.8    Define Project Activities
      1.9    Develop Project Schedule
      1.10   Prepare Project Budget
      1.11   Determine Project Staffing Requirements
      1.12   Establish Roles and Responsibilities
      1.13   Conduct Project Status Assessment

2.    **Training**
      2.1    Determine Training Requirements
      2.2    Identify and Acquire Tools
      2.3    Develop Training Plan
      2.4    Manage Training Activities
      2.5    Establish Budget Status Reporting Methods
      2.6    Establish Schedule Status Reporting Methods
      2.7    Conduct Project Status Assessment

3.    **Project Control**
      3.1    Monitor Project Progress
      3.2    Identify and Resolve Issues
      3.3    Manage Exception Situations
      3.4    Review and Revise Project Plan
      3.5    Conduct Project Status Assessment

4.    **Project Quality Procedures**
      4.1    Review Enterprise Documentation Standards
      4.2    Define Quality Objectives
      4.3    Define Product Quality Control Reviews
      4.4    Define Documentation Standards for Policies
      4.5    Define Documentation Standards for Procedures
      4.6    Develop Quality Plan
      4.7    Define Policy/Procedure Review Strategies
      4.8    Define Documentation Management Plan
      4.9    Identify/Define Support Tools and Procedures
      4.10   Conduct Project Status Assessment

5.    **Develop Policies**
      5.1    Document Definitions

*(continued)*

**Exhibit 4    Sample Decomposed WBS (continued)**

|   |   |
|---|---|
| 5.2 | Identify Required Policies |
| 5.3 | Identify Procedures, Standards Required |
| 5.4 | Determine Formatting |
| 5.5 | Outline Content |
| 5.6 | Develop and Define Policies |
| 5.7 | Develop and Define Standards |
| 5.8 | Develop and Define Guidelines |
| 5.9 | Develop and Define Procedures |
| 5.10 | Conduct Project Status Assessment |

**6.    Communications Planning**

|   |   |
|---|---|
| 6.1 | Identify Audiences |
| 6.2 | Determine Distribution Frequency Requirements |
| 6.3 | Determine Information Distribution Mechanisms |
| 6.4 | Develop Communications Plan |
| 6.5 | Define Performance Reporting Requirements |
| 6.6 | Conduct Project Status Assessment |

**7.    Project Closure**

|   |   |
|---|---|
| 7.1 | Complete Final Evaluations |
| 7.2 | Initiate Maintenance Process |
| 7.3 | Close Outstanding Project Work |
| 7.4 | Collect Project Feedback |
| 7.5 | Compile Project Closure Documents |

To develop a weighted-average estimate, have participants estimate each component of the activities list giving best-case, worst-case, and most likely estimates. This task should be completed individually; then a workshop can be conducted to consolidate and review the initial estimates. A determination of how the weighted average is calculated should be determined by the project manager or by team consensus. The weighted-average table shown in Exhibit 5 and its calculations are illustrative only and are not intended to represent the actual experience of any specific project.

The results should be reviewed with special attention paid to large variations between the best, worst, and most likely estimates given for the same activity. Reasons for the large variations should be determined and reconciled. Try to gain agreement among the estimators. The intention is not to arrive at the same value for the best, worst, and most likely cases, but to gain agreement on what the best, worst, and most likely cases are.

Once the estimates have been completed, they should be converted into practical estimates by allowing for nonproductive time such as sickness and vacation. This may be involve the application of a standard percentage value that is used to increase effort estimates. Be careful to avoid double-counting these items and inadvertently inflating the estimates.

**Exhibit 5   Sample Table of Weighted-Average Calculations**

| Category | Item | Best Case, in days (weight = 15 percent) | Most Likely Case, in days (weight = 55 percent) | Worst Case, in days (weight = 30 percent) | Weighted Average (rounded) |
|---|---|---|---|---|---|
| Information classification | Establish the team | 1 | 5 | 15 | 7 |
| Information classification | Develop the policy | 2 | 10 | 25 | 13 |
| Information classification | Determining confidential information | 5 | 20 | 80 | 36 |
| Information classification | Identifying information to be declassified or reclassified | 10 | 20 | 60 | 31 |

Weighted-average formula: $(BC \times 0.15) + (MLC \times 0.55) + (WC \times 0.30)$.

Estimates can be developed using both consensus and weighted-average techniques with the results compared to develop a single estimate. As the project progresses, estimates may be revised based on the actual performance to date and due to unplanned events such as scope changes, staff changes, and newly identified activities.

The WBS and activities list can be developed simultaneously and may be documented as a spreadsheet or used as input to an automated scheduling tool. An automated scheduling tool will allow the project manager to complete "what-if" scenarios such as when the work should be started if an arbitrary deadline is imposed on the project and how the schedule will be impacted if project resources are limited or expanded. The project schedule, or timeline, will serve as a basis for tracking progress against the plan.

## 9.4   Cost Management

The WBS and sequenced activities list developed during the beginning stages of the project are used to support the development of a cost estimate. A more-detailed WBS and activities list will support a more accurate estimate, but the level of detail required depends on the required degree of accuracy and the project manager's estimating experience. Keep in mind that a highly detailed WBS can be used to demonstrate the magnitude of the work involved and will provide support for the cost estimate. Each item on the activities list should include a labor and materials component. The cost of materials can often be overlooked when considering activities that appear to be labor intensive. For example, an activity identified as "training" may be estimated at 20 hours × $60/hour. The $1200 estimate will be too low if a graphics software package must be purchased to design the training material, printing and binding services are required, or organizational expectations are that participants will be served food and beverages during training.

## 9.5   Planning for Quality

Planning for quality requires that processes be in place to ensure that the policies and procedures created satisfy the needs for which they were developed. These processes include activities such as inspection reviews. These reviews are conducted to critique the policies or procedures to help ensure that management expectations and requirements have been met. Reviews also provide an opportunity to reduce the likelihood of errors, omissions, or misunderstandings. Results are documented and corrective action taken if necessary. Documentation standards, if any, should be reviewed to ensure that the policies and procedures developed are in compliance.

Review participants should include project team members as well as peers from other organization teams who have not been closely associated with the project. Management generally should not be included at preliminary reviews to ensure that the focus remains on the examination and tuning of the policies or procedures developed and not on the performance or status of the project itself.

## 9.6  Managing Human Resources

The primary objective of human resource management is to make the most effective use of the people involved with the project. Activities included are planning the organizational structure of the project, acquiring staff, and developing team members. The resources necessary to carry out the project and to ensure its success should be clearly defined and documented in terms of their roles and responsibilities. Reporting relationships can also be documented if necessary. All people in the project should understand their responsibilities and should have the time available to carry out those responsibilities.

When determining staffing requirements, the skills required for the activities to be performed and their associated time frames should be defined. The WBS and activities list should be used during this task. Organizational policies and a description of the existing available resource pool should also be reviewed. If it is determined that resources will be acquired from outside the organization, a plan for how these resources will be brought onto and removed from the project may need to be developed. Paying attention to how team members will be transitioned onto and off of a project can help contain costs by eliminating the tendency to create work to fill the time between assignments.

Team development includes activities that support the ability of team members to increase their individual contributions to the project and enhance the ability of the team to function effectively. The capabilities and skills of the project team should be assessed to help establish a plan to train members in any areas of deficiency. The types of training required should be documented so that a training plan can be developed. This training is specific to the project team and is in addition to the awareness training plan that should be developed to introduce the new policies and procedures to the enterprise. The time required to develop team skills should be included in the project schedule. Include a reference to the location of the training session plan.

## 9.7  Creating a Communications Plan

Managing security communications effectively ensures that timely and appropriate information is generated, updated, and disseminated to all who need to know. Lack of employee awareness will defeat the intentions of even the most comprehensive policies and procedures. The communications process ensures that critical connections are established among all individuals of an organization. These communication links are absolutely necessary for the successful implementation of security policies and procedures. Creating a communications plan will provide a framework from which to manage the communications process.

The structure of an organization will have a major effect on communications requirements. The information delivery mechanisms for an organization that houses staff in one central location may be very different from one that has employees distributed over several remote locations. Take time to determine the information needs for your organization. Consider who needs what information, when and how often they should receive it, and how it will be delivered to them. An analysis of the policies and procedures and the circumstances that they address will help determine how significant they are to the organization and how often they should be delivered. Analyzing the circumstances that the policies and procedures address will also help identify the intended audience.

Exhibit 6 contains recommended types of communications that can be established during the development of policies and procedures. The needs of the project and the expectations of the project sponsor and stakeholders will influence how adjustments should be made.

Exhibit 7 contains recommended types of communications to establish once policies and procedures have been approved and are ready to be disseminated to the organization. Responsibilities for delivery may be delegated; however, the sponsor should explicitly endorse all communications. The delivery mech-

**Exhibit 6  Sample Communications Plan (during Development of Planning and Preparation)**

| Communication Type | Audience | Frequency | Responsibility | Delivery Mechanism |
|---|---|---|---|---|
| Project kickoff* | Project sponsor Stakeholders Project team | At project start | Project manager | Meeting |
| Overall status report* | Project sponsor Stakeholders Project team | Monthly | Project manager | Document attachment via e-mail |
| Project review milestone Assessment* | Project sponsor | Quarterly | Project manager | Meeting |
| Project team meeting* | Project team | Weekly | Project manager | Meeting |
| Project newsletter | All affected (interested) parties | Monthly | Team members | Newsletter document via general mail |
| Task status | Project team Project manager | Weekly | Team members | Update commitment calendar |
| Issue identification | Project manager | As needed | All | Issue management process |
| History/inquiries about project | All | As needed | Project manager | Electronic project notebook accessible via Web page |
| Problem identification: internal | Project manager | As needed | All | Problem management process |

* Should be *required*.

**Exhibit 7  Sample Communications Plan (after Deployment)**

| Communication Type | Audience | Frequency | Responsibility | Delivery Mechanism |
|---|---|---|---|---|
| New or revised policy announcement* | All | As released, periodically thereafter | Sponsor | Broadcast mail<br>Broadcast e-mail<br>Broadcast voice-mail |
| New or revised procedure* | All affected (interested) parties | As released | Sponsor | Training |
| Complete policy manual* | All | Yearly and at new employee orientation | Sponsor | Manual<br>Intranet Web page |
| General security awareness | All | Quarterly | Information security team | Broadcast mail<br>Broadcast e-mail<br>Intranet Web page<br>Posters |
| Awareness newsletter | All | Semiannually or quarterly | Information security team | Departmental meetings<br>Broadcast mail |
| Employee security awareness day | All | Yearly or semiannually | Information security team | Promotional items<br>Employee contests<br>Topic discussions and demonstrations |

* *Required.*

anisms or frequencies should be revised to meet the needs of the organization or the urgency of the situations the policies were was designed to address. For example, a new policy that states that all company communications are subject to spontaneous monitoring may require more frequent delivery in a large organization with a high turnover rate than in an organization with a workforce that is relatively stable.

## 9.8  Summary

Managing the development of security policies and procedures as a project involves the application of a variety of skills, tools, experiences, and techniques. Project management processes help guide project activities to meet stakeholder needs and expectations. A primary objective of project management is to manage resources efficiently and effectively to deliver products on time and within budget while attaining a given level of quality. The intent of this chapter was to introduce a few key project management concepts that should be readily adaptable to a policies and procedures development project.

# Chapter 10

# Information Technology: Code of Practice for Information Security Management

The policies in the following sections are examples of what might be expected in each of the ten major areas of the ISO 17799. These are only examples; they will require edits that will make these examples your own.

When you review the sections, you will notice that there are nearly 700 suggestions on things to have and to include. Select what is needed and keep the rest for reference. Remember that policies, standards, and procedures are vital and active. They will need to be reviewed on a regular basis to see if they are still appropriate (Exhibit 1).

## 10.1   Scope

This standard gives recommendations for information security management for the use by those who are responsible for initiating, implementing, or maintaining security in their organization. *This is a non-action section.*

## 10.2   Terms and Definitions

This section defines:

■ Information security

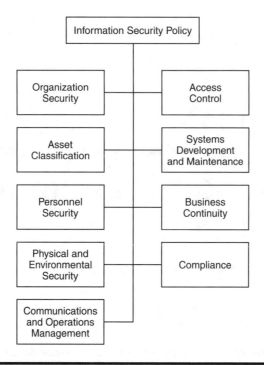

**Exhibit 1    ISO 17799 Structure**

- Confidentiality
- Integrity
- Availability
- Risk assessment
- Risk management

# 10.3    Information Security Policy

*Objective:* Company management must establish a clear direction and support for an enterprisewide information security program (Exhibit 2).

**Exhibit 2    Information Security Policy**

**Policy**

Information is a company asset and is the property of the Company. The Company information includes information that is electronically generated, printed, filmed, typed, stored, or verbally communicated. Information must be protected according to its sensitivity, criticality, and value, regardless of the media on which it is stored, the manual or automated systems that process it, or the methods by which it is distributed.

**Provisions**

To ensure that business objectives and customer confidence are maintained, all employees have a responsibility to protect information from unauthorized access, modification, disclosure, or destruction, whether accidental or intentional.

**Exhibit 2   Information Security Policy (continued)**

**Responsibilities**
1.  Senior management and the officers of the Company are required to employ internal controls designed to safeguard company assets, including business information. It is a management obligation to ensure that all employees understand and comply with the Company security policies and standards as well as all applicable laws and regulations.
2.  Employee responsibilities for protecting the Company information are detailed in the *Information Classification* policy.

**Compliance**
1.  Company management has the responsibility to manage corporate information, personnel, and physical property relevant to business operations, as well as the right to monitor the actual utilization of all corporate assets.
2.  Employees who fail to comply with the policies will be considered to be in violation of the Company *Employee Standards of Conduct* and will be subject to appropriate corrective action.

# 10.4   Organization Security

*Objective:* A management forum must be established to sponsor and champion an enterprisewide information security program. This group of senior executives will provide the direction, leadership, and resources to support such a program (Exhibit 3).

**Exhibit 3   Information Security Infrastructure**

**Policy**
A Management Steering Committee (MST) has been established to establish and approve policies supporting the Information Security Policy, assign security roles, and coordinate the implementation of security across the organization.

**Provisions**
Each Vice President shall appoint an employee who will administer an information protection program that appropriately classifies and protects corporate information under the Vice President's control and implement a program to ensure that all employees are aware of the importance of information and methods for its protection.

**Key Terms**
Security forum; security responsibilities; job descriptions; third-party access; outsourcing
**Responsibilities**
1.  Review and approve information security-related policies.
2.  Publish an Information Security Mission Statement.

*(continued)*

**Exhibit 3   Information Security Infrastructure (continued)**

3. Establish job descriptions for at least the following:
   a. Information Security Officer
   b. Information Security Administrator
   c. Organization Information Security Coordinator
4. Provide adequate funding and support for the information security program.
5. Review annual "State of Information Security" Report published by ISO each January.

**Compliance**
The Company MST must review security-related incident reports to ensure that appropriate corrective action is implemented.

## 10.5   Asset Classification and Control

*Objective:* A consistent process to classify and protect enterprise information assets must be established. This policy must include a discussion on the responsibility of management to protect the assets of the organization (Exhibit 4).

**Exhibit 4   Information Classification Policy**

**General**
Information is a corporate asset and is the property of the Company. This is true of all business information within the Company, regardless of how it is created, distributed, or stored and whether it is typed, handwritten, printed, computer-generated, or spoken.

The Company management is responsible for ensuring that all employees understand and adhere to this policy. Management is also responsible for noting variances from established information protection practices and for initiating corrective action. Employees found to be in violation of this policy are subject to disciplinary action as described in the Employee Standards of Conduct.

**Key Terms**
Accountability; inventory of assets; information labeling

**Information Protection**
Information must be protected according to its sensitivity, criticality, and value, regardless of the media on which it is stored, the manual or automated systems that process it, or the methods by which it is distributed.

Employees are responsible for protecting corporate information from unauthorized access, modification, destruction, or disclosure, whether accidental or intentional. To facilitate the protection of corporate information, employee responsibilities have been established at three levels: *Owner, Custodian,* and *User.*
- *Owner:* Company management of the organizational unit where the information is created, or management of the organizational unit that is the primary user of the information. Owners are responsible to:

**Exhibit 4   Information Classification Policy (continued)**

1. Identify the classification level of all corporate information within their organizational unit;
2. Define appropriate safeguards to ensure the confidentiality, integrity, and availability of the information resource;
3. Monitor safeguards to ensure they are properly implemented;
4. Authorize access to those who have a business need for the information; and
5. Remove access from those who no longer have a business need for the information.

■ *Custodian:* Employees designated by the owner to be responsible for maintaining the safeguards established by the owner.

■ *User:* Employees authorized by the owner to access information and use the safeguards established by the owner.

To ensure the proper protection of corporate information, the owner shall use a formal review process to classify information into one of the following classifications:

■ *Public:* Information, that has been made available for public distribution through authorized company channels.

■ *Confidential:* Information that, if disclosed, could violate the privacy of individuals, reduce the company's competitive advantage, or could cause significant damage to the Company.

■ *Internal Use:* Information that is intended for use by all employees when conducting company business. Most information used in the Company would be classified as internal use.

# 10.6   Personnel Security

*Objective:* Policies, standards. and procedures must be established to address the adequate screening of potential candidates for employment (Exhibit 5). Additional controls must be implemented for those individuals working in areas with access to sensitive or competitive-advantage information.

**Exhibit 5   Personnel Security Policy**

**Policy**
Individuals with access to Company information assets are expected to protect those assets. Security responsibilities are addressed during employee recruitment and activities are monitored throughout employment.

**Provisions**
Potential employees are to be adequately screened, especially for sensitive jobs. All employees and third-party users of Company information are subject to the contents of this policy.

**Key Terms**
Confidentiality agreements; terms and conditions of employment; security incidents; disciplinary process

*(continued)*

**Exhibit 5    Personnel Security Policy (continued)**

**Responsibilities**

1. Senior management and the officers of the Company are required to employ internal controls designed to safeguard company assets, including business information.
2. It is a management obligation to ensure that all employees have clear and concise job descriptions and that all qualifications are properly verified.
3. Employees and third-party users of Company information are required to read and sign a Confidentiality Agreement.

**Compliance**

1. Company management has the responsibility to document conditions required to obtain and maintain employment, as well as the right to monitor personnel activities.
2. Employees who fail to comply with the terms of the Confidentiality Agreement or who falsified resume (curriculum vitae) information are subject to appropriate disciplinary actions.

## 10.7    Physical and Environmental Security

*Objective:* It is a management responsibility to establish a safe and secure working environment (Exhibit 6). Access to enterprise locations must be restricted to those persons with a business need. Levels of protection must be commensurate with the value of the asset and vulnerability to identified risks.

**Exhibit 6    General Security**

**Policy**

It is the responsibility of Company management to provide a safe and secure workplace for all employees.

**Provisions**

1. Company offices will be protected from unauthorized access.
2. Areas within buildings, which house sensitive or high-risk equipment, will be protected against fire, water, and other hazards.
3. Devices that are critical to the operation of company business processes will be protected against power failure.

**Key Terms**

Security perimeter; entry controls; cabling security; secure disposal of equipment; clear desk policy

**Responsibilities**

1. Senior management and the officers of the Company are required to maintain accurate records and to employ internal controls designed to safeguard company assets and property against unauthorized use or disposition.

**Exhibit 6   General Security (continued)**

2. The assets of the Company include but are not limited to physical property, intellectual property, patents, trade secrets, copyrights, and trademarks.
3. Additionally, it is the responsibility of line management to ensure that staff is aware of, and fully complies with, Company security guidelines and all relevant laws and regulations.

**Compliance**
1. Management is responsible for conducting periodic reviews and audits to ensure the compliance of all policies, procedures, practices, standards, and guidelines.
2. Employees who fail to comply with the policies will be treated as being in violation of the *Employee Standards of Conduct* and will be subject to appropriate corrective action.

## 10.8   Communications and Operations Management

*Objective:* Employee responsibilities and procedures for the management and operation of all information-processing facilities and platforms must be established (Exhibit 7). This includes the implementation of effective operating instructions and incident response procedures.

**Exhibit 7   Operational Change Control**

**Policy**
All changes to the information processing system, facilities, production libraries, hardware, software, and applications must be controlled. Company management has implemented a formal *Change Control Process* for all platforms and systems.

**Standards**
1. The Changes Control Review Team (CCRT) prior to implementation must review all changes requests. For emergency changes, see *Emergency Change Control Process*.
2. CCRT review meeting will be held on the Wednesday of each week.
3. Approved requests will be scheduled within eight working days.

**Responsibilities**
1. Change Requestor:
   a. Complete all documentation and submit to CCRT for review;
   b. Complete "back out" procedure prior to scheduled implementation date; and
   c. Communicate details of change to all relevant persons.
2. CCRT
   a. Review all Requestor packages;
   b. Schedule formal reviews for next CCRT weekly session;
   c. Assess potential impact of change;
   d. Schedule approved changes; and
   e. Assess actual impact of change.

(continued)

**Exhibit 7    Operational Change Control (continued)**

**Compliance**

CCRT will maintain a log of all changes and report to Management Steering Team any deviations from this policy.

# 10.9    Access Control Policy

*Objective:* Business requirements for access control must be implemented (Exhibit 8). Access control rules and rights for each user or group of users must be clearly stated. Included in this section is a determination on establishing access rules based on a policy of "access must be generally forbidden unless expressly permitted" rather than the weaker rule that "information assets are generally open unless expressly closed."

**Exhibit 8    Access Control Requirements**

**Policy**

Access to all enterprise information assets must be for business- or mission-related purposes only.

**Provisions**

Access control rules and rights for the Owner of the information asset must establish each individual user or group of users (refer to *Information Classification Policy* for Owner definition).

**Key Terms**

Segregation of duties; separation of duties; rotation of assignments; capacity planning; malicious software; operator logs; network management; disposal of media; security of e-mail and information exchange

**Responsibilities**

1. MST is responsible for publishing access criteria.
2. Information Owners are responsible for approving business-related access to information assets under their control.
3. Individuals granted access must use the information asset in accordance with the Owner's specifications.

**Compliance**

1. Individuals who exceed or attempt to exceed approved authority are subject to having access revoked.
2. Repeat violations of this policy can lead to disciplinary actions as described in the *Employee Standards of Conduct*.

## 10.10 Systems Development and Maintenance

*Objective:* The business processes affected by a new application or system or an enhancement to an existing application or system must be reviewed to ensure that adequate controls are in place to ensure the continued availability of the business process (Exhibit 9). Controls to ensure the integrity of the output must be implemented.

**Exhibit 9   Application Development Policy**

**Policy**

A standard application development methodology is to be used when developing new or enhancing existing business applications. Appropriate controls and audit trails or activity logs must be designed into the application. These controls include but are not limited to the validation of input, internal processing, output preparation, and transmission of data where applicable.

**Key Terms**

Data validation; checks and balances; message authentication; output validation; non-repudiation services; audit logs

**General Guidelines**
1. Separate development and production environments and data have been established.
2. Security is an integral part of application development.
3. Test data is not to contain confidential information.
4. Use a secured language (e.g., Java rather than C, Tainted Perl rather than Perl).
5. All major new systems must be submitted to the Change Control Review Team for review and approval prior to production.

## 10.11 Business Continuity Planning

*Objective:* Implement controls and procedures that counteract interruptions to business activities and to protect critical business processes from the effects of major failures or disasters (Exhibit 10).

**Exhibit 10   Business Continuity Planning**

The business continuity plan (BCP) is a management-type control to ensure that *critical business functions* can be performed after a disruption to normal business operations. The scope of the BCP includes activities that should be performed before, during, and after such a disruption to business. But what does this have to do with information security? Many critical business functions are dependent on the availability of information assets. Each organization IS team should coordinate the development of a BCP that identifies the organization's critical business functions and the information required by those functions. Before writing the plan, a Business Impact Analysis should be done.

*(continued)*

**Exhibit 10    Business Continuity Planning (continued)**

**Key Terms**
Disaster recovery plan; emergency response plans; business impact analysis; plan exercises; hot site; cold site; recovery teams

**Performing a Business Impact Analysis**
The purpose of a business impact analysis (BIA) is to determine the effect on the organization of loss of critical business functions. The critical business functions directly support the primary goals of the organization and enable the fulfillment of its value-added role.

How to (see Information Classification Worksheet, Chapter 8):
1. Identify the critical business functions of the organization.
2. Establish the priority of each critical business function.
3. Determine how long the organization can do without each critical business function.
4. Identify the resources, especially information resources, required to support the critical business functions.
5. Estimate the tangible and intangible impacts on the organization of loss of each critical business function.

You may notice that the business impact analysis is similar to the information risk assessment. The main difference is that a threat-vulnerability analysis is not done here.

## 10.12 Compliance

*Objective:* Policies, standards, and procedures must be established to ensure that the enterprise and its employees do not breach any criminal and civil law, statutory, regulatory, or contractual obligations (Exhibit 11).

**Exhibit 11    Software Code of Ethics**

**Key Terms**
Copyright; intellectual property; privacy; regulations; evidence; compliance checking; audit

**Policy**
Unauthorized duplication of copyrighted computer software violates the law and is contrary to corporate standards of conduct. The Company prohibits such copying and recognizes the following principles as a basis for preventing its occurrence:
- The Company will neither commit nor tolerate the making or use of unauthorized software copies under any circumstances.
- The Company will provide legitimately acquired software to meet all legitimate software needs in a timely fashion and in sufficient quantities.
- All employees shall comply with all license or purchase terms regulating the use of any software acquired or used.

**Exhibit 11   Software Code of Ethics (continued)**

■ The Company will implement and enforce strong internal controls to prevent the making or use of unauthorized software copies, including effective measures to verify compliance with these standards.

# Chapter 11

# Review

In Chapter 1 we discussed the role of the information protection professional, which has changed over the past 25 years and will change again and again. Implementing controls to be in compliance with audit requirements is not the way in which a program such as this can be run. There are limited resources available for controls. To be effective, information owners and users must accept the controls. To meet this end, it is necessary for information protection professionals to establish partnerships with their constituency. Work with your owners and users to find an appropriate level of controls. Understand the needs of the business or the mission of your organization. Make certain that information protection supports those goals and objectives.

In Chapter 2 we discussed the writing mechanics and concepts to be used to get the message out to the reader. Included in this discussion were:

- Attention span
- Keeping the topic up-front
- Amount of time before we lose the reader
- Writing concepts
- Identifying the objective
- Knowing the audience
- Finding a hook
- Knowing the subject
- Asking for what is needed from the reader
- Keeping sentences clear and precise
- Using established forms of documents
- Using an active voice
- Reading other policies
- Using a conversational style
- Topic sentence and thesis statements
- Writing don'ts

When you need to write policies, standards, and procedures, you will have an overwhelming desire to start writing. But take the time to determine what needs to be done and how you will do it. Do your research. There are no new policies. Whatever you need to write about, you should be able to find an example that can be used to guide you along in your development. Try to avoid the temptation of taking an existing policy and just changing the names. It might work, but the odds that this kind of quick fix will meet the specific business objectives of your organization are very small.

In Chapter 3 we discussed that the policy is the cornerstone of the information security architecture of an organization; that the policy is important to establish both internally and externally the position of an organization on a particular topic.

We then looked at what a policy is and what it is not. There was discussion on the definitions of:

- Policy
- Standard
- Guideline
- Procedure

Next, there was an examination of the key elements of a policy:

- Be easy to understand
- Be applicable
- Be "doable"
- Be enforceable
- Be phased in
- Be proactive
- Avoid absolutes
- Meet business objectives

There was a review of what the policy format might be, and then we discussed the three basic types of policy:

- Program policy
- Topic-specific policy
- Application-specific policy

Finally we examined five actual policy statements and critiqued them based on the checklist and some helpful hints and pitfalls to avoid.

In Chapter 4 we discussed that the mission statement should ensure that the security of the information and communication processing resources of the corporation are sufficient to reduce risk to a level acceptable to the management of the corporation.

Responsibilities:

- To recommend policies, standards, and procedures that foster the protection of information and information-processing resources

- To assist units and divisions in the selection and implementation of the protective measures required in their areas of responsibility
- To evaluate new technology and recommend security strategies to protect it
- To identify areas of potential risk in the protection of corporate computer and information assets and to alert management once those areas have been identified
- To provide training for security control requirements during all phases of application and system development
- To develop programs to increase security awareness at all levels of the corporation
- To develop a liaison between the corporate security and audit staffs to ensure that security efforts are coordinated and resources are conserved by preventing duplication of effort
- To coordinate and assist in the development of business resumption plans for all data centers supporting critical business functions
- To work with the local ISSO to ensure that corporate-mandated programs are cost-effective and operationally effective
- To act as a consultant to all areas on the security of information and computer systems
- To monitor changes in laws and regulations as well as changes in technology and corporate goals and to determine the impact of these changes on corporate security requirements
- To review new system access and information protection products and make recommendations on these products to ensure they meet minimum corporate requirements
- To provide account administration across all platforms
- To provide consulting support for all application development projects.
- To act as audit liaison for all information and computer security-related matters
- To assist in the investigation and reporting of computer thefts, intrusions, viruses, and breaches of information protection controls
- To assist in the development of effective monitoring programs to ensure that corporate information is protected as required

In Chapter 5 we discussed the standard. In the introduction we examined where it fit in the scheme of written documents and found that it is needed to provide a policy with direction. It was strongly recommended that the standards not be made part of the policy. This was mainly due to the process required to get policies modified and approved.

On the other hand, it is quite permissible to have policies found in a standards manual. When developing a standards manual, it will be necessary to have an overview (topic-specific or application/system-specific policy) provide the introduction to the topic and then have supporting standards.

We also discussed where the standard fits in the process of documentation for employee use and why policies are not enough. We reviewed what a standard is and examined examples of standards and how they can work in your enterprise. Finally, we discussed the ISO 17799 International Standard for information security and how it is actually guideline document.

To assist you in understanding what might be necessary in developing a security manual, Appendix A has a Policy Baseline Checklist that identifies 71 key elements to be considered when developing your information security documentation.

In Chapter 6 we discussed that, when writing procedures, it is best to keep the language as simple as possible. Attempt to stay away from flowery phrases and multi-syllable words. Keep the sentences short and the terms crisp. Identify each role in the procedure, and find the style that best meets the needs of your organization.

In this chapter we reviewed the definitions of policy, procedure, standard, and guideline and discussed the writing "Ten Commandments."

We then examined the key elements of procedures:

- Identify the procedure need
- Identify the target audience
- Establish the scope of the procedure
- Describe the intent of the procedure

We examined a procedure twelve-point checklist, and then examined six styles of procedures:

- Headline
- Caption
- Matrix
- Narrative
- Flowchart
- Playscript

In Chapter 7 we discussed the elements of information classification. We reviewed why it is necessary to classify information and discussed the structure of a topic-specific policy. We reviewed the need to restrict the number of categories for better use and what constitutes confidential information. We then discussed the need for a methodology to score information in order to place it in its proper classification level and the need for an information handling standards matrix. Finally we examined the need for a policy on employee responsibilities, especially: owner, custodian, and user.

In Chapter 8 we discussed how information security is more than just polices, standards, procedures, and guidelines. It is more than audit comments and requirements. It is a cultural change for most employees. Before employees can be required to be compliant with a security program, they first must become aware of the program. Security awareness is an ongoing program that employees must have contact with on at least an annual basis.

Information security awareness does not require huge cash outlays. It does require time and proper project management. Keep the message in front of the employees. Use different methods and means. Bring in outside speakers whenever possible and use videos to your best advantage.

In Chapter 9 we discussed managing the development of security policies and procedures as a project, involving application of a variety skills, tools, experiences, and techniques. Project management processes help guide project activities to meet or exceed stakeholder needs and expectations. A primary objective of project management is to manage resources efficiently and effectively to deliver products on time and within budget while attaining a given level of quality. The intent of this chapter was to introduce a few key project management concepts that should be readily adaptable to a policies and procedures development project.

In Chapter 10 we discussed the ISO 17799 document and gave examples of a policy for each section. We discussed the objectives and key terms. When you review the ten sections of ISO 17799, you will notice that there are nearly 700 suggestions on things to have and to include. Select what is needed and keep the rest for reference. Remember that policies, standards, and procedures are vital and active. They will need to be reviewed on a regular basis to see if they are still appropriate.

# APPENDICES

# Appendix A

# Policy Baseline Checklist

## Policy Baseline

Best practices indicate that the following elements should be addressed when developing policy-related documentation for a client. The 71 requirements denote technical requirements for which technology-specific procedures are required for their implementation.

| Section | Explanation |
|---|---|
| **Security Management Policy** | |
| *Data Classification Directive* | This directive describes requirements for a program to classify information resources by sensitivity, including designation of information owners, establishment of levels of classification by sensitivity, and periodic review of information. |
| ■ Information Ownership Requirement | Ensure that there is a written requirement that an owner is identified for all information processed on company systems. This should include individual files as well as collective files/records grouped in directories, databases, and data sets. |
| ■ Classification Levels Requirement | This section describes and provides examples of the various classification levels implemented for company data (e.g., confidential, sensitive, and restricted). |
| ■ Classification Designation Requirement | Include a section that outlines the process for original designating of data by information owners. |
| ■ Classification Review Requirement | Include a requirement that data classification be reviewed by information owners on a periodic basis (e.g., annually) to ensure that the assigned level is still appropriate. |

| Section | Explanation |
|---|---|
| **System Monitoring Policy** | This section describes policies related to monitoring system activities for unauthorized activities to ensure that security controls are not tampered with or bypassed. This includes requirements for reporting observed violations, monitoring network security, use of intrusion detection systems, and response to security-related incidents. |
| *Violation Reporting Directive* | This addresses requirements for reporting security-related events in a timely fashion. |
| ■ Customer Reporting Requirements | Establish requirements that customers are responsible for reporting any suspected security breaches or violations. |
| ■ Timeliness of Reporting Requirements | Address requirements that security breaches be reported in a timely manner based on the severity of the incident and the nature of the data involved. |
| *Network Security Monitoring Directive* | This documents company policy and standards for monitoring network activity. This includes identification of who can monitor, how monitoring is authorized, restrictions on monitoring, activities that will be monitored, information that is to be recorded, and procedures for reviewing recorded audit trail information. |
| ■ Authority to Monitor Requirements | Create a requirement that ensures users are aware of the company authority to monitor network traffic. |
| ■ Monitoring Policy Publication Requirement | To maximize the effectiveness of auditing, establish a requirement for the company to publicize the fact that it is policy to audit network activity. |
| ■ Authorization of Monitoring Activities Requirement | Define requirements that the company must formally authorize all monitoring activities. |
| ■ Control of Monitoring Devices Requirement | This section should identify requirements that only authorized personnel are allowed to use network diagnostic test hardware and software, such as sniffers and monitoring devices, to monitor traffic on the company network. |
| ■ Activities to be Monitored Requirements | Establish requirements that define the types of system activities that will be monitored (e.g., failed log-on attempts). |
| ■ Audit Trail Content Requirements | Define requirements for the elements of information that will be recorded for each event in the audit trail (e.g., userid, date/time). |
| ■ Audit Trails Retention Requirements | Identify requirements that audit trails will be maintained in accordance with previously established company rules pertaining to retention of sensitive information. |
| ■ Audit Trails Protection Requirements | Establish requirements for protecting audit trails from disclosure to personnel who do not have a need to access them, and from inadvertent deletion, destruction, or modification. |

| Section | Explanation |
|---|---|
| ■ Information Sharing Requirements | Establish a requirement that, as part of the approval process for connecting to the company network, network partners must agree to share audit trail data in the event of an incident. |
| ■ Audit Trail Review Requirements | Address requirements for the regular and frequent review of the contents of the audit trail data. |
| *Use of Intrusion Detection Systems (IDS) Directive* | This provides requirements for the use of automated intrusion detection systems to provide real-time monitoring of network activities. |
| ■ Real-Time Monitoring Requirement | This section outlines requirements for the use of intrusion detection systems to perform real-time analysis of network traffic patterns to detect attempted attacks. |
| ■ Use of IDS with Public Access Systems Requirement | Identify requirements that publicly accessible systems (e.g., external Web sites) must utilize system monitoring tools that provide real-time alerts whenever suspicious user activity is detected |
| *Incident Response Directive* | This establishes a process for responding to security violations and incidents to limit further damage to information resources and to permit identification and prosecution of violators. |
| ■ Notification Requirements | Identify requirements for officials and organizations that must be notified in the event of an incident. |
| ■ Isolation Requirements | Provide requirements to take action to limit the effects of an incident through isolation of the problem as narrowly as possible. |
| ■ Documentation Requirements | Establish requirements for documenting the incident. |
| ■ Investigation Requirements | Define requirements for investigating the incident to include external law enforcement as well as internal investigative capabilities. |
| ■ Reporting Requirements | Address requirements for providing reports to officials, agencies who need them, including time frames for submission. |
| ■ Follow-Up Requirements | Establish requirements for tracking resolution of incidents and following up on any pending corrective actions. |
| **User Account Administration Policy** | This section establishes policy for administering the accounts of system users to include user ids, passwords, privilege management, user transfer/termination, and application system access controls. |
| *User Identification Directive* | This section establishes a directive governing the management of user accounts and identification numbers. |
| ■ Sponsorship of Users Requirements | Identify a requirement that the relevant business unit must identify the process to verify a user's identity as a condition for providing credentials, or for utilizing any credentials (such as digital certificates) the user may already possess. |

| Section | Explanation |
|---|---|
| ■ Issuance of User ids Requirements | Define a requirement for a user to provide sufficient identifying information upon registration that the sponsoring business function can verify user's business relationship to the company and the appropriate information access permissions. |
| ■ User id Composition Requirements | Establish a requirement that user ids will consist of a minimum of four alphanumeric characters, with no maximum other than system-imposed limits. |
| ■ Inactive Accounts Requirements | Create a requirement that user accounts that have been inactive for more than 60 days will be disabled, until the specified user requests that the account be re-enabled, and provides proof of identity, including proof that the user's business relationship with the company has not changed. |
| ■ Sharing/Group Accounts Requirements | Establish a requirement that although a single user id may be shared across multiple systems and applications, the use of group ids will be prohibited. |
| ■ Default Accounts Requirements | There should be a requirement that default user ids shipped with software be disabled. |
| ■ Privileged Accounts Requirements | Define a requirement that users who are granted privileged access (i.e., access to system security mechanisms, etc.) will use a different account name from that of normal user. |
| ■ Least Privilege Requirements | There should be a requirement that the level of access granted will be appropriate for the business purpose and is consistent with organization security policy (e.g., does not compromise segregation of duties). |
| ■ Auditing Accounts Requirements | On a quarterly basis, system administrators should be required to conduct an audit of current user accounts to ensure that the accounts of unauthorized users have been removed. |
| ■ Last Login/Logout Notification Requirements | Where technically feasible, upon login, the user should be required to present with date and time of last login and logout, along with contact information if the user wishes to report a discrepancy with the user's records. |
| ■ Failed Access Attempts Requirements | There should be a requirement that three successive failures within a 24-hour period will result in a user's account being locked. Additionally, user's should not be able to login until their account is unlocked. |
| ■ Protection of User Identification Information | Identify requirements for safeguarding user identification information from unauthorized disclosure. |
| *Password Management Directive* | This establishes requirements for user passwords. |
| ■ Password Storage Requirements | There should be a requirement for user passwords to be stored on computer systems in encrypted form only, and password entry should be masked. |

| Section | Explanation |
|---|---|
| ■ Password Composition Requirements | Password composition requirements should call for passwords to consist of a minimum of six alpha and numeric characters and not to contain the user's name or user id. |
| ■ Password Composition Standards | In this section, identify minimum requirements for password composition (i.e., length, alphanumeric, special characters, and examples of weak passwords). |
| ■ User Selection of Passwords Requirements | Establish a requirement that, when technically feasible, users should be provided with the capability to change their password on the login interface after authentication. |
| ■ Password Expiration Requirements | Requirements for passwords for normal user accounts should include expiration after a maximum of 60 calendar days and a new password should be created at that time. Passwords for privileged user accounts (e.g., root, administrator, supervisor) should be required to expire after a maximum of 30 calendar days. |
| ■ Password History Requirements | Detail requirements designed to ensure that users must select a unique password and avoid reuse of previously selected passwords. |
| ■ Password Issuance Requirements | Identify a requirement that when a user is provided with an initial password, this password must be changed the first time a user logs into a service (one-time password). |
| ■ Password Reset Requirements | User password resets should be performed when requested by the user, after verification of identity. There should be a requirement for the relevant business group to be responsible for defining the verification credentials. The new password should be a one-time password. |
| ■ Password Reset Procedures | Identify here the procedures for obtaining a new password in the event that a user-selected password is forgotten or expires. |
| ■ Default Passwords Requirements | There should be a requirement that default passwords shipped with software should be disabled or changed. |
| ■ Password Confidentiality Requirements | There should be a requirement for user passwords to remain confidential and not to be shared, posted, or otherwise divulged in any manner. |
| *Privilege Management Directive* | This documents the process for approval, issuance, and management of discretionary access to systems, directories, and files. |
| ■ Need-to-Know Requirements | Identify requirements for privileges to be allocated to individuals on a "need-to-use" basis and on an "event-by-event" basis (i.e., the minimum requirement for their functional role only when needed). |
| ■ Authorization Requirements | An authorization process should be required and a record of all privileges allocated should be made. Privileges should not be granted until the authorization process is complete. |

| Section | Explanation |
|---|---|
| ■ Management by Platform Requirements | Establish a requirement that the privileges associated with each system product (e.g., operating system, database management system) be identified, as well as the categories of staff to which they need to be allocated. |
| ■ Special Privileges Requirements | There should be a requirement for users that are assigned high privileges for special purposes to use a different user identity for normal business use. |
| *User Termination Directive* | This provides guidance on actions to be taken in the event an authorized user is terminated. |
| ■ Revocation Requirements | Identify a requirement that all ids and passwords are revoked upon termination of customer personnel and that access be revoked or modified upon transfer of responsibilities. |
| ■ Customer Function Change Notification Requirements | Customers should be required to notify company management of changes in the customer's status in order to ensure that access privileges are appropriately adjusted. |
| ■ Customer Clearance Requirements | Establish requirements that PCs, keys, ID cards, software, data, documentation, manuals, etc. of terminated customers be returned to the company. |
| ■ Involuntary Termination Requirements | There should be a requirement that procedures for the removal of customers terminated for cause be established. |
| **Workstation Security Policy** | This section provides policy on the security of company information processed, stored, or transmitted on desktop and laptop computer systems. |
| *Ownership of Software Directive* | This establishes requirements related to the ownership of company developed, owned, or licensed software. |
| ■ Proprietary Software Control Requirements | Identify a requirement that authorization is to be obtained from business management before distributing proprietary software that is owned by the company to a third party. |
| ■ Software Licensing Agreements Requirements | Address requirements for all users to adhere to package software license agreements and copyright laws. Users will be required to copy package software only in accordance with license agreement (e.g., a backup copy for protection). |
| ■ Vendor Use Review Requirements | Establish requirements for the periodic review of vendor use of proprietary, company-owned software. |
| *Data Backup/Recovery Directive* | This addresses user requirements for backing up data in relation to system backup activities. |

| Section | Explanation |
| --- | --- |
| ■ User Responsibilities Requirements | Establish a requirement that users ensure that all data on their workstations are backed up regularly. The preferred manner of ensuring that this is accomplished should be to save or copy data to a directory that is routinely backed up by the system administrator. Where this is not possible, users should back up data files to diskette. |
| ■ System Administrator Backup Requirements | Identify a requirement for system administrators to ensure that backups of software on the servers are performed, and that off-site storage procedures are followed. |
| *Virus Prevention Directive* | This documents requirements for the prevention, detection and eradication of malicious software on workstations. |
| ■ Approved Products Use Requirements | Identify a requirement that only standard/approved products that have been obtained from authorized suppliers will be installed onto workstations. |
| ■ Scanning Software Use Requirements | Establish a requirement that virus filters and/or detection programs be used prior to installing any software on a workstation. |
| ■ Virus Response Requirements | There should be a requirement that if a virus is suspected, the system administrator will disconnect the workstation from the network immediately, will notify management, and will remove the virus prior to any reconnection to network services. |
| *File Server Access Directive* | This covers requirements necessary to provide additional security to servers. |
| ■ Server Physical Access Requirements | Establish a requirement that file servers will be secured in locked cabinets, closets, or offices and access will be limited to individuals with a documented business need for such access. |
| ■ Server Identification and Authentication Requirements | Identify a requirement that system administrators will utilize system security features for identification and authentication of individuals attempting file server access, and for recording and review of unsuccessful file server access attempts. |
| **Network Security Policy** | This section provides direction on the security of networked company information resources. |
| *Network Operations Directive* | This documents requirements for gaining access to the network or network routers, logging of activities, and greeting and warning screen content and location. |
| ■ Greeting Screen Requirements | Establish a requirement restricting the display of a greeting of any kind to any external network connection until the user is authenticated and authorized through a sign-on sequence. |
| ■ Warning Message Requirements | Where technically feasible, require that a message be displayed on all external network connections warning potential users that unauthorized use is prohibited. |

| Section | Explanation |
|---|---|
| ■ Network Access Requirements | Ensure that system administrators require that the host operating system validate each user prior to allowing network access. Once verified, users should be required to be automatically directed to applications for which they have been authorized. |
| ■ Router Access Requirements | Create a requirement that only authorized administrators be allowed logical access to routers. |
| ■ Activity Logging Requirements | Require that all network infrastructure platforms implement security-related event logging. |
| ■ Confidentiality of Network Addresses Requirements | Ensure that there is a requirement that the internal addresses, configurations, and related system design information for networked computer systems be restricted so that external systems and users cannot access this information without explicit management approval. |
| ■ Avoidance of Trust Relationships Requirements | Ensure that wherever possible trust relationships are strictly avoided between systems with different risk profiles. |
| *Network Privacy Directive* | This establishes requirements designed to assure the privacy of data transmitted on the network to include restriction to business use only, restriction on user browsing, consideration of e-mail as official correspondence, and requirements for backing up e-mail for potential legal use. |
| ■ Business Use Only Notification Requirements | Require that there be notification that company computers are to be used for valid business reasons only. |
| ■ Restrictions on Browsing Requirements | Establish a requirement for each user to avoid accessing areas on company networks for which the user does not have a valid business need, and that it is each user's responsibility to exercise judgment regarding the information accessed. |
| *Confidentiality Controls Directive* | This provides guidance on implementing controls designed to protect the confidentiality of transmitted information. |
| ■ Message Authentication Requirements | Create a requirement that message authentication will be employed for applications where the integrity of message content is vital. Hardware and/or software mechanisms should be implemented to detect unauthorized changes to, or corruption of the contents of a transmitted electronic message. Message authentication should be used along with encryption to reduce further the potential for eavesdropping. |
| ■ Encryption Requirements | Establish a requirement that information that is classified as highly sensitive should be encrypted while passing through the network using encryption software or hardware approved by the information security function. |

| Section | Explanation |
|---|---|
| ■ Device Identification Requirements | Require that the physical component and, where possible, the location of the logical access request be identified to the system being accessed. Devices may include terminals, lines, communication nodes, controllers, remote processors, and personal computers. |
| *Network Acceptable Use Directive* | This section provides to users rules related to acceptable use of the network. |
| ■ Lack of Public Network Confidentiality Awareness Requirements | Establish a requirement that any messages sent over the Internet are not considered secure unless additional measures are taken to protect such information (e.g., encryption). Users should communicate via e-mail as they would in a public meeting (e.g., if you are not comfortable saying something to a room of people, it should not be said via e-mail). |
| ■ Internet Rules of Behavior Requirements | There should be a requirement that states that using company facilities or equipment to make abusive, unethical or "inappropriate" use of the Internet will not be tolerated and may be considered grounds for disciplinary action, including termination of employment. |
| ■ Control of Sensitive Data Requirements | Sensitive information should not be transmitted over the Internet without prior management approval and reasonable security measures (such as encryption or other appropriate method) in place. Credit card numbers, telephone calling card numbers, login passwords, and other parameters that can be used to gain access to goods or services should not be sent over the Internet in readable form. |
| **Software Security Policy** | This section provides direction on security aspects of software development and maintenance. |
| ■ Proprietary Property Protection Requirements | Establish a requirement that information systems resources under development (e.g., programs, files, and documentation) be considered company assets that will be provided protection as would be applicable to the finished product. |
| ■ Licensing Agreement Compliance Requirements | All developers should be required to adhere to package software license agreements and copyright laws. They should only copy package software products in accordance with license agreement (e.g., a backup copy for protection). |
| ■ Authorization to Copy Requirements | Require that written authorization from the vendor be obtained to copy products licensed to run on a specific computer or at a particular onto another computer or another site. |
| **Security of Third-Party Services Policy** | |
| ■ Customer Nondisclosure Requirement | Establish requirements for customers to sign nondisclosure arrangements and/or confidentiality agreements. All customer personnel will be informed in a written statement of the importance of data processing security. |

| Section | Explanation |
|---------|-------------|
| ■ Customer Statement of Awareness Requirement | Ensure that customers are required to acknowledge their awareness of company information security policies, and their responsibility for adhering to them. |
| ■ Customer Violation Reporting Requirements | Define requirements to ensure that customers are aware of their responsibility for immediately informing the manager responsible for the contract of any security breaches, including unauthorized access to or compromise of company data or resources. |
| ■ Provisions for Sofware Ownership Requirements | Establish requirements to ensure that contract agreements define company ownership of software developed under the contract. |

# *Appendix B*

# Sample Corporate Policies

## Conflict of Interest

### Policy

Company employees are expected to adhere to the highest standards of conduct. To assure adherence to these standards, employees must have a special sensitivity to conflict-of-interest situations or relationships, as well as the inappropriateness of personal involvement in them. Although not always covered by law, these situations can harm Your Company or its reputation if improperly handled.

### Provisions

1. A conflict of interest occurs when an employee's personal interests conflict with the company interests. Conflicts of interest may also involve relationships between members of the employee's immediate family and the company. In conflict-of-interest situations, employees are expected to act in the best interests of the company.
2. The following standards for ethical behavior in conflict-of-interest situations are established for all employees:
   a. When actual or potential conflict-of-interest situations arise, or where there is an appearance of such conflict, employees shall remove themselves from involvement in the matter. In no case should employees become involved to the extent where they are or could be influenced to make decisions that are not in the best interest of the company.
   b. Employees shall not solicit or accept personal gain, privileges, or other benefits through involvement in any matters on behalf of Your Company.

c. Employees shall direct their efforts to company business while at work, and shall use company resources only for management-approved activities. Resources include, but are not limited to, equipment, supplies, corporate information, and company-paid time.

## *Responsibilities*

1. Whenever faced with an actual or potential business-related conflict-of-interest situation, employees shall seek guidance from their supervisors.
2. When conflict-of-interest questions cannot be resolved within the organizational unit, employees may request advice from the General Auditor.
3. When requested, employees shall also disclose actual and potential conflict-of-interest situations to the General Auditor.
4. The General Auditor shall review each situation and advise the organizational unit of any recommended action the employee should take.

## *Common Conflict-of-Interest Situations*

The specific situations described in this section are common, but are not all-inclusive of business-related conflict-of-interest situations that may arise for Company employees.

1. **Gifts, etc.:** Giving gifts, providing meals and entertainment, and offering site tours and product samples are common business practices. Because the intent of these practices is to build relationships and influence business decisions, such practices can result in conflict of interest. Company expenses incurred in any of the following situations are subject to organizational approval.
   a. *Gifts:* Gifts generally benefit the employee, but not the company. In dealing with suppliers, customers, or others outside the company, employees shall not accept or give money or gifts, except an occasional, unsolicited, nonmonetary item of a token nature, such as an advertising novelty of nominal value.
   b. *Meals and entertainment:* In dealing with suppliers, customers, or others outside the company, employees shall not accept or provide meals or entertainment, except when there is a business purpose. The provider of the meal or entertainment should be present at the occasion. Frequent or repeated acceptance of meals and entertainment may be an indicator of the employee's personal gain, and could raise questions about the legitimacy of the business purpose for such occasions. When there is a business purpose for frequent meals or entertainment, the company encourages reciprocation.
   c. *Travel:* When there is a business purpose for travel, the company should pay travel expenses. Employees should not accept air trans-

portation offered by vendors or others outside the company when convenient commercial transportation is available. Generally, the company should pay for lodging expenses.

d. *Product samples:* If Your Company wants a sample product or service of more than nominal value, Your Company should pay for it.

2. **Outside work:** Employees who have another job outside of Your Company shall not represent themselves as performing work for Your Company when doing such jobs. Furthermore, they may not use Your Company resources in performing the other job. Employees shall not be employed by competitors of Your Company.

3. **Interest in outside business organizations:** Employees shall avoid significant financial or management interest in any business that does or seeks to do business with Your Company if such involvement could cause employees to make business decisions that are not in Your Company's best interest.

4. **Use of confidential or proprietary information:** Employees entrusted with such information shall restrict access and use to authorized individuals inside and outside the company who have a clear business need to know this information.

5. **Insider trading:** No employee who has material nonpublic ("insider") information relating to the company may use that information in buying and selling securities of Your Company, either directly or indirectly. Furthermore, employees may not engage in other actions to take personal advantage of that information or pass it on to others. Even the appearance of an improper transaction must be avoided to preserve the reputation of the company for adhering to the highest standards of conduct.

The conflict-of-interest situations item 4. discusses that the use of confidential or proprietary information must be controlled to those with an identified business need for access. Wherever possible, have the corporate policies support the information security policy.

# Employee Standards of Conduct

## Policy

Company employees are expected to conduct themselves in a professional and business manner at all times when on company property or when representing Your Company.

## Provisions

Company employees are expected to adhere to the following standards of conduct:

1. Employees shall act in an ethical manner, and shall avoid actions that have the *appearance* of being unethical.
2. Employees shall abide by applicable laws, regulations, and professional standards.
3. Employees shall avoid conflict-of-interest situations. (See Conflict of Interest policy for more information.)
4. Employees shall meet individual performance expectations.
5. Employees shall abide by company and organizational policies and practices.
6. Employees shall accurately and honestly record and report corporate information in a timely manner.
7. Employees shall also maintain the confidentiality of corporate information. (See Information Classification policy.)
8. Employees shall treat co-workers and others with dignity and respect.

## Responsibilities

Employees who violate these standards of conduct are subject to disciplinary action up to and including discharge. In some cases, employees may also be subject to criminal charges.

1. Employees are expected to use intelligence, common sense, and good judgment in applying these standards of conduct.
2. When in doubt, employees shall direct questions relating to the standards of conduct to their supervisors.
3. Employees who observe conduct that does not appear consistent with these standards of conduct should discuss the matter with their supervisor. The supervisor shall report fraudulent activity to the General Auditor.
4. Any employee who has suffered a violation of the standards of conduct should immediately report the matter to his or her supervisor or to the Vice President of Human Resources.
5. All complaints shall be investigated in as discreet a fashion as possible. Once the investigation is complete, appropriate action will be taken.

6. Supervision shall provide appropriate feedback to those who report misconduct.

7. Your Company will not retaliate against employees who report suspected misconduct.

8. Company management has the responsibility to manage corporate information, personnel, and physical properties relevant to its business operations, as well as the right to monitor the actual utilization of all corporate assets.

9. If an employee becomes involved in a legal matter arising· out of employment with Your Company, and if, in the opinion of the General Counsel, the employee was acting in good faith, within the scope of the job responsibilities, the company shall provide or select legal counsel and indemnify that employee and legal counsel if indemnification is not otherwise available to the employee.

## Unacceptable Conduct

1. Supervisors shall follow appropriate disciplinary procedures, up to and including discharge, for employees whose work performance or behavior does not meet the standards of conduct. Some examples of unacceptable conduct are shown below. This list is not all-inclusive.

    a. Work performance
       i. Failure to meet job requirements
       ii. Unacceptable work performance

    b. Attendance and tardiness
       i. Absence without notice or permission
       ii. Failure to notify as required
       iii. Excessive tardiness or excessive absence

    c. Conduct — General
       i. Alcohol or substance abuse when on company premises or business
       ii. Conflict-of-interest activities
       iii. Dishonesty
       iv. Failure to maintain acceptable appearance and hygiene standards
       v. Gambling or operating a lottery while on the job
       vi. Possession of unauthorized weapons or cameras on company property
       vii. Sleeping on the job
       viii. Unauthorized use or possession of company property
       ix. Insubordination
       x. Violation of a copyright or software licensing agreement, including the introduction of non-company-approved software or code into any company system

## *Harassment*

Harassment can take many forms in words or actions that are either implied or clear and direct. It is not limited by position, sex, or race. Harassment includes, but is not limited to, sexual harassment, verbal abuse, or threatening others.

Sexual harassment refers to behavior of a sexual nature that is unwelcome and offensive and is a form of misconduct that undermines the integrity of the employment relationship. Sexual harassment means unwelcome sexual advances, requests for sexual favors, and other verbal or physical conduct or communication of a sexual nature when:

1. Such conduct or communication has the purpose or effect of substantially interfering with an individual's employment or creating an intimidating, hostile, or offensive work environment
2. Submission to such conduct or communication is made a term or condition either explicitly or implicitly to obtain employment
3. Submission to, or rejection of, such conduct or communication by an individual is used as a factor in decisions affecting such individual's employment

## *Compliance*

1. Company management has the responsibility to:
   a. Ensure that all employees are aware and understand their obligation to behave in an ethical and proper manner.
   b. Note variance from established conduct standards and initiate corrective action as appropriate, including:
2. Employees who commit any of the following will normally be subject to immediate discharge. This list is not all-inclusive. An employee may be discharged for serious offenses or for any reason management deems appropriate, including:
   a. Absence without notice for three consecutive work days
   b. Defrauding company
   c. Falsifying company records
   d. Physical assault
   e. Possessing, selling, distributing, dispensing, manufacturing, or using illegal drugs while on company premises or business
   f. Theft of company, employee, customer, or supplier information resources, or other property
   g. Willfully destroying company, employee, customer, or vendor information resources, or other property

# External Corporate Communications

## *Policy*

Your company is committed to building good relationships by effectively communicating with clients and the general public. All employees are required to obtain approval from Your Company regarding interaction with these groups.

## *Scope*

All external company communications shall be:

1. Truthful, credible, and consistent with the company's performance and actions
2. In accordance with applicable legal and regulatory requirements

This policy includes, but is not restricted to, white papers, articles, speeches, articles, books, summaries, and software.

## *Definitions*

Your Company employees can create different types of written documents, to include:

1. *Executive overview* — a one-page summary of materials presented in-depth somewhere else
2. *Articles* — documents printed by some third party that may assume copyright control over the material
3. *White paper* — detailed, authoritative report with an informed conclusion
4. *External communication* —
   a. Your Company is open, honest, and willing to help media and others seeking information about the company. However, each employee shall take care not to disclose information that violates the privacy of employees and customers. Each employee shall also take care not to disclose information that is proprietary (Confidential or Internal Use) or could be of strategic or competitive business value to others.
   b. The CIO shall designate employees that have authority to sign correspondence or other external communications or issue public statements on behalf of the company. Formal communications to audiences on behalf of the company, such as speeches, technical papers, and brochures, shall be approved prior to release or publication by Your Company.
   c. The CIO shall approve all communication with the media, such as newspapers, radio, television, news groups, and magazines. Only senior management may release written communications to the media.

## Responsibilities

Your Company management has the responsibility to:

1. Ensure that all employees understand their rights and obligations relating to external communication.
2. Review employee documents to ensure protection of company proprietary resources.

Your Company employees have responsibility to:

1. Protect your company proprietary resources, especially when communicating to third parties.
2. Use the appropriate white paper format available through Corporate Communications.
3. Ensure a proper copyright statement is included in all documents made available to third parties (© Your Company, all rights reserved).
4. Ensure that appropriate Your Company management reviews the contents prior to distribution.

## Compliance

Your Company management has the responsibility to:

1. Ensure that all employees are aware of this policy and are in compliance.
2. Report any variances to Corporate Communications and to take appropriate corrective action.

Company employees have responsibility to:

1. Be in compliance with this policy.
2. Report to Your Company management any noncompliant situations.

# Information Protection

## Policy

Information is a company asset and is the property of Your Company. Your Company information includes information that is electronically generated, printed, filmed, typed, stored, or verbally communicated. Information must be protected according to its sensitivity, criticality, and value, regardless of the media on which it is stored, the manual or automated systems that process it, or the methods by which it is distributed.

## Provisions

To ensure that business objectives and customer confidence are maintained, all employees have a responsibility to protect information from unauthorized access, modification, disclosure, and destruction, whether accidental or intentional.

## Responsibilities

1.  Senior management and the officers of Your Company are required to employ internal controls designed to safeguard company assets, including business information.
2.  It is a line management obligation to ensure that all employees understand and comply with Your Company security policies and standards, as well as all applicable laws and regulations.
3.  Employee responsibilities for protecting Your Company information are detailed in the Information Classification policy.

## Compliance

1.  Company management has the responsibility to manage corporate information, personnel, and physical property relevant to business operations, as well as the right to monitor the actual utilization of all corporate assets.
2.  Employees who fail to comply with the policies will be considered to be in violation of Your Company Employee Standards of Conduct and will be subject to appropriate corrective action.

# General Security

## *Policy*

It is the responsibility of Your Company management to provide a safe and secure workplace for all employees.

## *Provisions*

1. Your Company offices will be protected from unauthorized access.
2. Areas within buildings that house sensitive or high-risk equipment will be protected against fire, water, and other hazards.
3. Devices that are critical to the operation of company business processes will be protected against power failure.

## *Responsibilities*

1. Senior management and the officers of Your Company are required to maintain accurate records and to employ internal controls designed to safeguard company assets and property against unauthorized use or disposition.
2. The assets of the company include but are not limited to physical property, intellectual property, patents, trade secrets, copyrights, and trademarks.
3. Additionally, it is the responsibility of line management to ensure that staff is aware of, and fully complies with, the company security guidelines and all relevant laws and regulations.

## *Compliance*

1. Management is responsible for conducting periodic reviews and audits to ensure the compliance of all policies, procedures, practices, standards, and guidelines.
2. Employees who fail to comply with the policies will be treated as being in violation of the Employee Standards of Conduct and will be subject to appropriate corrective action.

# Appendix C

# List of Acronyms

## A

| | |
|---|---|
| **AAL** | ATM Adaptation Layer |
| **AARP** | AppleTalk Address Resolution Protocol |
| **ABR** | Area Border Router |
| **AC** | Access Control (Token Ring) |
| **ACK** | Acknowledgment |
| **ADSL** | Asymmetric Digital Subscriber Line |
| **ADSP** | AppleTalk Data Stream Protocol |
| **AFP** | AppleTalk File Protocol |
| **AM** | Amplitude Modulation |
| **AMI** | Alternate Mark Inversion (T1/E1) |
| **ANSI** | American National Standards Institute |
| **API** | Application Programming Interface |
| **APPN** | Advanced Peer-to-Peer Networking |
| **ARP** | Address Resolution Protocol |
| **ARPA** | Advanced Research Projects Agency |
| **AS** | Autonomous System |
| **ASBR** | Autonomous System Boundary Router |
| **ASCII** | American Standard Code for Information Interchange |
| **ASIC** | Application-Specific Integrated Circuit |
| **ASK** | Amplitude Shift Keying |
| **ASP** | AppleTalk Session Protocol |
| **ATM** | Asynchronous Transfer Mode |
| **ATP** | AppleTalk Transaction Protocol |
| **AUI** | Attachment Unit Interface |
| **AURP** | AppleTalk Update-Based Routing Protocol |

# B

| | |
|---|---|
| **BDR** | Backup Designated Router |
| **BECN** | Backward Explicit Congestion Notification (Frame Relay) |
| **BER** | Bit Error Rate |
| **BGP** | Border Gateway Protocol |
| **BIA** | Burned-In Address |
| **B-ISDN** | Broadband ISDN |
| **BIT** | Binary digit |
| **BOOTP** | Bootstrap Protocol |
| **BPDU** | Bridge Protocol Data Unit |
| **BPS** | Bits Per Second |
| **BRI** | Basic Rate Interface (ISDN) |

# C

| | |
|---|---|
| **CBR** | Constant Bit Rate |
| **CCITT** | Consultative Committee for International Telegraph and Telephone |
| **CCO** | Cisco Connection Online |
| **CCP** | Compression Control Protocol |
| **CCS** | Common Channel Signaling |
| **CD** | Carrier Detect |
| **CDDI** | Copper Distributed Data Interface |
| **CDP** | Cisco Discovery Protocol |
| **CHAP** | Challenge Handshake Authentication Protocol |
| **CIDR** | Classless InterDomain Routing |
| **CIR** | Committed Information Rate |
| **CLP** | Cell Loss Priority |
| **CLNP** | Connectionless Network Protocol |
| **CLNS** | Connectionless Network Services |
| **CMI** | Coded Mark Inversion |
| **CO** | Central Office |
| **CPE** | Customer Premise Equipment |
| **CPU** | Central Processing Unit |
| **CRC** | Cyclical Redundancy Check |
| **CSMA/CD** | Carrier Sense Multiple Access/Collision Detect |
| **CSNP** | Complete Sequence Number PDU |
| **CSPDN** | Circuit-Switched Public Data Network |
| **CSU/DSU** | Channel Service Unit/Digital Service Unit |
| **CTS** | Clear To Send |
| **CUD** | Caller User Data (X.25) |

# D

| | |
|---|---|
| **DA** | Destination Address |
| **DAC** | Dual Attached Concentrator |

**DARPA** Defense Advanced Research Projects Agency
**DAS** Dual Attachment Station (FDDI, CDDI)
**DCE** Data Circuit-Terminating Equipment
**DDP** Datagram Delivery Protocol (AppleTalk)
**DDR** Dial-on-Demand Routing
**DES** Data Encryption Standard
**DHCP** Dynamic Host Configuration Protocol
**DIX** Digital-Intel-Xerox
**DLC** Data Link Control
**DLCI** Data Link Connection Identifier (Frame Relay)
**DMT** Discrete Multitone
**DNA SCP** Digital Network Architecture Session Control Protocol (DECnet)
**DNIC** Data Network Identification Code (X.25)
**DNS** Domain Name Server
**DQDB** Distributed Queue Dual Bus (SMDS)
**DR** Designated Router
**DRAM** Dynamic Random Access Memory
**DS-0** Digital Signal Level 0 (64 kb)
**DS-1** Digital Signal Level 1 (1.544 Mb)
**DS-3** Digital Signal Level 3 (45 Mb)
**DSAP** Destination Service Access Point (LLC)
**DSE** Data Switching Equipment
**DSL** Digital Subscriber Line
**DSR** Data Set Ready
**DSS 1** Digital Subscriber Signaling System 1
**DSU** Data Service Unit
**DTE** Data Terminal Equipment
**DTR** Data Terminal Ready
**DUAL** Diffused Update Algorithm (EIGRP)

# E

**EBCDIC** Extended Binary Encoded Decimal Interchange Code
**EBGP** Exterior Border Gateway Protocol
**EDI** Electronic Data Interchange
**EEPROM** Electrically Erasable Programmable Read-Only Memory
**EGP** Exterior Gateway Protocol
**EIA** Electronic Industries Association
**EIGRP** Enhanced Interior Gateway Routing Protocol
**EOT** End of Transmission
**EPROM** Erasable Programmable Read-Only Memory
**ESF** Extended Super Framing (T1/E1)
**ET** Exchange Termination
**ETSI** European Telecommunication Standards Institute

## F

| | |
|---|---|
| **FC** | Frame Control (Token Ring) |
| **FCC** | Federal Communications Commission |
| **FCS** | Frame Check Sequence |
| **FD** | Feasible Distance (EIGRP) |
| **FDDI** | Fiber Distributed Data Interface |
| **FDM** | Frequency Division Multiplexing |
| **FECN** | Forward Explicit Congestion Notification |
| **FEP** | Front-End Processor |
| **FIFO** | First In/First Out |
| **FMBS** | Frame-Mode Bearer Service |
| **FRAD** | Frame Relay Access Device |
| **FSIP** | Fast Serial Interface Processor |
| **FSK** | Frequency Shift Keying |
| **FTP** | File Transfer Protocol |

## G

| | |
|---|---|
| **GIF** | Graphics Interchange Format |
| **GNS** | Get Nearest Server (Novell) |
| **GOSIP** | Government OSI Profile (U.S.) |
| **GRE** | Generic Routing Encapsulation |
| **GZL** | Get Zone List (AppleTalk) |

## H

| | |
|---|---|
| **HDLC** | High-Level Data Link Control |
| **HSRP** | Hot Standby Routing Protocol |
| **HSSI** | High-Speed Serial Interface |
| **HTML** | Hypertext Markup Language |
| **HTTP** | Hypertext Transfer Protocol |

## I

| | |
|---|---|
| **IA** | Intra-Area (OSPF) |
| **IBGP** | Interior Border Gateway Protocol |
| **ICMP** | Internet Control Message Protocol |
| **IDN** | Integrated Digital Network |
| **IEEE** | Institute of Electrical and Electronics Engineers |
| **IETF** | Internet Engineering Task Force |
| **IGP** | Interior Gateway Protocol |
| **IGRP** | Interior Gateway Routing Protocol |
| **IOS** | Internetwork Operating System |
| **IP** | Internet Protocol |

| | |
|---|---|
| **IPC** | Interprocess Communications (Vines) |
| **IPX** | Internet Packet Exchange |
| **IRB** | Integrated Routing and Bridging |
| **IS** | Intermediate System |
| **ISDN BRI** | Integrated Services Digital Network–Basic Rate Interface |
| **ISDN PRI** | Integrated Services Digital Network–Primary Rate Interface |
| **ISIS** | Intermediate System–Intermediate System (OSI standard routing protocol) |
| **ISO** | International Organization for Standardization |
| **ISP** | Internet Service Provider |
| **ITU** | International Telecommunications Union |
| **ITU-T** | ITU Telecommunication Standardization Sector |

# J

| | |
|---|---|
| **JPEG** | Joint Photographic Experts Group |

# L

| | |
|---|---|
| **LAN** | Local Area Network |
| **LAPB** | Link Access Procedure — Balanced |
| **LAPD** | Link Access Procedure on the D channel |
| **LAPF** | Link Access Procedure for Frame-Mode Bearer Services |
| **LAT** | Local Area Transport |
| **LCN** | Logical Channel Number (X.25) |
| **LCP** | Link Control Protocol (X.25) |
| **LDN** | Local Dial Number (ISDN) |
| **LLC** | Logical Link Control |
| **LMI** | Local Management Interface (Frame Relay) |
| **LSA** | Link-State Advertisement |
| **LSP** | Link State Packet |
| **LT** | Local Termination |

# M

| | |
|---|---|
| **MAC** | Media Access Control |
| **MAN** | Metropolitan Area Network |
| **MAP** | Manufacturing Automation Protocol |
| **MAU** | Media Attachment Unit |
| **MIB** | Management Information Base |
| **MIDI** | Musical Instrument Digital Interface |
| **MW** | Multichannel Interface Processor |
| **MLP** | Multilink PPP |
| **MMP** | Mulitchassis Multilink PPP |

**MOP**      Maintenance Operation Protocol
**MP**        Multilink Protocol
**MPEG**     Motion Picture Experts Group
**MPR**      Multiprotocol PC-based Routing
**MRRU**     Maximum Received Reconstructed Unit (PPP)
**MSAU**     Multistation Access Units (Token Ring)
**MTU**      Maximum Transmission Unit


# N

**NAT**       Network Address Translation
**NAUN**     Nearest Active Upstream Neighbour
**NBMA**     Non-Broadcast Multiaccess
**NBP**       Name Binding Protocol (AppleTalk)
**NCP**       NetWare Core Protocol
**NCP**       Network Control Protocol (PPP)
**NDIS**      Network Driver Interface Specification
**NETBIOS** Network Basic I/O System
**NFS**       Network File System
**NIC**       Network Information Center
**NLPID**    Network Level Protocol Identifier
**NLSP**      NetWare Link Service Protocol
**NNI**       Network to Network Interface (ATM, Frame Relay)
**NOS**       Network Operating System
**NT-1**      Network Termination 1
**NTN**       Network Terminal Number (X.25)
**NTP**       Network Time Protocol
**NVE**       Network-Visible Entity
**NVRAM**   Nonvolatile Random Access Memory


# O

**OC**        Optical Circuit
**ODI**        Open Datalink Interface
**OSI**        Open System Interconnection
**OSPF**      Open Shortest Path First
**OUI**        Organizationally Unique Identifier


# P

**PAD**       Packet Assembler/Disassembler
**PAP**       Password Authentication Protocol
**PAP**       Printer Access Protocol (AppleTalk)
**PBX**       Private Branch Exchange

| | |
|---|---|
| **PCM** | Pulse Code Modulation |
| **PDN** | Public Data Network |
| **PDU** | Protocol Data Unit |
| **PING** | Packet Internet Groper |
| **PLP** | Packet Level Protocol (X.25) |
| **PMD** | Physical Medium Dependent |
| **POP** | Point of Presence |
| **POP** | Post Office Protocol |
| **POTS** | Plain Old Telephone Service |
| **PPP** | Point-to-Point Protocol |
| **PRI** | Primary Rate Interface (ISDN) |
| **PROM** | Programmable Read-Only Memory |
| **PSDN** | Packet-Switched Data Network |
| **PSK** | Phase Shift Keying |
| **PSN** | Packet Switched Network |
| **PSNP** | Partial Sequence Number PDU |
| **PSPDN** | Packet-Switched Public Data Network |
| **PSTN** | Public Switched Telephone Network |
| **PTT** | Post, Telephone, and Telegraph |
| **PVC** | Permanent Virtual Circuit |

# Q

| | |
|---|---|
| **QAM** | Quadrature Amplitude Modulation |
| **QoS** | Quality of Service |

# R

| | |
|---|---|
| **RADIUS** | Remote Authentication Dial-In User Service |
| **RAM** | Random Access Memory |
| **RARP** | Reverse Address Resolution Protocol |
| **RBOC** | Regional Bell Operating Companies |
| **RCP** | Remote Copy Protocol |
| **RFC** | Request For Comments |
| **RIP** | Routing Information Protocol |
| **RISC** | Reduced Instruction Set Computer |
| **RJE** | Remote Job Entry |
| **RLP** | Remote Location Protocol |
| **RMON** | Remote Monitoring |
| **ROM** | Read-Only Memory |
| **RPC** | Remote Procedure Call |
| **RTMP** | Routing Table Maintenance Protocol (AppleTalk) |
| **RTP** | Routing Update Protocol (Vines) |

# S

| | |
|---|---|
| **SA** | Source Address |
| **SABM** | Set Asynchronous Balanced Mode |
| **SABME** | Set Asynchronous Balanced Mode Extended |
| **SAP** | Service Access Point |
| **SAP** | Service Advertisement Protocol (Novell) |
| **SAS** | Single Attached Station |
| **SDH** | Synchronous Digital Hierarchy |
| **SDLC** | Synchronous Data Link Control |
| **SDU** | Service Data Unit |
| **SF** | Super Framing (T1/E1) |
| **SIP** | SMDS Interface Protocol |
| **SLARP** | Serial Link Address Resolution Protocol |
| **SLIP** | Serial Line Interface Protocol |
| **SMDS** | Switched Multimegabit Data Service |
| **SMTP** | Simple Mail Transfer Protocol |
| **SNA** | Systems Network Architecture |
| **SNAP** | SubNetwork Access Protocol |
| **SNMP** | Simple Network Management Protocol |
| **SOF** | Start of Frame |
| **SONET** | Synchronous Optical Network |
| **SPF** | Shortest Path First |
| **SPID** | Service Provider Identifier (ISDN) |
| **SPP** | Sequenced Packet Protocol (Vines) |
| **SPX** | Sequenced Packet Exchange (Novell) |
| **SQL** | Standard Query Language |
| **SRAM** | Static RAM |
| **SRB** | Source Route Bridging |
| **SRT** | Source Route Transparent Bridging |
| **SRTP** | Sequenced Routing Update Protocol (Vines) |
| **SS7** | Signaling System 7 |
| **SSAP** | Source Service Access Point (LLC) |
| **SVC** | Switched Virtual Circuit |

# T

| | |
|---|---|
| **TA** | Terminal Adapter |
| **TACACS** | Terminal Access Controller Access Control System |
| **TA/NT1** | Terminal Adapter/Network Termination 1 (ISDN) |
| **TCP** | Transmission Control Protocol |
| **TCP/IP** | Transmission Control Protocol/Internet Protocol |
| **TDM** | Time Division Multiplexing |
| **TE** | Terminal Equipment |
| **TE1 & TE2** | Terminal Endpoints |
| **TFTP** | Trivial File Transfer Protocol |

**TIFF**    Tagged Image Format
**TTL**    Time to Live

# U

**UART**    Universal Asynchronous Receiver/Transmitter
**UDP**    User Datagram Protocol
**UNI**    User Network Interface
**UTP**    Unshielded Twisted Pair

# V

**VBR**    Variable Bit Rate
**VC**    Virtual Circuit
**VCI**    Virtual Channel Identifier (X.25)
**VCN**    Virtual Circuit Number (X.25)
**VLSM**    Variable-Length Subnet Mask
**VTAM**    Virtual Terminal Access Method

# W

**WAIS**    Wind Area Information Server
**WAN**    Wide Area Network
**WDM**    Wavelength-Division Multiplexing
**WFQ**    Weighted Fair Queuing
**WWW**    World Wide Web

# X

**XNS**    Xerox Network Systems
**XOT**    X.25 over TCP

# Z

**ZIP**    Zone Information Protocol (AppleTalk)
**ZIT**    Zone Information Table (AppleTalk)

# Appendix D

# Sample Security Policies

## Network Security Policy

### Preamble

This document establishes the network security policy for the University of Telephone.

The network security policy is intended to protect the integrity of campus networks and to mitigate the risks and losses associated with security threats to campus networks and network resources.

Like many other universities, the University of Telephone has experienced and will continue to experience an increase in unauthorized access or attempts to access its network and computer systems. Several incidents have resulted in break-ins. In addition, computer systems on campus have been used as platforms to launch attacks on systems on the Internet at large. These incidents represent a responsibility and potential legal liability for the university and could tarnish its reputation.

Attacks and security incidents constitute a risk to the university's academic mission. The loss or corruption of data or unauthorized disclosure of information on research and instructional computers, student records, and financial systems could greatly hinder the legitimate activities of university staff, faculty, and students. The university also has a legal responsibility to secure its computers and networks from misuse. Failure to exercise due diligence may lead to financial liability for damage done by persons accessing the network from or through the university. Moreover, an unprotected university network open to abuse might be shunned by parts of the larger network community. This policy will allow the University of Telephone to handle network security responsibly.

This policy is subject to revision and will be evaluated as the university gains experience with this policy. Procedures and guidelines associated with this policy will be posted on the Computer Security Administration Web Page.

## Goals

The goals of this network security policy are to:

- Establish university-wide policies to protect the university's networks and computer systems from abuse and inappropriate use.
- Establish mechanisms that will aid in the identification and prevention of abuse of university networks and computer systems.
- Provide an effective mechanism for responding to external complaints and queries about real or perceived abuses of university networks and computer systems.
- Establish mechanisms that will protect the reputation of the university and will allow the university to satisfy its legal and ethical responsibilities with regard to its network and computer system connectivity to the worldwide Internet.
- Establish mechanisms that will support the goals of other existing policies, e.g., Appropriate Use of Information Technology and Student Code of Conduct.

*Note:* Any violation of the network security policy will also be deemed a violation of the above listed policies, as appropriate.

## Policy Statement

The University of Telephone provides network resources to its divisions, faculties, and departments in support of its Academic Mission. This policy puts in place measures to prevent or at least minimize the number of security incidents on the campus network without impacting the academic mission or the integrity of the university's many different computing communities.

The responsibility for the security of the university's computing resources rests with the system administrators who manage those resources. Computing and Networking Services (CNS) and the Computer Security Administration (CSA) group will help system administrators to carry out these responsibilities according to this policy.

The Provost has overall responsibility for this policy.

The Academic Advisory Committee (AcAC) of the Computer Management Board will review and respond to formal complaints resulting from the implementation of this policy. Computing and Networking Services (CNS) will prepare an annual report for AcAC relating experience with this policy and AcAC will recommend improvements to the Provost.

In support of this policy, all departments that administer LANs connected to the backbone will:

- Provide Computing and Networking Services (CNS) with the names, e-mail addresses, and telephone numbers for at least two different contacts: a management contact; and a primary technical contact (usually the System Administrator). An alternate contact should be provided in situations where both the management contact and the primary technical contact are one and the same person.

- Endeavor to assign to an individual the authority to connect systems to the departmental network(s).
- Endeavor to keep this information accurate and up-to-date.

Computing and Networking Services (CNS) will:

- Monitor, in real time, backbone network traffic, as necessary and appropriate, for the detection of unauthorized activity and intrusion attempts.
- Carry out such monitoring in compliance with the university's statement on Personal Privacy in the Appropriate Use of Information Technology.
- Seek the cooperation of the appropriate contacts for the systems and networks involved when a security problem (or potential security problem) is identified to resolve such problems, but in the absence or unavailability of such individuals be prepared to act unilaterally to contain the problem, up to and including temporary isolation of systems or devices from the network, and to notify the responsible system administrator when this is done.
- Publish security alerts, vulnerability notices and patches, and other pertinent information in an effort to prevent security breaches.
- Carry out and review the results of automated network-based security scans of the systems and devices on university networks to detect known vulnerabilities or compromised hosts.
- Inform the departmental system administrators of planned scan activity, providing detailed information about the scans, including time of scan, originating machine, and vulnerabilities tested for. The security, operation, or functionality of the scanned machines should not be endangered by the scan.
- Report the results of scans that identify security vulnerabilities only to the departmental system administrator contact responsible for those systems.
- Report recurring vulnerabilities over multiple scans to departmental management.
- If identified security vulnerabilities, deemed to be a significant risk to others and which have been reported to the relevant system administrators, are not addressed in a timely manner, take steps to disable network access to those systems or devices until the problems have been rectified.
- Prepare summary reports of its network security activities for the AcAC on a quarterly basis.
- Prepare recommendations and guidelines for network and system administrators, to be posted at the Computer Security Administration Web Page.
- Provide assistance and advice to system administrators to the extent possible with available resources.

■ Issue semiannual requests to verify the accuracy of departmental contact information.

The Computer Security Administration group within CNS will:

■ Coordinate all CNS network security efforts and act as the primary administrative contact for all related activities.
■ Coordinate investigations into any alleged computer or network security compromises, incidents, or problems; to ensure that this coordination is effective, security compromises should be reported to Computer Security Administration — e-mail: security.admin@uTelephone.edu or telephone 416-978-1354.
■ Cooperate in the identification and prosecution of activities contrary to university policies and the law; actions will be taken in accordance with relevant university Policies, Codes and Procedures with, as appropriate, the involvement of the Campus Police or other law enforcement agencies.
■ In consultation with system administrators, develop procedures for handling and tracking a suspected intrusion, and deploy those procedures in the resolution of security incidents.

System Administrators will:

■ Endeavor to protect the networks and systems for which they are responsible.
■ Endeavor to employ CNS recommended practice and guidelines where appropriate and practical.
■ Cooperate with CNS in addressing security problems identified by network monitoring.
■ Address security vulnerabilities identified by CNS scans deemed to be a significant risk to others.
■ Report significant computer security compromises to Computer Security Administration.

Network users will:

■ Abide by the Appropriate Use of Information Technology policy of the university.
■ Abide by departmental policies governing connection to departmental networks.

## Definitions

■ *Network Resources* — Network resources include any networks connected to the University of Telephone backbone, any devices attached to these networks, and any services made available over these networks.

Devices and services include network servers, peripheral equipment, workstations, and personal computers (PCs), UTORdial, UTORmail, etc.

- *Departments* — Department is used as a generic term to signify an academic or administration unit.
- *System Administrator* — The individual who is responsible for system and network support for computing devices in a local computing group. In some instances, this may be a single person whereas in others the responsibility may be shared by several individuals, some of whom may be at different organizational levels.

## Contact

For information about this policy or for clarification of any of the provisions of this policy, please contact the Manager of Computer Security Administration at security.admin@uTelephone.edu.

# Business Continuity Planning

Continuity of important business processes shall be guaranteed through disaster planning and information classification.

## *Availability of Computerized Information*

Business processes that could affect Business Continuity require high availability. The owner of these processes should define the availability required and ensure that the IT staff implement it.

## *System Redundancy*

Systems of operating class may require some form of hardware, service, or system redundancy. See the system requirements for the Availability classes (Standards) and the Mechanisms Standards.

## *Security Crisis/Disasters*

If a serious attack or disaster occurs:

- The *Firecall* team should take charge.
- The concerned machine should be disconnected from the network.
- Document every single action taken, events, evidence found (with time and date).
- Analyze the system: What files were changed? What programs/accounts were added or modified? If modifications are found, check for these modifications on similar systems.
- Notify administrators, management, and law enforcement authorities as required.
- If you discuss details of the attack with anyone via e-mail, use encrypted e-mail with signatures.
- Report the incident to a CERT/FIRST if necessary.

# Dial-In Access

All incoming dial-up connections (via PSTN or ISDN) should use a strong one-time password authentication system (such as SecurID).

Dial-in access to the corporate network should only be allowed where necessary and where the following conditions are met:

- Assurance

  The dial-in server configuration shall be accurately documented.

  It shall be subjected to yearly audits.
- Identification and Authentication

  All incoming dial-up connections (via PSTN or IDSN) shall use a strong authentication system: one-time passwords, challenge-response, etc.

  Administrator log-in shall not send passwords in cleartext.

  In addition, the call-back or closed user groups features should be used, where possible.
- Accountability and Audit

  Users shall be accountable for their actions.

  Dial-up servers shall provide detailed logging and auditing of connections.

  Logs shall be automatically analyzed, with critical errors generating alarms.

  Logs shall be archived for at least one year.

  The nontrivial log entries shall be examined daily.

  Statistics on usage should be available.

  The servers shall be subject to regular monitoring (weekly) and yearly audits.
- Access Control

  Dial-up servers shall not share file or printer resources with other internal machines; that is, they shall not be file or printer servers.

  Only administrative personnel shall be allowed to log on locally.

  Users shall *not* be able to log on directly to these machines (from the inside).

  Dial-up servers shall be installed in a physically secured (locked) room.

  A list should be kept of those users with modems. If possible, the telephone network should be regularly scanned for unauthorized modems.

  Switch off modems at night if not needed (a $5 timer is available to do this).
- Accuracy: no requirements.
- Data Exchange

  Use encrypted password communication (e.g., encrypted Telnet, SSH), if possible, especially for remote administrator access.

  Nonrepudiation of origin and receipt is not required.

- Reliability of Service

  Dial-up servers shall have all unnecessary services stopped.

  Dial-up servers shall be robust multi-tasking machines (e.g., UNIX, VAX, or NT).

  Dial-up servers shall offer the following availability: $7 \times 24$, maximum downtime four hours (during office hours), maximum frequency twice per month. Maintenance window: Wednesday evening after office hours.

- Change Management

  Updates and configuration changes shall be logged and carried out according to Quality processes.

- Alerts should be raised if important processes crash.
- Regular backups shall be made where necessary.

# Access Control

- All users should be authorized.
- Users should be able to set the privileges of objects belonging to them in their environment.
- Users should be prevented from deleting other user files in shared directories.
- Consider allowing root log-in only via the console.
- It should be possible to control user access to all objects on the system (files, printers, devices, databases, commands, applications, etc.) according to a stated policy.
- Users should not be able to examine the access control granted to other users.
- It should be possible to label data with a classification.
- Mandatory access control should be provided.

# Communications Security Policy

## Statement

The complex and highly sophisticated communications networks used with information technology systems require security arrangements specifically tailored to them. To ensure that the communications systems of the university are appropriately protected, the following physical security policies shall be followed:

- The primary data communications site located within campus shall be physically secured via a card swipe access system. Access to this area is restricted to those personnel given access by the Vice President for Administration and Finance.
- All employees and guests of Computing and Communications Services (OCCS) shall be provided badges. The badges shall be appropriately displayed at all times by the individuals while they are within the secured facilities.
- All wiring closets containing the campus-area network equipment consisting of distributed ATM and Ethernet switches throughout the university should be secured at minimum via a cipher push-button lock. Access to these facilities shall be appropriately limited to only those individuals requiring access in the performance of their job responsibilities.
- As budgetary constraints allow, the wiring closets should be protected by a card swipe system with access logging.
- Wiring closets should not be shared with other university functions such as housekeeping, elevator access, etc. They should be dedicated, single-use spaces.
- Physical connections to campus networks shall only be made by Computing and Communications (OCCS) Network Services personnel for OCCS-owned networks.
- Subnetworks owned and operated by other university departments will be maintained by the owning department and appropriately protected by the same type of security measures as described above.
- All connections to external networks, including but not limited to dial-in facilities (RAS, access servers, modems, etc.) shall only be made by OCCS staff or with the written authorization of the Director of Communications and Network Services.

## Network Access Control Procedures

OCCS Network Services personnel are responsible for researching, recommending, and/or requesting funding to use appropriate technology to accomplish network security. Advancements in these ever-changing technologies mandate ongoing research and advising of the university's Vice President for Administration and Finance of the risks and possible strategies to reduce any identified risk.

OCCS is responsible for the development and recommendation of access control policies, given budgetary constraints and resource allocations. The development of procedures to implement approved policies is also the responsibility of OCCS.

Resources owned by other university departments shall be appropriately secured via departmental staff.

The university will comply with all existing state and federal laws governing network access and attached resources.

To facilitate ongoing network maintenance and assist in law enforcement efforts, all networked resources will display a banner similar to the following at all log-in prompts:

> You are entering a University of Telephone System, which may be used only for authorized purposes. Unauthorized modification of any information stored on this system may result in criminal prosecution. University of Telephone may monitor and audit the usage of this system, and all persons are hereby notified that use of this system constitutes consent to such monitoring and auditing. For security purposes, and to ensure that this service remains available to all users, this University of Telephone computer system employs software programs to monitor network traffic to identify unauthorized attempts to upload or change information or to otherwise cause damage, including attempts to deny service to authorized users. Attempts to upload or change information on this service without authorization or to download and copy with the intent to defraud are strictly prohibited and may be punishable under the Computer Fraud and Abuse Act of 1986 and the National Information Infrastructure Protection Act.

## Network Contingency Plan

OCCS Network Services personnel are responsible for the formulation of a network contingency plan for the university-owned networks, including the ATM backbone and external network connections. This plan should identify critical networked resources for administrative, teaching, and research needs. The plan shall be contained in the University Central Computing Disaster Recovery and Contingency Plan.

# Software Development Policy

Security should be an integral part of new systems. When functional requirements are designed, security requirements should be formulated corresponding to the sensitivity and availability of data to be handled by the system.

## *General Guidelines*

- Separate development and production environments and data.
- Consider security to be an integral part of application development.
- Assure that test data does not contain confidential information.
- Consider using a secured language (e.g., Java rather than C, Tainted Perl rather than Perl).
- Consider having major new systems ITSEC approved.

# System and Network Security Policy

## *Network Security*

A network security policy is definitely required before implementing an intranet. People will tend to treat the intranet as they do the Internet — a free-for-all — unless a few guidelines are established. In addition, most intranets contain corporate information, many times proprietary. Users should understand how they should use the intranet, as well as how they can contribute feedback to its improvement as a productivity tool.

The security of the network will be provided by the installation of a firewall router. The firewall should perform the following tasks:

- Shield all local IP addresses and hostnames from the outside world.
- Be transparent to internal users so that they are able to perform FTP, Telnet, etc. as they are used to.
- Allow applications from outside only if the particular remote user and remote host address are registered.
- Identify the of network addresses that are authorized to log into the firewall.
- Reject "finger" requests from outside.
- Block inbound and outbound r-commands (e.g., rlogin, rsh, rcp, rwho, etc.).
- Provide remote user advanced authentication (one-time passwords).
- Prevent NIS and NFS from leaving the local network.
- Log all valid and invalid log-ins to the firewall.
- Permit or deny services to specific host systems.

The following public access services will be located outside the firewall:

- World Wide Web services such as the NSRC home pages and related documents
- Anonymous FTP
- Domain name resolution (DNS)

## *Host Security*

- Create a corn job to remove all .rhost entries defining trusted hosts not belonging to NSRC. These file permissions must only be read/write by owner.
- Disable TFTP.
- Make sure no /etc/hosts.equiv are used.
- Make sure that all accounts have passwords. Make sure that no dictionary words are used for passwords. Implement password aging.
- Keep track of checksum values of all setuid root programs.
- Limit the number of failed log-in attempts and increase the time interval between consecutive log-in attempts.

## Electronic Communication Policy

The Company maintains a voice-mail system and an electronic-mail (e-mail) system to assist in the conduct of business within the Company. These systems, including the equipment and the data stored in the system, are and remain at all times the property of the Company. As such, all messages created, sent, received, or stored in the system are and remain the property of the Company.

Messages should be limited to management-approved activities.

The Company reserves the right to retrieve and review any message composed, sent, or received. Please note that even when a message is deleted or erased, it is still possible to recreate the message; therefore, ultimate privacy of messages cannot be ensured to anyone. Although voice mail and electronic mail may accommodate the use of passwords for security, confidentiality cannot be guaranteed. Messages may be reviewed by someone other than the intended recipient. Moreover, all passwords must be made known to the Company. The reason for this is simple: your system may need to be accessed by the Company when you are absent.

Messages may not contain content that may reasonably be considered offensive or disruptive to any employee. Offensive content would include, but would not be limited to, sexual comments or images, racial slurs, gender-specific comments, or any comments that would offend someone on the basis of his or her age, sexual orientation, religious or political beliefs, national origin, or disability.

Employees learning of any misuse of the voice-mail or electronic-mail system or violations of this policy shall notify the Director of Human Resources immediately. Failure to abide by this policy will be viewed as "unacceptable behavior" as discussed in the Employee Standards of Conduct Policy (see Exhibit 1).

## Exhibit 1   The Company Contract Personnel Confidentiality Agreement

This confidentiality agreement entered into on this  \_\_\_\_ day of _____ ,
                                                                                (date)                    (month)

_____ , is between the Company, located at  _____ , and
  (year)

_____ , a Contract Personnel for  _____ , a company
(contract personnel's name)                                    (contract provider)

located at _____ .
                        (contracting company address)

The Contract Personnel acknowledges and agrees that:

1. The work covered by this contract may include, but is not limited to, the Company (and its vendor's) software programs, computer code, software documentation, methodology documentation, reference manuals, business models, data models, and other valuable business and technological information (referred to herein collectively as "proprietary information and technology").

2. The Contract Personnel shall keep strictly confidential all such proprietary information and technology solely for the purpose of evaluating the Company, its business, and its products. The Contract Personnel agrees that any and all proprietary information and technology provided by the Company, or prepared by the Contract Personnel under this agreement, is (and shall remain) the proprietary and confidential information and property of the Company. The Contract Personnel may not use any of the proprietary information and/or technology of the Company for any purpose other than that which has been defined in the scope of work section of this document, without the prior written consent of the Company.

3. The Contract Personnel shall not introduce, or cause to have introduced, any non-Company-approved software, or computer code, into any Company computer system.

4. Depending on the extent of the Contract Personnel's assignment responsibilities, a background check may be required.

5. Upon request of the Company, the Contract Personnel agrees to return (within three business days) originals and all copies of any such proprietary information and technology, which was previously obtained. The termination of this contract does not relieve the Contract Personnel from his or her obligation to keep strictly confidential all such proprietary information and technology.

   The Contract Personnel's obligations, as to the proprietary information and technology, shall not apply to the following:

   a. That which the Contract Personnel at present has knowledge, or which is in the Contract Personnel's possession on the date hereof, and which was not obtained through contact with the Company previous to the date hereof;

   b. That which is at present publicly available, or a matter of public knowledge generally;

*(continued)*

**Exhibit 1    The Company Contract Personnel Confidentiality Agreement (continued)**

    c.  That which is lawfully received by the Contract Personnel from a third party who is (or was), to the best of the Contract Personnel's knowledge, not bound in any confidential relationship to the Company;

    d.  That which is independently developed by the Contract Personnel, and does not contain any Company proprietary information;

    e.  That which requires disclosure by applicable law.

6.  The Company grants no license, by implication or otherwise, under any of its copyrights, patents, trade secrets, trademarks, or trade names rights, as a result of the disclosure of the proprietary information and technology to the Contract Personnel under this agreement. The Contract Personnel shall not decompile, reverse-engineer, or disassemble any portion of the Company software products, or its vendor's products, except to the extent necessary to perform services required under this agreement.

7.  The Contract Personnel may be required to sign additional confidentiality agreements, due to vendors of the Company (and other companies) that have developed separate confidentiality agreements pertaining to products that may be used by the Contract Personnel during assignment at the Company.

8.  The Contract Personnel acknowledges that the Company shall not have an adequate remedy in the event that the Contract Personnel breaches this agreement, and that the Company will suffer irreparable damage and injury in such event, and the Contract Personnel agrees that the Company, in addition to any other available rights and remedies, shall be entitled to seek an injunction restricting the Contract Personnel from committing, or continuing, any violation of this agreement. The Contract Personnel agrees to submit the items outlined in sections 1 through section 5 of this agreement, for the purpose of interpreting or enforcing, *any* of the provisions of this agreement. This agreement shall be governed by the laws of the State of _____ .

9.  The Contract Personnel has received training in regard to the Company policies and procedures, which may include (but are not limited to) the following:

    a.  The Company proprietary information and technology rights

    b.  The Company policies regarding Information Protection and Personnel Standards of Conduct

    c.  The Information Protection Workstation Reference Guide

    d.  Standards of Conduct pertaining to the Contract House

    e.  The Company Contract Personnel Confidentiality Agreement

    f.  The Company information security awareness training material

    g.  The Company Safety Handbook

The parties do hereby sign and execute this Company confidentiality agreement as of the date written below:

**Exhibit 1   The Company Contract Personnel Confidentiality Agreement (continued)**

Name and address of Contract Provider:        Name and address of the Company
                                              Supervisor:

_____        _____

_____        _____

Printed Name of Contract Personnel:          Printed Name of the Company Supervisor:

Signature of Contract Personnel:             Signature of the Company Supervisor:

_____        _____

Date: _____

## Sign-On Banner

This system is for the use of authorized users only. Individuals using this computer system without authority, or in excess of their authority, are subject to having all activities on this system monitored and recorded by system personnel.

In the course of monitoring, individuals improperly using this system, or in the course of system maintenance, the activities of authorized users may also be monitored.

Anyone using this system expressly consents to such monitoring and is advised that if such monitoring reveals possible evidence of criminal activity, a report will be made to Management and all evidence will be turned over to the appropriate authorities.

# Standards of Conduct for Electronic Communications

The Company policies regarding Employee Standards of Conduct, Conflict of Interest, Equal Employment Opportunity and Diversity in the Workplace, Communication and Information Protection also apply to electronic messages (e-mail), telephone messages (voice mail), and other internal and external electronic communications, including, but not limited to, computer bulletin boards, newsgroups, and the Internet.

Transmitted messages are to be created, handled, distributed, and stored with the same care as any other business document. This includes complying with information-access prohibitions, accessing information only for legitimate business purposes, and protecting information from access by unauthorized persons.

Users should be aware that these systems, and the information stored within them, are the property of the Company and are to be used only for Company-approved activities. The Company maintains the right to monitor the operation of these systems.

Since confidentiality is not assured, these systems are to be used only for transmitting information considered "Public" or for "Internal Use." (The definitions for "Public," "Internal Use," and "Confidential" many be found in the Company Policy on Information Classification.) "Confidential" information should not be communicated using these electronic systems. The Company prohibition of derogatory and offensive comments also applies to messages communicated through these systems. Special care should be given to ensure that the style and tone of messages are appropriate.

Every effort should be made to send messages only to those who "need to know." The Company Policy on Communication details the approvals required before distributing information externally or internally through the use of company mailing lists.

Employees are responsible for using these systems appropriately. Inappropriate use could result in disciplinary action.

# E-Mail Access Policy

## Purpose

To establish guidelines for employees when accessing electronic mail (e-mail) services using Club computers. This policy is meant to augment e-mail policy statements contained in the employee handbooks for each of the entities in the Club family of organizations.

Benefits from complying with e-mail policies include the following:

- Assurance that people cannot send messages that appear to have you as the sender
- Business continuity during unexpected absences without compromising your password
- Confidentiality of information that could affect customers or employees of the company

## Scope

The Club supports two different e-mail systems:

- Host-based or TAO e-mail
- Client/server-based or Outlook e-mail

The Club also provides access to Internet e-mail services from both the TAO and Outlook e-mail systems on an as-needed basis.

The rules and obligations described in this policy apply to all employees who use the Club's computer network, wherever they may be located.

## Policy Statements

### Authorized Usage

It is every employee's duty to use the Club's computer e-mail systems responsibly, professionally, ethically, and lawfully. Only Club-provided, authorized e-mail software may be used. The computer e-mail systems are the property of the Club and may be used for legitimate business purposes. Employees should limit the use of e-mail for sending personal messages. Employees are permitted access to the Club's e-mail systems to assist them in performance of their jobs. Use of the e-mail systems is a privilege that may be revoked at any time.

As a guide for use, e-mail is generally acceptable for the following types of communication:

- Confirm appointments and meetings
- Remind others of deadlines
- Provide informal and brief progress reports

- Convey nonconfidential information to others quickly
- Stay in touch with business partners
- Share concerns and suggestions with others

## *Prohibited Activities*

Material that is fraudulent, harassing, embarrassing, sexually explicit, profane, obscene, intimidating, defamatory, or otherwise unlawful or inappropriate may not be sent by e-mail, or displayed, or stored on the Club's computer systems. Employees encountering or receiving this kind of material should immediately report the incident to their supervisor and the Information Systems Security Manager.

The Club's e-mail systems may not be used for dissemination or storage of commercial or personal advertisements, solicitations, promotions, destructive programs (i.e., viruses), political material, charitable endeavors, private business activities, or any other unauthorized use.

Employees may not deliberately perform acts that waste computer resources or unfairly monopolize resources to the exclusion of others. These acts include, but are not limited to, sending mass mailings or chain letters.

Unless expressly authorized by the Club, sending, transmitting, or otherwise disseminating proprietary data, trade secrets, or other confidential information of the Club is strictly prohibited. Unauthorized dissemination of this information may result in substantial civil liability as well as severe criminal penalties under the Economic Espionage Act of 1996.

## Internet E-Mail

Mail sent and received via the Internet using Club addresses is for conducting Club business only. E-mail via the Internet should be treated in much the same manner that one would treat mailings on official Club stationery. Your e-mail address represents the organization, and thus must be confined to official Club business. The Club reserves the right to access and disclose all electronic messages, documents, and data sent or received via Internet e-mail.

Internet e-mail messages are sent over public networks and therefore you should not use e-mail for confidential information. All file attachments to e-mail messages received over the Internet must be scanned for viruses prior to execution or opening the file.

Having an e-mail address on the Internet may lead to receipt of unsolicited e-mail containing annoying or offensive content. Receipt of unsolicited and unwanted information of this nature should be reported to the IS Security Manager. Employees accessing the Internet do so at their own risk.

### Computer Passwords

Employees are responsible for their e-mail account and the messages sent from this account. Computer passwords provide access control to employee e-mail accounts. Therefore, employees must not share computer passwords. Employees must not allow anyone else to send e-mail using their accounts. This includes their supervisors, secretaries, assistants, and any other subordinates.

Once an employee has shared the password with another person, the other person can log on to e-mail in the employee's name, send messages from the employee's name, read the employee's incoming messages (including confidential messages), and access the employee's e-mail files.

### No Expectation of Privacy

The computers and e-mail accounts given to employees are to assist them in performance of their jobs. Employees should be aware that e-mail communications could be forwarded, intercepted, printed, and stored by others. Therefore, employees should not have an expectation of privacy in anything they create, store, send, or receive on the computer system. E-mail communications systems and all messages generated on or handled by e-mail communications systems, including backup copies, are considered to be the property of the Club.

Employees consent to allowing personnel of the Club to access and review all materials employees create, store, send, or receive on the computer or through the Internet or any other computer network. It is the policy of the Club not to regularly monitor the content of electronic communications. However, the content of electronic communications may be monitored and the usage of e-mail communications will be monitored to support operational, maintenance, auditing, security, and investigative activities. Users should structure their electronic communications in recognition of the fact that the Club will from time to time examine the content of electronic communications. Employees understand that the Club may use manual or automated means to monitor use of its e-mail systems.

## Incidental Disclosure

It may be necessary for technical support personnel to review the content of an individual employee's communications during the course of problem resolution. Technical support personnel may not review the content of an individual employee's communications out of personal curiosity or at the behest of individuals who have not gone through proper approval channels.

## Policy Enforcement

Employees must also comply with all other computer access and use requirements, including those described in the Employee Computer Security Handbook. See the e-mail section of the Employee Handbook for additional details on the Club's e-mail policy.

Violations of standards, procedures, or guidelines established in support of this policy should be reported to management for appropriate action. Violations to this policy will be taken seriously and may result in disciplinary action, including possible termination, and civil and criminal liability.

## Responsibilities

- Staff Officers
  Approve access to the Internet e-mail for use by individuals in their business unit per this policy.
- Business Unit Management
  Approves access to internal e-mail for use by individuals in its business unit per this policy.
  Assists Information Systems Security in ensuring that each of its employees is aware of and understands this policy.
  Assists Information Systems Security in ensuring that employees comply with this policy.
  Reports violations that are detected within its assigned area of control to the Manager, Information Systems Security.
- Information Systems Security Department
  Has primary responsibility for the establishment, implementation, and maintenance of this policy to assist management in the protection of company information assets.
  Will develop and, with the concurrence of management, publish standards, procedures, and guidelines needed to assure adequate security is maintained within the scope of this policy.

- Enterprise Systems and Networks Department
  Establishes e-mail accounts for employees as required by business requirements.
  Installs and maintains network e-mail system, firewall, content filtering software, and virus protection software.
- Internet and Human Resource Systems Department
  Establishes Internet access upon receipt of approved request.

## Policy Exceptions

Exceptions to this policy require written authorization from the Vice President and CIO, Information Systems.

# Software Usage

Organization software usage guidelines are detailed in Exhibit 2, employee usage guidelines are shown in Exhibit 3, and employee home software usage guidelines are listed in Exhibit 4.

**Exhibit 2   Organization Software Usage Guidelines**

1. **General Statement of Policy.** It is the policy of [Organization] to respect all computer software copyrights and to adhere to the terms of all software licenses to which [Organization] is a party. [Organization] will take all steps necessary to prohibit users from duplicating any licensed software or related documentation for use either on [Organization] premises or elsewhere unless [Organization] is expressly authorized to do so by agreement with the licensor. Unauthorized duplication of software may subject users and/or [Organization] to both civil and criminal penalties under the United States Copyright Act.

   [Organization} must not permit any employee to use software in any manner inconsistent with the applicable license agreement, including giving or receiving software or fonts from clients, contractors, customers, and others.
2. **User Education.** [Organization] must provide and require a software education program for all of its software users (to be crafted by the software manager). Upon completion of the education program, users are required to sign the [Organization] Employee Personal Computer Software Usage Guidelines. New users will be provided the same education program within 10 days of the commencement of their employment.
3. **Budgeting for Software.** When acquiring computer hardware, software, and training, [Organization] must budget accordingly to meet the costs at the time of acquisition. When purchasing software for existing computers, [Organization] must charge the purchases to the department budget for information technology or an appropriate budget set aside for tracking software purchases.
4. **Acquisition of Software.** All software acquired by [Organization] must be purchased through the [MIS, purchasing, or other appropriate] designated department. Software may not be purchased through user corporate credit cards, petty cash, travel or entertainment budgets. Software acquisition channels are restricted to ensure that [Organization] has a complete record of all software that has been purchased for [Organization] computers and can register, support, and upgrade such software accordingly. This includes software that may be downloaded or purchased from the Internet.

(*continued*)

**Exhibit 2    Organization Software Usage Guidelines (continued)**

5. **Registration of Software.** When [Organization] receives the software, the designated department [MIS, purchasing, etc.] must receive the software first to complete registration and inventory requirements before installation. In the event the software is shrink-wrapped, the designated department is responsible for completing the registration card and returning it to the software publisher. Software must be registered in the name of [Organization] and department in which it will be used. Due to personnel turnover, software will never be registered in the name of the individual user. The designated department maintains a register of all [Organization] software and will keep a library of software licenses. The register must contain (a) the title and publisher of the software; (b) the date and source of software acquisition; (c) the location of each installation as well as the serial number of the hardware on which each copy of the software is installed; (d) the existence and location of backup copies; and (e) the serial number of the software product.

6. **Installation of Software.** After the registration requirements above have been met, the software will be installed by the software manager. Once installed, the original media will be kept in a safe storage area maintained by the designated department. User manuals, if provided, will either reside with the user or reside with the software manager.

7. **Home Computers.** [Organization] computers are organization-owned assets and must be kept both software legal and virus free. Only software purchased through the procedures outlined above may be used on [Organization] machines. Users are not permitted to bring software from home and load it onto [Organization] computers. Generally, organization-owned software cannot be taken home and loaded on a user's home computer if it also resides on [Organization] computer. If a user is to use software at home, [Organization] will purchase a separate package and record it as an [Organization]-owned asset in the software register. However, some software companies provide in their license agreements that home use is permitted under certain circumstances. If a user needs to use software at home, he or she should consult with the software manager or designated department to determine if appropriate licenses permit home use.

8. **Shareware.** Shareware software is copyrighted software that is distributed via the Internet. It is the policy of [Organization] to pay shareware authors the fee they specify for use of their products. Under this policy, acquisition and registration of shareware products will be handled the same way as for commercial software products.

9. **Quarterly Audits.** The software manager or designated department will conduct a quarterly audit of all [Organization] PCs and servers, including portables, to ensure that [Organization] is in compliance with all software licenses. Surprise audits may be conducted as well. Audits will be conducted using an auditing software product. Also, during the quarterly audit, [Organization] will search for computer viruses and eliminate any that are found. The full cooperation of all users is required during audits.

**Exhibit 2    Organization Software Usage Guidelines (continued)**

10. **Penalties and Reprimands.** According to the U.S. Copyright Act, illegal reproduction of software is subject to civil damages of as much as U.S.$100,000 per title infringed, and criminal penalties, including fines of as much as U.S.$250,000 per title infringed and imprisonment of up to five years. An [Organization] user who makes, acquires, or uses unauthorized copies of software will be disciplined as appropriate under the circumstances. Such discipline may include termination of employment. [Organization] does not condone the illegal duplication of software and will not tolerate it.

I have read [Organization] anti-piracy statement and agree to bind the [Organization] accordingly. I understand that violation of any above policies may result in both civil liability and criminal penalties for the [Organization] and/or its employees.

_____

Signature


_____

Title


_____

Date


Published by the SPA Anti-Piracy. (You are given permission to duplicate and modify this policy statement so long as attribution to the original document comes from SPA Anti-Piracy.)

**Exhibit 3    Employee Usage Guidelines for [Organization]**

Software will be used only in accordance with its license agreement. Unless otherwise provided in the license, any duplication of copyrighted software, except for backup and archival purposes by software manager or designated department, is a violation of copyright law. In addition to violating copyright law, unauthorized duplication of software is contrary to [Organization] standards of conduct. The following points are to be followed to comply with software license agreements:

1. All users must use all software in accordance with its license agreements and the [Organization] software policy. All users acknowledge that they do not own this software or its related documentation, and unless expressly authorized by the software publisher, may not make additional copies except for archival purposes.

2. [Organization] will not tolerate the use of any unauthorized copies of software or fonts in our organization. Any person illegally reproducing software can be subject to civil and criminal penalties including fines and imprisonment. All users must not condone illegal copying of software under any circumstances and anyone who makes, uses, or otherwise acquires unauthorized software will be appropriately disciplined.

3. No user will give software or fonts to any outsiders including clients, customers, and others. Under no circumstances will software be used within [Organization] that has been brought in from any unauthorized location under [Organization] policy, including, but not limited to, the Internet, the home, friends, and colleagues.

4. Any user who determines that there may be a misuse of software within [Organization] will notify the Certified Software Manager, department manager, or legal counsel.

5. All software used by [Organization] on [Organization]-owned computers will be purchased through appropriate procedures.

I have read the [Organization] software code of ethics. I am fully aware of our software compliance policies and agree to abide by them. I understand that violation of any above policies may result in my termination.

_____

Employee Signature

_____

Date

Published by the SPA Anti-Piracy. (You are given permission to duplicate and modify this policy statement so long as attribution to the original document comes from SPA Anti-Piracy.)

## Exhibit 4　Employee Home Software Usage Guidelines

**Purpose**

Consistent with paragraph seven (7) of [Organization] Software Use Guidelines, Employees use of [Organization] software at home is strictly prohibited unless express permission is received from [Organization] software manager or designated department. If the software manager or designated department determines home use is permissible under the relevant software license agreement, then in exchange for the privilege of home use, I expressly agree to the following terms and conditions of home software use:

1. To install only the permissible number of copies of [Organization] software to my home computer as determined by [Organization] software manager or designated department under the relevant software license agreement ;

2. To use the [Organization] software consistently with the software's license agreement and [Organization] software policy, including, but not limited to, restricting the software's use to [Organization] business only; AND

3. To subject my home computer with [Organization] software to periodic software audits to ensure the [Organization] software compliance, consistent with paragraph nine (9) of [Organization] Software Use Guidelines (see http://www.spa.org/piracy/programs/empguide2.htm).

4. To remove the [Organization] software from my computer and return any materials that I may have relating to [Organization] software back to [Organization] should I cease to work for [Organization]. I understand that continued use of the software may subject me to potential civil liability.

I have read [Organization] Software Use Guidelines and the preceding terms applying to the home use of [Organization] software. I am fully aware of the software compliance policies and agree to abide by them. I understand that violation of any of the [Organization] software use policies, including, but not limited to, the terms above, may result in my termination.

_____

Employee Signature

_____

Date

Published by the SPA Anti-Piracy. (You are given permission to duplicate and modify this policy statement so long as attribution to the original document comes from SPA Anti-Piracy.)

# Appendix E

# Job Descriptions

## Chief Information Officer (CIO)

### CIO Mission

To provide technology vision and leadership for developing and implementing IT initiatives that create and maintain leadership for the enterprise in a constantly changing and intensely competitive marketplace.

### Reporting Relationship

To a senior functional executive (President, EVP, CFO) or CEO. This is a key management position for the organization responsible for IT policy and alignment of IT strategy with business objectives.

### Responsibilities

- Sponsor collaborative business technology planning processes.
- Coordinate new and existing application development initiatives between IT and business units.
- Ensure IT infrastructure and architecture continue to meet enterprise business needs.
- Certify "make versus buy" decisions relative to outsourcing versus in-house provisioning of IT services, skills, and products.
- Establish strategic relationships with key IT suppliers and consultants.
- Provide enabling technologies to make it easier for customers and suppliers to conduct business with the enterprise as well as increase revenue and profitability.
- Interact with internal and external clients to ensure continuous customer satisfaction.

- Provide training for all IT personnel and users to ensure productive use of existing and new systems.

## Skills Required

- Strong business orientation, broad experience in the IT sector, and related activities (i.e., consulting and vendor activities).
- Demonstrated ability to bring the benefits of IT to solve business issues while effectively managing costs and risks.
- Skill at identifying and evaluating new technological developments and gauging their appropriateness for the enterprise.
- Ability to communicate with and understand the needs of nontechnical internal clients.
- Exceptional organization skills to ensure proper management of central IS resources and applications and to coordinate business unit initiatives and resources.
- Ability to conceptualize, launch, and deliver multiple IT projects on time and within budget.
- Ability to blend with the existing management team by being an effective listener, team builder, and an articulate advocate of the IT vision.

## Personal Qualities

- Superb leadership, communication, and interpersonal skills; ability to function in a collaborative and collegial environment; sensitivity to others; high integrity and intelligence; excellent judgment; a conceptual thinker, strategically as well as pragmatically; and ability to generate trust and build alliances with co-workers.

# Information Security Manager

## *Primary Responsibilities*

Provides strategic direction for the protection of company information assets. Reports to the Corporate Information Officer (CIO).

## *Job Scope*

Develop strategic direction for the protection of information assets. Provide programs to meet management's fiduciary and legal responsibilities. Develop security solutions that facilitate the strategic business needs of the company. Implement processes to identify threats to the company information assets and computer resources. Assist information owners in identifying and implementing controls to mitigate threats to company information assets and computer resources. Develop policies on information asset protection. Implement formal information protection programs and employee awareness training. Identify and recommend security solutions based on changing technology. Implement proactive computer virus, copyright compliance, business continuity planning, emergency response programs.

## *Required Skills, Experience, and Competencies*

Must have a Bachelor's degree from a recognized college or university in Management Information Systems, Business, or Computer Science, and a minimum of three years job-related experience supporting information protection activities; or an Associate's degree in Management Information Systems, Business, or Computer Science, and a minimum or five years job-related experience; or seven years supporting information protection activities. Ability to understand and correlate information protection controls to business needs. Proven project management skills. Proven team-building and leading skills. Solid communication skills, both oral and written. Ability to work without direct supervision. Proven ability to develop key relationships needed to support strategic direction.

## *Additional Desired Competencies*

CISSP and CDRP preferred. Recogntion as an industry expert by peers. Proven ability to work with senior management of private, public, and academic organizations. Proven ability to influence security profession. Established network of contacts throughout the information security profession.

# Security Administrator

## Primary Responsibilities

Maintains standard information protection policies and procedures. Monitors conformance to these standards. Reports to Information Security Manager.

## Job Scope

- Implement proactive programs to meet fiduciary and legal responsibilities of management.
- Administer security solutions that facilitate the company strategic business needs.
- Conduct security assessment and risk analysis to identify threats to the company information assets and computer resources.
- Assist information owners in identifying and implementing controls to mitigate threats to company information assets and computer resources.
- Monitor compliance to policies on information asset protection.
- Conduct formal information protection programs and employee awareness training.
- Implement security solutions based on changing technology.
- Administer proactive computer virus, copyright compliance, business continuity planning, and computer emergency response programs (CERT).

## Required Skills, Experience, and Competencies

- Must have a Bachelor's degree from a recognized college or university in Management Information Systems, Business, or Computer Science, and a minimum of one year job-related experience supporting information protection activities; or an Associate's degree in Management Information Systems, Business, or Computer Science, and a minimum or three years job-related experience; or five years supporting information protection activities.
- Ability to understand and correlate information protection controls to business needs.
- Proven level of oral and written communication skills.
- Experience in developing and guiding effective, results-oriented, team-based projects.
- Business, research, and computer experience.
- Ability to create environment that fosters people and team growth in response to customer needs.
- Ability to represent the organization internally and externally.
- Ability to translate information security objectives and business strategic plans.

## *Additional Desired Competencies*

- CISSP and Project Management Professional (PMP) preferred.
- Comprehensive knowledge of information security field.
- In-depth knowledge of business unit functions and cross-relationships.
- Lead technical review process to select new technology solutions.

# Firewall Administrator, Information Security

## Primary Responsibilities

- Provides technical support for remote system access controls.
- Reports to Security Administrator.

## Job Scope

- Support the operation, administration, and maintenance of the corporate Internet firewall.
- Develop, maintain, and implement procedures to generate and distribute Internet access usage reports.
- Assist in the support and maintenance of the Internet access usage policies and guidelines.
- Respond to critical firewall alarms and take corrective measures.
- Keep abreast of CERT advisories, firewall product announcements, and new Internet technology to improve the protection of the corporate network and information systems.
- Assist in the setup and maintenance of corporate home pages (internal and external).
- Provide assistance in Internet-related issues to internal customers.
- Monitor the firewall components and provide input into the performance and capacity planning for the effective operation of the Internet connection.

## Required Skills, Experience, and Competencies

- Minimum of three years experience in supporting computer and communications architecture (both hardware and software) including a minimum of one year of UNIX system administration.
- Must have a working knowledge in the installation, configuration, and implementation of Internet firewall technologies.
- Must be familiar with Internet protocols, services, and applications.
- Must have a working knowledge in designing, developing, and supporting an environment that protects computer systems and information from unauthorized access.
- Must be able to work effectively with people at all levels both within and outside the company.
- Must communicate effectively, both orally and in writing.
- Must be able to work flexible hours.

# Appendix F

# Security Assessment

## I.    Security Policy

A security policy is the basis of any security effort, and provides a framework with which to assess the rest of the organization.

It is, therefore, the starting point for a Security Assessment.

| Factors | Rating/Value 1 2 3 4 | Prelim Score | Action Item | Comments | Final Score |
|---|---|---|---|---|---|
| **A. Policy**   1 = Clearly; 2 = Fairly Clearly; 3 = Somewhat Unclear; 4 = Unclear. | | | | | |
| 1. Is there an information security policy in place? (Yes = 1, No = 4) | 1 2 3 4 | | | | |
| 2. Does the policy state what is and is not permissible? | 1 2 3 4 | | | | |
| 3. Does the scope of the policy cover all facets of information? | 1 2 3 4 | | | | |
| 4. Does the policy define and identify what is classed as "information"? | 1 2 3 4 | | | | |
| 5. Does the policy support the business objectives or mission of the enterprise? | 1 2 3 4 | | | | |
| 6. Does the policy identify management and employee responsibilities? | 1 2 3 4 | | | | |

| Factors | Rating/Value 1 2 3 4 | Prelim Score | Action Item | Comments | Final Score |
|---|---|---|---|---|---|
| 7. Does the policy make clear the consequences of noncompliance? | 1 2 3 4 | | | | |

**B. Procedures** 1 = Completed; 2 = Being Implemented; 3 = In Development; 4 = Have Not Begun.

| Factors | Rating/Value 1 2 3 4 | Prelim Score | Action Item | Comments | Final Score |
|---|---|---|---|---|---|
| 1. Are procedures in place to implement the information security policy? | 1 2 3 4 | | | | |
| 2. Are the policies and procedures continually evaluated against current enterprise business needs? | 1 2 3 4 | | | | |
| 3. Are standards in place to supplement the policies and procedures? | 1 2 3 4 | | | | |
| 4. Are the procedures and standards evaluated to determine their level of impact to the business process? | 1 2 3 4 | | | | |
| 5. Does the project management methodology uphold the security practices? | 1 2 3 4 | | | | |

**C. Document Handling** 1 = Completed; 2 = Being Implemented; 3 = In Development; 4 = Have Not Begun.

| Factors | Rating/Value 1 2 3 4 | Prelim Score | Action Item | Comments | Final Score |
|---|---|---|---|---|---|
| 1. Is there a reasonable and usable information classification policy? (Y = 1, N = 4) | 1       4 | | | | |
| 2. Does the information classification policy address all enterprise information? | 1 2 3 4 | | | | |
| 3. Is the information classification policy followed? | 1 2 3 4 | | | | |
| 4. Is an information classification methodology in place to assist employees in identifying levels of information within the business unit? | 1 2 3 4 | | | | |
| 5. Is there an information-handling matrix that explains how specific information resources are to be handled? | 1 2 3 4 | | | | |

| Factors | Rating/Value 1 2 3 4 | Prelim Score | Action Item | Comments | Final Score |
|---|---|---|---|---|---|

**D. Security Handbook** 1 = Completed; 2 = Being Implemented; 3 = In Development; 4 = Have Not Begun.

| Factors | Rating/Value |
|---|---|
| 1. Is there an information security employee handbook in place? (Y = 1, N = 4) | 1   4 |
| 2. Does the handbook cover the entire policy? | 1 2 3 4 |
| 3. Does the handbook identify the importance of the security policy? | 1 2 3 4 |
| 4. Does the handbook address the employee's responsibilities? | 1 2 3 4 |
| 5. Does the handbook stress the degree of employee personal accountability? | 1 2 3 4 |
| 6. Does the handbook make clear the consequences of noncompliance? | 1 2 3 4 |

**Other Factors**

1.     1 2 3 4

**Security Policy**     **Total Score:**

**Interpreting the total score:** Use this table of Risk Assessment questionnaire score ranges to assess resolution urgency and related actions.

| If the Score is ... | And | The Assessment Rate Is ... | Actions Might Include ... |
|---|---|---|---|
| 23 to 40 | ■ Most activities have been implemented ■ Most employees are aware of the program | Superior | ■ Information Protection (IP) policy is implemented ■ Supporting standards and procedures are integrated into the workplace ■ Information classification policy and methodology have been implemented |

| If the Score is ... | And | The Assessment Rate Is ... | Actions Might Include ... |
|---|---|---|---|
| 41 to 58 | ■ Many activities have been implemented<br>■ Many employees are aware of the program and its objectives | Solid | ■ IP policy is being introduced<br>■ Supporting standards and procedures are being developed<br>■ Employee awareness has begun |
| 59 to 76 | ■ Some activities are under development<br>■ Most management endorses IP objectives | Fair | ■ IP policy and supporting documents are being developed<br>■ An IP team has been identified |
| 77 to 92 | ■ Policies, standards, procedures are missing or not implemented<br>■ Management and employees are unaware of the need for a program | Poor | ■ Management has expressed a need for IP policies and procedures<br>■ Audit comments are pending |

## II.   Organizational Suitability

Security policies and procedures can be rendered useless if the organization does not support the information security program.

Rating Scale: 1 = Yes 4 = No

| Factors | Rating/Value 1   4 | Prelim Score | Action Item | Comments | Final Score |
|---|---|---|---|---|---|
| **A. Organizational Suitability** | | | | | |
| 1. Does senior management support the information security program? | 1   4 | | | | |
| 2. Are employees able to perform their duties efficiently and effectively while following security procedures? | 1   4 | | | | |
| 3. Does the information security program have its own line item in the budget? | 1   4 | | | | |
| 4. Are resources adequate to fund and staff an effective information security program? | 1   4 | | | | |

| Factors | Rating/Value 1 | 4 | Prelim Score | Action Item | Comments | Final Score |
|---|---|---|---|---|---|---|
| 5. Does the security group have the authority to submit needed security policy changes throughout the enterprise? | 1 | 4 | | | | |
| 6. Is an annual report on the level of information security compliance issued to management? | 1 | 4 | | | | |

**B. Personnel Issues**

| Factors | Rating/Value 1 | 4 | Prelim Score | Action Item | Comments | Final Score |
|---|---|---|---|---|---|---|
| 1. Does the enterprise have enough employees to support current business goals? | 1 | 4 | | | | |
| 2. Are employees and project managers aware of their responsibilities for protecting information resources? | 1 | 4 | | | | |
| 3. Are employees properly trained to perform their tasks? | 1 | 4 | | | | |
| 4. Does the enterprise have sufficient expertise to implement an information security awareness program? | 1 | 4 | | | | |
| 5. Are contractor personnel subject to confidentiality agreements? | 1 | 4 | | | | |
| 6. Are contract personnel subject to the same policies as employees? | 1 | 4 | | | | |
| 7. Is access to sensitive/confidential information by contract personnel monitored? | 1 | 4 | | | | |

**C. Training and Education**

| Factors | Rating/Value 1 | 4 | Prelim Score | Action Item | Comments | Final Score |
|---|---|---|---|---|---|---|
| 1. Do employees know the business goals and direction? | 1 | 4 | | | | |
| 2. Do employees receive security-related training specific to their responsibilities? | 1 | 4 | | | | |

| Factors | Rating/Value 1 | Rating/Value 4 | Prelim Score | Action Item | Comments | Final Score |
|---|---|---|---|---|---|---|
| 3. Are employees receiving both positive and negative feedback related to security on their performance evaluations? | 1 | 4 | | | | |
| 4. Is security-related training provided periodically to reflect changes and new methods? | 1 | 4 | | | | |
| 5. Are system administrators given additional security training specific to their jobs? | 1 | 4 | | | | |
| 6. Is there a regular security awareness and training program in place? | 1 | 4 | | | | |
| **D. Oversight and Auditing** | | | | | | |
| 1. Are the security policies and procedures routinely tested? | 1 | 4 | | | | |
| 2. Are exceptions to security policies and procedures justified and documented? | 1 | 4 | | | | |
| 3. Are audit logs or other reporting mechanisms in place on all platforms? | 1 | 4 | | | | |
| 4. Are errors and failures tracked? | 1 | 4 | | | | |
| 5. When an employee is found to be in noncompliance with the security policies, has appropriate disciplinary action been taken? | 1 | 4 | | | | |
| 6. Are audits performed on a regular basis? | 1 | 4 | | | | |
| 7. Are unscheduled/ surprise audits performed? | 1 | 4 | | | | |
| 8. Has someone been identified as responsible for reconciling audit results? | 1 | 4 | | | | |

| Factors | Rating/Value 1 4 | Prelim Score | Action Item | Comments | Final Score |
|---|---|---|---|---|---|
| **E. Application Development and Management** | | | | | |
| 1. Has an application development methodology been implemented? | 1    4 | | | | |
| 2. Are appropriate/key application users involved with developing and improving application methodology and implementation process? | 1    4 | | | | |
| 3. Is preproduction testing performed in an isolated environment? | 1    4 | | | | |
| 4. Has a promotion to production procedures been implemented? | 1    4 | | | | |
| 5. Is there a legacy application management program? | 1    4 | | | | |

**Organizational Suitability**      **Total Score:**

**Interpreting the total score:** Use this table of Risk Assessment questionnaire score ranges to assess resolution urgency and related actions.

| If the Score Is … | And | The Assessment Rate Is … | Actions Might Include … |
|---|---|---|---|
| 23 to 40 | ■ Most activities have been implemented<br>■ Most employees are aware of the program | Superior | ■ CIO and mission have been chartered<br>■ Employee training is an ongoing process<br>■ Awareness training program is in place<br>■ IP objectives are reviewed annually |
| 41 to 58 | ■ Many activities have been implemented<br>■ Many employees are aware of the program and its objectives | Solid | ■ CIO is being considered<br>■ Mission statement is under development<br>■ Initial employee awareness process has begun |

| If the Score Is … | And | The Assessment Rate Is … | Actions Might Include … |
|---|---|---|---|
| 59 to 76 | ■ Some activities are under development<br>■ Most management endorses IP objectives | Fair | ■ Search for a CIO has begun<br>■ IP group has been identified<br>■ Employees have been informed that changes are under way |
| 77 to 92 | ■ Policies, standards, procedures are missing or not implemented<br>■ Management and employees are unaware of the need for a program | Poor | ■ Management has a plan for an IP program<br>■ Audit has identified the need |

# III. Physical Security

The security of the equipment and the buildings used by an organization is as important as the security of a specific platform.

Rating Scale: 1 = Yes 2 = Being Implemented 3 = In Development 4 = No

| Factors | Rating/Value 1 2 3 4 | Prelim Score | Action Item | Comments | Final Score |
|---|---|---|---|---|---|
| **A. Physical and Facilities** | | | | | |
| 1. Is access to buildings controlled? | 1 2 3 4 | | | | |
| 2. Is access to computing facilities controlled? | 1 2 3 4 | | | | |
| 3. Is there an additional level of control for after-hours access? | 1 2 3 4 | | | | |
| 4. Is there an audit log to identify the individual and the time of access for nonstandard hours access? | 1 2 3 4 | | | | |
| 5. Are systems and other hardware adequately protected from theft? | 1 2 3 4 | | | | |
| 6. Are procedures in place for the proper disposal of confidential information? | 1 2 3 4 | | | | |
| **B. After-Hours Review** | | | | | |
| 1. Are areas containing sensitive information properly secured? | 1 2 3 4 | | | | |
| 2. Are workstations secured after hours? | 1 2 3 4 | | | | |
| 3. Are keys and access cards properly secured? | 1 2 3 4 | | | | |
| 4. Is confidential information properly secured? | 1 2 3 4 | | | | |
| 5. Are contract cleaning crews activities monitored? | 1 2 3 4 | | | | |

| Factors | Rating/Value<br>1 2 3 4 | Prelim<br>Score | Action<br>Item | Comments | Final<br>Score |
|---|---|---|---|---|---|
| **C. Incident Handling** | | | | | |
| 1. Has an Incident Response Team (IRT) been established? | 1 2 3 4 | | | | |
| 2. Have employees been trained regarding when the IRT should be notified? | 1 2 3 4 | | | | |
| 3. Has the IRT been trained in evidence gathering and handling? | 1 2 3 4 | | | | |
| 4. Are incident reports issued to appropriate management? | 1 2 3 4 | | | | |
| 5. After an incident, are policies and procedures reviewed to determine if modifications need to be implemented? | 1 2 3 4 | | | | |
| **D. Contingency Planning** | | | | | |
| 1. Has a Business Impact Analysis (BIA) been conducted on all systems, applications, and platforms? | 1 2 3 4 | | | | |
| 2. Is there a documented data center Disaster Recovery Plan (DRP) in place? | 1 2 3 4 | | | | |
| 3. Has the data center DRP been tested within the past 12 months? | 1 2 3 4 | | | | |
| 4. Are system, application, and data backups sent to a secure off-site facility on a regular basis? | 1 2 3 4 | | | | |
| 5. Are service level agreements (SLA) that identify processing requirements in place with all users and service providers? | 1 2 3 4 | | | | |

| Factors | Rating/Value<br>1 2 3 4 | Prelim<br>Score | Action<br>Item | Comments | Final<br>Score |
|---|---|---|---|---|---|
| 6. Have departments, business units, groups, and other such entities implemented business continuity plans that supplement the data center DRP? | 1 2 3 4 | | | | |
| 7. Have emergency response procedures (ERP) been implemented? | 1 2 3 4 | | | | |
| 8. Have ERPs been tested for effectiveness? | 1 2 3 4 | | | | |
| **Physical Security** | **Total Score** | | | | |

**Interpreting the total score:** Use this table of Risk Assessment questionnaire score ranges to assess resolution urgency and related actions.

| If the<br>Score Is... | And | The<br>Assessment<br>Rate Is ... | Actions Might Include ... |
|---|---|---|---|
| 23 to 40 | ■ Most activities have been implemented<br>■ Most employees are aware of the program | Superior | ■ Access to sensitive areas is restricted via automated mechanism<br>■ An incident response team has been implemented<br>■ Contingency plans have are tested annually |
| 41 to 58 | ■ Many activities have been implemented<br>■ Many employees are aware of the program and its objectives | Solid | ■ Access to sensitive areas is generally restricted<br>■ Employees are aware of fire safety procedures<br>■ Contingency plans have been developed |
| If the<br>Score Is... | And | The<br>Assessment<br>Rate Is ... | Actions Might Include ... |
| 59 to 76 | ■ Some activities are under development<br>■ Most management endorses IP objectives | Fair | ■ Access to sensitive areas requires sign-in<br>■ Employees contact the help desk when there is a problem<br>■ Contingency plans are being developed |

| 77 to 92 | ■ Policies, standards, procedures are missing or not implemented<br>■ Management and employees are unaware of the need for a program | Poor | ■ Access to sensitive areas is being defined<br>■ Incidents are handled locally<br>■ Backups are sent off site |

# IV. Business Impact Analysis, Continuity Planning Processes

The ability to recover time-critical processes and supporting systems and other resources is important to every organization. To be successful, an enterprise must establish a method to rank processes, applications, systems, networks, facilities, etc. and to recover them in a timely manner.

Rating Scale: 1 = Yes 2 = Being Implemented 3 = In Development 4 = No

| Factors | Rating/Value 1 2 3 4 | Prelim Score | Action Item | Comments | Final Score |
|---|---|---|---|---|---|
| **A. Business Impact Analysis (BIA)** | | | | | |
| 1. A business impact analysis (BIA) has been conducted for all business processes, applications, systems, networks, and facilities. | 1 2 3 4 | | | | |
| 2. Continuity planning includes identification of all time-critical data, programs, documentation, and supporting resources required in performance of essential tasks during recovery period. | 1 2 3 4 | | | | |
| 3. The BIA is reviewed and updated regularly with attention to new technologies, migration of applications to alternative platforms, business process, and organizational changes, etc. | 1 2 3 4 | | | | |
| 4. Critical time frames have been identified for all support resources (i.e., applications, systems, networks, facilities, business units, etc.). | 1 2 3 4 | | | | |
| 5. Executive management has reviewed and approved the prioritized list of time-critical recovery requirements. | 1 2 3 4 | | | | |

| Factors | Rating/Value 1 2 3 4 | Prelim Score | Action Item | Comments | Final Score |
|---|---|---|---|---|---|
| **B. Enterprise Continuity and Crisis Management Plans** | | | | | |
| 1. An enterprise continuity and crisis management planning infrastructure coordinator has been named and a mission statement identifying scope and responsibilities has been formalized. | 1 2 3 4 | | | | |
| 2. *Worst-case* scenario continuity plans (both IT and business operations) and crisis management infrastructure designed for timely recovery of operations within prescribed time frames has been implemented, tested, and is maintained. | 1 2 3 4 | | | | |
| 3. *Emergency response procedures* that detail actions in emergency situations (i.e., fire, bomb threat, flood, electrical outages, hacker and virus incidents, etc.) are formalized and strategically located throughout the facility and at off-site locations and appropriate employee training and awareness programs are in place. | 1 2 3 4 | | | | |
| 4. The remote recovery facilities (i.e., IT, business operations, emergency operations centers, etc.) are located in a geographical location unlikely to be affected by the same disruption as the primary facilities. | 1 2 3 4 | | | | |

| Factors | Rating/Value<br>1 2 3 4 | Prelim<br>Score | Action<br>Item | Comments | Final<br>Score |
|---|---|---|---|---|---|
| 5. Contracts for outsourced activities have been amended to include service providers' responsibilities for continuity planning. | 1 2 3 4 | | | | |
| 6. Continuity and crisis management plans are in place to ensure that adequate supplies of time-critical inventory inventories (i.e., hardware, software, communications, facilities, people, working space, documentation, data, transportation, etc.) are in place. | 1 2 3 4 | | | | |
| 7. Lead times for IT and business operations communication lines and equipment, specialized devices, power hookups, construction, firewalls, computer configurations, and LAN implementation have been factored into the continuity plans. | 1 2 3 4 | | | | |
| 8. At least one copy of each of the continuity plans is stored at the backup site and is updated regularly. | 1 2 3 4 | | | | |
| 9. Automatic restart and recovery procedures are in place to restore IT data files in the event of a processing failure. | 1 2 3 4 | | | | |
| 10. Contingency arrangements are in place for hardware, software, communications, software, facilities, business operations, and supporting staffing. | 1 2 3 4 | | | | |

| Factors | Rating/Value 1 2 3 4 | Prelim Score | Action Item | Comments | Final Score |
|---|---|---|---|---|---|
| **C. Testing, Maintenance, and Awareness** | | | | | |
| 1. Continuity and crisis management plans recovery activities and tasks are defined with appropriate responsibilities assigned members of the recovery team infrastructure for each plan. | 1 2 3 4 | | | | |
| 2. Training sessions are conducted for all relevant personnel on backup, recovery, crisis management, and contingency operating procedures. | 1 2 3 4 | | | | |
| 3. Continuity and crisis management plan recovery team members have an active role in creating and reviewing control reliability and recovery provisions for relevant processes, applications, systems, networks, etc. | 1 2 3 4 | | | | |
| 4. Appropriate recovery team representatives participate in continuity and crisis management tests. | 1 2 3 4 | | | | |
| **D. Other Issues** | | | | | |
| 1. Provisions are in place to maintain the security of business operations and IT processing functions in the event of an emergency. | 1 2 3 4 | | | | |
| 2. Insurance coverage for losses incurred as a result of a disaster to the enterprise is in place. | 1 2 3 4 | | | | |
| **Business Impact Analysis, Continuity Planning Processes** | **Total Score:** | | | | |

**Interpreting the total score:** Use this table of Risk Assessment questionnaire score ranges to assess resolution urgency and related actions.

| If the Score Is ... | And | The Assessment Rate Is ... | Actions Might Include ... |
|---|---|---|---|
| 21 to 36 | ■ Most activities have been implemented<br>■ Most employees are aware of the program | Superior | ■ Continuity and crisis management plans are in place and have been tested<br>■ Employees are trained in continuity and crisis management plans roles<br>■ BIAs are reviewed annually<br>■ Continuity and crisis management plan coordinator(s) has been identified |

| If the Score Is ... | And | The Assessment Rate Is ... | Actions Might Include ... |
|---|---|---|---|
| 37 to 52 | ■ Many activities have been implemented<br>■ Many employees are aware of the program and its objectives | Solid | ■ Continuity and crisis management plans are written<br>■ Employees are aware of their roles in the continuity and crisis management plans<br>■ Management supports and has budgeted for the continuity and crisis management planning business process |
| 53 to 67 | ■ Some activities are under development<br>■ Most management endorses information protection objectives | Fair | ■ Continuity and crisis management plans task force has been formed<br>■ Time-critical processes, systems, applications, network, etc. assessment has begun<br>■ Time-critical resources are being identified<br>■ Backups are stored off site |
| 68 to 84 | ■ Policies, standards, procedures are missing or not implemented<br>■ Management and employees are unaware of the need for a program | Poor | ■ Audit has identified a weakness in continuity and crisis management planning process<br>■ Management is aware of its responsibility |

## V.    Technical Safeguards

Technical safeguards enforce the security policies and procedures throughout the network infrastructure.

Rating Scale: 1 = Yes 2 = Being Implemented 3 = In Development 4 = No

| Factors | Rating/Value 1 2 3 4 | Prelim Score | Action Item | Comments | Final Score |
|---|---|---|---|---|---|
| **A. Network Infrastructure** | | | | | |
| 1. Is the network environment partitioned? | 1 2 3 4 | | | | |
| 2. Are the desktop platforms secured? | 1 2 3 4 | | | | |
| 3. Are host systems and servers as well as application servers secured? | 1 2 3 4 | | | | |
| 4. Are passwords and/or accounts being shared? | 1 2 3 4 | | | | |
| 5. Are unsecure user accounts (e.g., guest) still active? | 1 2 3 4 | | | | |
| 6. Are temporary user accounts restricted and disabled in a timely fashion? | 1 2 3 4 | | | | |
| 7. Have employees been trained on proper password management? | 1 2 3 4 | | | | |
| 8. Are users of all company-provided network resources required to change the initial default password? | 1 2 3 4 | | | | |
| 9. Are the passwords required to use current tools as secure as the tools allow them to be? | 1 2 3 4 | | | | |
| 10. Do network and system administrators have adequate experience to implement security standards? | 1 2 3 4 | | | | |
| 11. Are report logs reviewed and reconciled on a regular basis? | 1 2 3 4 | | | | |
| 12. Are "permissions" being set securely? | 1 2 3 4 | | | | |

| Factors | Rating/Value<br>1 2 3 4 | Prelim<br>Score | Action<br>Item | Comments | Final<br>Score |
|---|---|---|---|---|---|
| 13. Are administrators using appropriate tools to perform their jobs? | 1 2 3 4 | | | | |
| 14. Is there a current network diagram available? | 1 2 3 4 | | | | |
| 15. Are access control lists (ACL) maintained on a regular basis? | 1 2 3 4 | | | | |
| 16. Is there a remote access procedure in place? | 1 2 3 4 | | | | |
| 17. Are critical servers protected with appropriate access controls? | 1 2 3 4 | | | | |
| 18. Is the network infrastructure audited on a regular basis? | 1 2 3 4 | | | | |
| 19. Are network vulnerability assessments conducted? | 1 2 3 4 | | | | |
| 20. Are changes/ improvements made in a timely fashion following network vulnerability assessments? | 1 2 3 4 | | | | |
| **B. Firewalls** | | | | | |
| 1. Are protocols allowed to go across the firewall? | 1 2 3 4 | | | | |
| 2. Has a risk analysis been conducted to determine if the protocols allowed maintain an acceptable level of risk? | 1 2 3 4 | | | | |
| 3. Has the firewall been tested to determine if outside penetration is possible? | 1 2 3 4 | | | | |
| 4. Are other products in place to augment the firewall level of security? | 1 2 3 4 | | | | |
| 5. Are the firewalls maintained and monitored around the clock? | 1 2 3 4 | | | | |
| 6. Have services offered across the firewall been documented? | 1 2 3 4 | | | | |

| Factors | Rating/Value 1 2 3 4 | Prelim Score | Action Item | Comments | Final Score |
|---|---|---|---|---|---|
| 7. Has a demilitarized zone (DMZ) or perimeter network (a segment of network between the router that connects to the Internet and the firewall) been implemented? | 1 2 3 4 | | | | |

| Technical Safeguards | Total Score: |
|---|---|

**Interpreting the total score:** Use this table of Risk Assessment questionnaire score ranges to assess resolution urgency and related actions.

| If the Score Is ... | And | The Assessment Rate Is ... | Actions Might Include ... |
|---|---|---|---|
| 23 to 40 | ■ Most activities have been implemented<br>■ Most employees are aware of the program | Superior | ■ Network security policies and standards are implemented<br>■ System and LAN administrators are trained in security issues<br>■ Firewalls are implemented and monitored |
| 41 to 58 | ■ Many activities have been implemented<br>■ Many employees are aware of the program and its objectives | Solid | ■ Network security policy is being approved<br>■ Network and desktop standards are under development<br>■ Firewall administrator job description has been developed |
| 59 to 76 | ■ Some activities are under development<br>■ Most management endorses IP objectives | Fair | ■ Subject matter experts have been identified<br>■ Policy and procedures development team has been identified<br>■ Firewall implementation is under way |
| 77 to 92 | ■ Policies, standards, procedures are missing or not implemented<br>■ Management and employees are unaware of the need for a program | Poor | ■ Management has expressed a concern for network security<br>■ Internet connection is being considered |

## VI.   Telecommunications Security

Enterprises must take precautions to protect their information when being transmitted via various telecommunication processes.

Rating Scale: 1 = Yes 2 = Being Implemented 3 = In Development 4 = No

| Factors | Rating/Value 1 2 3 4 | Prelim Score | Action Item | Comments | Final Score |
|---|---|---|---|---|---|
| **A. Policy** | | | | | |
| 1. There is a published policy on the use of organizational telecommunications resources. | 1 2 3 4 | | | | |
| 2. All employees have been made aware of the telecommunications policy. | 1 2 3 4 | | | | |
| 3. Employees authorized for Internet access are made aware of the proprietary information of the organization and what they can discuss in open forums. | 1 2 3 4 | | | | |
| 4. Employees using cellular or wireless phones are briefed on the lack of privacy of conversations when using unsecured versions of this technology. | 1 2 3 4 | | | | |
| 5. Terminating employees have their calling cards and voice-mail passwords disabled. | 1 2 3 4 | | | | |
| 6. Temporary and contract personnel have their calling cards and voice-mail passwords disabled when their assignment ends. | 1 2 3 4 | | | | |
| 7. The organization has a published policy on prosecution of employees and outsiders if found guilty have serious premeditated criminal acts against the organization. | 1 2 3 4 | | | | |

| Factors | Rating/Value 1 2 3 4 | Prelim Score | Action Item | Comments | Final Score |
|---|---|---|---|---|---|
| **B. Standards** | | | | | |
| 1. A threshold is established to monitor and suspend repeated unsuccessful dial-in attempts. | 1 2 3 4 | | | | |
| 2. Access to databases reachable via dial-in has an access control in place to prevent unauthorized access. | 1 2 3 4 | | | | |
| 3. Financial applications available via dial-in have audit trails established to track access and transaction usage. | 1 2 3 4 | | | | |
| 4. Are audit trails reviewed and corrective action taken on a regular basis? | 1 2 3 4 | | | | |
| 5. Wherever possible, the mainframe security program is used to control dial-in access to specific applications. | 1 2 3 4 | | | | |
| 6. Company proprietary data stored on portable computers is secured from unauthorized access. | 1 2 3 4 | | | | |
| 7. Users of all company-provided communication systems are required to change the default or initial password. | 1 2 3 4 | | | | |
| **C. Practices** | | | | | |
| 1. Security, application, and network personnel actively work to ensure control inconvenience is as minimal as possible. | 1 2 3 4 | | | | |
| 2. Personnel independent of the operations staff and/or security administration review tamper-resistant logs and audit trails. | 1 2 3 4 | | | | |

| Factors | Rating/Value<br>1 2 3 4 | Prelim<br>Score | Action<br>Item | Comments | Final<br>Score |
|---|---|---|---|---|---|
| 3. Special procedures and audited "firecall" user ids have been established for application, system, and network troubleshooting activities. | 1 2 3 4 | | | | |
| 4. Telephone usage logs are reviewed on a regular basis to discover potential usage abuse. | 1 2 3 4 | | | | |
| 5. Messages and transactions coming in via phone lines are serially numbered, time-stamped, and logged for audit investigation and backup purposes. | 1 2 3 4 | | | | |
| 6. Employees are made aware of their responsibility to keep remote access codes secure from unauthorized access and/or usage. | 1 2 3 4 | | | | |
| 7. Portable computer users are provided with a mechanism to allow backup of appropriate sensitive information or critical application to a server or to portable storage media. | 1 2 3 4 | | | | |
| 8. Removal of portable computers from the company location must be done through normal property removal procedures. | 1 2 3 4 | | | | |
| 9. Employees are briefed on their responsibility to protect the property (physical and logical) of the company when working away from the company environment. | 1 2 3 4 | | | | |

**Telecommunications Security**   **Total Score:**

**Interpreting the total score:** Use this table of Risk Assessment questionnaire score ranges to assess resolution urgency and related actions.

| If the Score Is ... | And | The Assessment Rate Is ... | Actions Might Include ... |
|---|---|---|---|
| 21 to 36 | ■ Most activities have been implemented | Superior | ■ Telecommunications security policies and standards are implemented |

| If the Score Is ... | And | The Assessment Rate Is ... | Actions Might Include ... |
|---|---|---|---|
| | ■ Most employees are aware of the program | | ■ Telecom administrators are trained in security issues<br>■ Usage reports are monitored<br>■ Discrepancies are investigated |
| 37 to 52 | ■ Many activities have been implemented<br>■ Many employees are aware of the program and its objectives | Solid | ■ Telecommunications security policy is being approved<br>■ Standards are under development<br>■ System and report logs are being generated |
| 53 to 67 | ■ Some activities are under development<br>■ Most management endorses IP objectives | Fair | ■ Subject matter experts have been identified<br>■ Policy and procedures development team has been identified<br>■ Telecom standards implementation is under way |
| 68 to 84 | ■ Policies, standards, procedures are missing or not implemented<br>■ Management and employees are unaware of the need for a program | Poor | ■ Management has expressed a concern for telecommunication security<br>■ Audit has identified weaknesses in telecommunications security |

# Appendix G

# References

1. Bryson, Lisa. Protect your boss and your job: Due care in information security. *Computer Security Alert*. Number 146, May 1995, pp. 4 and 8.
2. d'Agenais, J. and J. Carruthers. *Creating Effective Manuals*. Cincinnati, OH: South-Western Publishing Co., 1985.
3. DeMaio, H. *Information Protection and Other Unnatural Acts*. New York: AMACOM, 1992.
4. Frank, Milo O., *How to Get Your Point Across in 30 Seconds or Less*. New York: Pocket Books, 1986.
5. Frank, Stanley D., *The Evelyn Wood Seven-Day Speed Reading and Learning Program*. New York: Barnes & Noble Books, 1990.
6. Fine, N. The economic espionage act: Turning fear into compliance. *Competitive Intelligence Review*. Volume 8, Number 3, Fall 1997.
7. Fites, P. and M. Kratz. *Information Systems Security: A Practitioner's Reference*. New York: Van Nostrand, 1993.
8. Guttman, B. and E. Roback. *An Introduction to Computer Security: The NIST Handbook*. Gaithersburg, MD: U.S. Department of Commerce, 1995.
9. Jordan, K. Ethics and compliance programs: Keeping your boss out of jail and your company off of the front pages. *Betterley's Risk Management*. April, 1998.
10. Krause, M. and H. Tipton (editors). *Handbook of Information Security Management*. New York: Auerbach, 1998.
11. Lincoln, J. A. EPA's policy on incentives for self-policing, federal sentencing guidelines and other carrots and sticks. *Forum for Best Management Practices*. 1997.
12. Navran, F. A decision maker's guide to the federal sentencing guidelines for ethics violations. *Navran Associates' Newsletter*. March 1996.
13. Palmer, I. and G. Potter. *Computer Security Risk Management*. New York: Van Nostrand Reinhold, 1989.
14. Peltier, T. *Policies and Procedures for Data Security*. San Francisco, CA: Miller Freeman, 1991.
15. Peltier, Thomas R., *Information Security Policies and Procedures: A Practitioner's Reference*. Boca Raton, FL: CRC Press, 1999.
16. Tomasko, R. *Rethinking the Corporation: The Architecture of Change*. New York: AMACOM, 1993.

17. Information-Technology — Code of Practice for Information Security Managment. ISO/IEC, 2000.
18. Banking and Related Financials Services — Information Security Guidelines. ISO, 1997.

# About the Author

**Thomas R. Peltier, CISSP,** is in his fourth decade of computer technology experience as an operator, applications and systems programmer, systems analyst, and information systems security officer. Currently, he is president of Peltier & Associates. Prior to that he was Director of Policies and Administration for the Netigy Corporation's Global Security Practice; the National Director for Consulting Services for CyberSafe Corporation; and the Corporate Information Protection Coordinator for Detroit Edison. This program has been recognized for excellence in the field of computer and information security by winning the Computer Security Institute's Information Security Program of the Year for 1996. Previously he was the Information Security Specialist for General Motors Corporation and was responsible for implementing an information security program for GM's worldwide activities.

Tom has had a number of articles published on various computer and information security issues, including developing policies and procedures, disaster recovery planning, copyright compliance, virus management, and security controls. He has published books titled *Information Security Risk Analysis, Information System Security Policies and Procedures: A Practitioners' Reference, The Complete Manual of Policies and Procedures for Data Security*, and is a contributing author for the *Computer Security Handbook*, both the third and fifth edtions, and for *Data Security Management*.

Tom has been the technical advisor on a number of security films from Commonwealth Films. He is the past chairman of the Computer Security Institute (CSI) advisory council, the chairman of the 18th Annual CSI Conference, founder and past-president of the Southeast Michigan Computer Security Special Interest Group, and a former member of the board of directors for (ISC)2, the security professional certification organization. He was the 1993 "Lifetime Award" recipient at the 20th Annual CSI conference. He also received the 1999 Information Systems Security Association's Individual Contribution to the Profession Award and the CSI Lifetime Emeritus Membership Award. He conducts numerous seminars and workshops on various security topics and has led seminars for CSI, Crisis Management, American Institute of Banking, the American Institute of Certified Public Accountants, Institute of Internal Auditors, ISACA, and Sungard Planning Solutions. Tom was also an Associate Professor at the graduate level for Eastern Michigan University.

# Index

computer security objectives, 55–56
examples
 corporate data processing department, 59
 corporate information security administration, 59, 60
 global manufacturing company, 57–58
 information protection group, 67, 72
 information security department, 62–63
 medium-sized manufacturing company, 59–62
 North American manufacturing company, 58–59
 format, 56
 ISO 17799 standard, 53, 56–57
 management support for, 63–64
 stakeholder involvement in making, 54
 standards and, 71, 72
Monitoring policy, 196–197
 ISO 17799 standards, 80
 sign-on banner policy, 242
Multinational organizations, 3

# N

Narrative style for procedures, 88, 92, 94–100
Network acceptable use, 203
Network security, 97
 access, information handling procedures matrix, 124
 contingency plan, 235
 definitions, 228
 ISO 17799 standards, 78–79
 policy, 201–203, 225–229, 234–235, 237
 privacy policy, 202
 security assessment checklist, 278–279
Nondisclosure policy, 203–204

# O

Open Systems Interconnection (OSI), 23
Operational change control, 181–182
Organizational culture, 3
Organizational structure, management levels and responsibilities, 64–65

# P

Passcode, 97
Passwords
 e-mail policy, 246

example standard, guideline, and procedure statements, 26
management policy, 198–199
security assessment checklist, 278
user authorization example, 75
Personal identification number (PIN), 97, 98
Personnel security, 179–180
 ISO 17799 standards, 77–78
Physical security, 180–181, 214
 ISO 17799 standards, 78
 security assessment checklist, 269–272
 staff, 5
PIN, 97, 98
Planning for quality, 170
Playscript style for procedures, 88, 101–102
Policy
 defined, 83
 differentiating from standards, guidelines, and procedures, 25
 information security, See Information security policy
 mission statement and, 56
 writing mechanics, See Writing mechanics
Policy and procedures implementation, See Project management
Power company, security program policy example, 35
Printing security, 142
Privacy, 48
 e-mail policy, 246–247
Privilege management policy, 199–200
Procedures, 25, 83–106
 creating, 105
 definition, 26, 83–84
 development checklist, 86–87
 elements of, 190
 hierarchy of policies, standards, and procedures, 70
 providing safe and secure environment, 27
 purposes for writing, 86
 restricted information access, 26
 security assessment checklist, 262
 styles, 88–105
  caption, 88, 91, 93
  flowchart, 88, 100–101
  headline, 88, 89–91
  matrix, 88, 92, 93
  narrative, 88, 92, 94–100
  playscript, 88, 101–102
  tree, 102–105
 topic-specific policy format and elements, 30–31
 writing guidelines, 84–86, 190
  getting started, 87–88
  styles, 88–105